THE FATHERS
OF THE CHURCH

A NEW TRANSLATION

VOLUME 1

THE FATHERS
OF THE CHURCH

A NEW TRANSLATION

GENERAL FOREWORD

THE FATHERS OF THE CHURCH* lived in an age when a new world, a Christian world, was emerging out of the civilization of Greco-Roman antiquity. Retaining all that was good in the ancient culture, they struggled not only against the various opponents of the Church, but also against the heresies which arose within the Church itself. Over against a decadent paganism they stressed unceasingly the ethical teachings of Christ's gospel. As spiritual leaders they confronted at first a hostile worldly power; they stood their ground with equal firmness when the state had turned Christian but was only too often inclined to infringe upon the rights of the Church. These manifold controversies and tensions have left us an unusually rich literature; monuments of far-reaching influence in the history of Christian thought, monuments to which Councils and theologians have turned at all times for guidance; monuments whose constructive value is being acutely realized in a special way today, at a time when so many social and philosophical systems have proved futile. Serious thinkers, therefore, are seeking to find in these writings the path by which humanity can perhaps retrace its steps to the solidarity it has lost.

Accordingly, the demand for new translations of the works of the Fathers has been growing more insistent from year to year. The old translations are not only difficult to obtain, but frequently fail to convey to the reader, as they ought, the results of modern scholarship.

---

* *The Fathers of the Church*, a title similar to Migne's *Patrologia*, has been chosen as a collective name for this series of the works of the Early Christian Writers represented in the present project.

GENERAL FOREWORD

This series of seventy-two volumes will present outstanding patristic writings and include some works never translated before. The translations, although done by American Catholic scholars, are destined neither for scholars only, nor exclusively for Catholics, but for the entire English-speaking world. They will be kept as close as possible to the meaning and the spirit of the original as is compatible with the character of modern English. Introductions will familiarize the reader with the life and works of the authors. While all annotations will be brief, a select bibliography may serve as means for further study.

In the summer of 1936 I first conceived the plan of publishing a series of the Fathers in English. In this venture I was encouraged by my old teacher and friend, the great scholar A. Dyroff. I am well aware of the great responsibility I took upon myself in finally launching the project and of the great labor it involves. I cannot but be grateful for the splendid comments the announcement of the series has received in the secular as well as in the religious press. The assistance of a distinguished and experienced Editorial Board and the collaboration of eminent and competent men engaged in the translations encourage my hope that this series may become, with the help of Almighty God, one of the great monuments of Christian scholarship in America.

March 12, 1946   LUDWIG SCHOPP

SUPPLEMENTARY STATEMENT

Twenty-three years have elapsed since Dr. Schopp, the founder of this series and its first Editorial Director, wrote his challenging General Foreword. Since then a close approach has already been made to the early goal of seventy-two volumes, and our sights have been set on a total of not less than a hundred volumes. More important is a change in policy in respect of our translators. Whatever could have been said at the time for a restriction observed in the earlier volumes, it should now be stated that for some years the series has been enriched by the collaboration of scholars who were neither American nor Roman Catholic. We welcome the collaboration of any who would join us in making the Fathers of the Church better known to readers of English. This important policy revision apart, Dr. Schopp's General Foreword still serves to declare the aim and scope of our undertaking.

BERNARD M. PEEBLES
Editorial Director

February 25, 1969

THE
APOSTOLIC FATHERS

TRANSLATED

by

FRANCIS X. GLIMM

JOSEPH M.-F. MARIQUE, S.J.

† GERALD G. WALSH, S.J.

THE CATHOLIC UNIVERSITY OF AMERICA PRESS
Washington, D.C.

NIHIL OBSTAT:

JOHN M. FEARNS, S.T.D.
CENSOR LIBRORUM

IMPRIMATUR:

✠ FRANCIS CARDINAL SPELLMAN
ARCHBISHOP OF NEW YORK

April 3, 1947

Library of Congress Catalog Card No.: 47-31345
ISBN-13: 978-0-8132-1549-5 (pbk)

Copyright © 1947 by
THE CATHOLIC UNIVERSITY OF AMERICA PRESS, INC.
All rights reserved
Second Printing 1948
Third Printing 1962
Fourth Printing 1969
Fifth Printing 1981
First paperback reprint 2008

INTRODUCTION

WORLD WAR II was hardly over before the movement of Christian intellectual reconversion was far on its way. One of the first signs of this new life was the effort of Dr. Ludwig Schopp to interest American scholars in a new translation of the classics of early Christian literature. His general policy and preliminary plans had, in fact, been already formulated before the outbreak of the war.

Dr. Schopp's dream was of a collaborative effort—both American and Catholic—in which the best available scholarship in theology, patristics, history and classical philology could combine to produce an accurate, readable, moderately priced and thoroughly modern rendering of the precious literature of the first seven centuries of the Christian era.

The present volume, *The Apostolic Fathers,*[1] is the first of a projected series of seventy-two. It contains but a sample—though a notable one—of the treasury of wisdom, culture, heroism and holiness revealed in early Christianity. The volume should make an appeal to every Christian mind and heart—and, not least, to those who, by the vicissitudes of later history, have become separated from the center of Catholic unity. The Apostolic Fathers wrote at a time when heresy and schism had, indeed, begun their perennial work of religious corrosion, but long before the great constitutional revolts of Constantinople and Canterbury from Rome had wrought their seemingly irreparable damage to the seamless robe. In these primitive writings, as in a mirror, all Christians whose minds and wills and souls are wholly set on the Truth

---

1 The Apostolic Fathers is a collective name, in use since the 17th century, for a group of Christian writers who either were or were believed to be disciples of the Apostles. Cf. Bihlmeyer, *Die apostolischen Väter* (Tübingen 1924) VIIf.

and Way and Life of Jesus Christ will find a dogmatic creed, a moral code, an ecclesiastical constitution and, above all, an inward character of devotional, supernatural, sacramental life that are self-authenticating. In the presence of martyrs, saints, scholars and simple souls like Pope Clement of Rome or Bishop Ignatius of Antioch or Polycarp of Smyrna or the author of the *Didache* or the *Shepherd* or the *Letter to Diognetus* no one will feel inclined to apply such labels as 'Romanism' or 'Byzantinism,' or 'Protestantism.' And, on the other hand, there is no Christian who will not feel that he has the right—and still more the duty—to ask himself whether his heart burns, as these early Christian hearts burned, with love for Jesus Christ, our Lord; whether his mind is as clear as these minds were clear in regard to the Mystery of the Blessed Trinity, the Divinity of Jesus Christ, the necessity of inward communion with the Holy Spirit and of outward communion with the government of one, holy, Catholic and Apostolic Church; whether his soul is nourished, as these souls were nourished, with the sacraments—and, especially, the Eucharistic sacrament—of which there is here such unmistakable witness.

As subsequent volumes of this series are published, it should become clearer not only to Christians but to others as well that, during the first seven centuries that followed the passion and resurrection of Jesus Christ, men of towering genius and of heroic mold, born in many lands and in different ages, men of diverse character, education, racial origin and political background, men inclined to defend their own brilliant and original opinions and the cherished customs of their own locality sought and found a common life, a common bond of love, a common source of spiritual strength that leveled frontiers and made them members of a single family.

Men who do not admit the full claims of Christianity will read these documents with some interest. Even those who take pride in the 'modern mind' and the 'contemporary mood' will feel little sense of intellectual superiority when they meet the minds of men like Athanasius, Basil or Augustine. It will be still harder to entertain any feeling of moral superiority in the presence of men like Ignatius of Antioch, Cyprian of Carthage or Chrysostom of Constantinople. Those who imagine that Christianity involves some kind of passive conformism will be startled by the aggressive tenacity of men like Irenaeus, Hippolytus or Jerome. And those who insist that convictions should emerge from genuine debate will learn something from the subtle and vigorous polemics with heretics as skillful as Novatian, Sabellius, Donatus, Arius, Eunomius, Macedonius, Apollinaris, Pelagius and Nestorius. There was every reason in (or, at least, of) the world why the Fathers might have been tempted to abandon or modify the dogmatic, moral and sacramental tradition of the Apostles. There is here an intellectual and religious problem that no man of good will can dismiss without, at least, the courtesy of inquiry.

As for modern sectarian Christianity, the shibboleths of controversy lose their force in the face of this massive evidence. Phrases like 'corruptions in doctrine and discipline' look rather ridiculous when the 'corruptions' are traced back, in an unbroken line, from the seventh, to the fourth, to the first century. Or, to take an obvious example, who can be inclined to accuse a thoroughly Oriental bishop of the first century like Ignatius of Antioch of, let us say, 'the later legal constitutionalism' of the Latin spirit? Yet no Latin Father was ever so strong for the hierarchic position of bishops and no modern 'Romanist' was ever more flattering in speaking of the primacy of Rome than the Syrian bishop of Antioch.

In general, these Fathers will prove to be a reproach to all narrowness and exclusivism. If we are inclined to minimize theological speculation in the interests of religious activism, we have the long tradition of the Greek Fathers to reproach us. Or, again, if we tend to emphasize personal feeling at the expense of public ecclesiastical order, we have the equally authentic tradition of the Latin Fathers. If humanistic culture should seem to us a danger to the purity of Christian convictions, we have the *Letter to Diognetus,* the *Octavius* of Minucius Felix, the exhortations of St. Basil to correct our 'puritanism.' If ever we forget the part that Christian poetry has played in the propagation of Christian truth, we have only to recall the hymns and lyric lines of Ambrose, Ephraem, Pope Damasus, Prudentius and Boethius. If discussion and dogmatic debate seem to us a violation of Scriptural simplicity and of Christian charity, almost any of these volumes—and particularly any of the volumes which cover the fourth century—will serve to shock us from our intellectual inertia. And if we think that the last word has been said on any matter of Christian love, or life or learning, we need only note the never-ending effort of these followers of the Apostles to develop (without deforming) the meaning of all the Apostles said and did and suffered.

THE EDITORS

CONTENTS

THE LETTER

OF

ST. CLEMENT OF ROME

TO THE CORINTHIANS

Translated

by

FRANCIS X. GLIMM, S.T.L.

Seminary of the Immaculate Conception

Huntington, N. Y.

INTRODUCTION

THE REPUTATION of St. Clement, the third successor
of St. Peter as Bishop of Rome, was so great that
even in antiquity numerous legends grew up about
him and apocryphal writings were circulated under his name.
We are here concerned only with the few authentic facts
about him that are known through ancient authors. It is possible that he is the 'fellow-worker' mentioned by St. Paul in
the Epistle to the Philippians (4.3), as both Origen and
Eusebius assert. The ancient lists of the Popes, including that
found in Irenaeus,[1] agree in showing him as the third successor of St. Peter. A detail added by Tertullian[2] and taken
for granted by numerous apocryphal writings attributed to
Clement is that he was ordained by St. Peter and was a kind
of auxiliary bishop to St. Linus and St. Cletus, his immediate
papal predecessors. His own pontificate, extending from about
A.D. 90 to 99, would fall within the reigns of Domitian, Nerva,
and Trajan. Efforts to identify him with the imperial house
of the Flavii and with the consul Titus Flavius Clemens,
cousin of Domitian, have been futile. The story of his exile
and martyrdom in the Tauric Chersonese is likewise a late
legend. The exact date and the manner of his death are unknown. His feast is celebrated on November 23. Excavations
have made it seem probable that the Basilica of St. Clement
at Rome, one of the earliest *tituli* or parish churches of the
city is actually built on the site of his home.

---

1 Irenaeus, *Adversus haereses* 3.3.3.
2 Tertullian, *De praescriptione* 32.

3

We know of only one authentic writing of St. Clement,
the *Epistle to the Corinthians.* In form it is a letter of the
Church of Rome to the Church of Corinth, and in its body
the name of Clement does not appear. It is not, however,
as Kirsopp Lake suggests,[3] anonymous. In fact, all the known
manuscripts, six in number, attribute it to Clement, who is,
moreover, named as its author by Dionysius of Corinth, Origen, Irenaeus, and Eusebius. Other citations from the second
and third centuries attest to its early circulation and popularity.

The occasion of the letter was a schism in the Church of
Corinth. This unfortunate incident must have caused wide-
spread repercussions at the time, since both Irenaeus and
Eusebius speak of it retrospectively as a matter of general
concern. The names of the leaders of the schism, however,
have not come down to us, nor have any details about the
specific issues involved. From St. Clement's letter we gather
that a group of lay persons had succeeded in ousting all or
most of the higher clergy, or had persuaded a large portion
of the community to alienate themselves from the presbyters,
an action declared to be not only unauthorized but unjustified.
The letter insists, moreover, that the lives of these presbyters
had so far been blameless and that the cause of the quarrel
was simply 'envy and jealousy.'

The letter is very lengthy and carefully planned. An appeal
is made to the whole congregation at Corinth, in the name of
charity and for the sake of Christ, to end this scandal. In
great detail the obedience and humility of the saints of the
Old Testament are brought forward as examples. Then
Christ's obedience to His Father and the heroic submission
of the recent martyrs, and particularly Sts. Peter and Paul,

---

3 K. Lake, *The Apostolic Fathers* (Loeb Classical Library, London and
New York 1912) 1. 337.

are all reviewed in order to bring the Corinthians to a sense of obedience to God and the officers of His Church.

In the course of this long appeal Clement advances in support of his reasons for unity and charity a great deal of incidental information which gives his letter great importance among the Apostolic Fathers.

In this letter the Roman Church is seen as holding an impressive position of authority, intervening as it did in the internal affairs of the Corinthian Church without being requested to do so (47.6-7). The language used in the letter is more than once threatening. A delegation of three men brought the letter to Corinth, and the Corinthians were instructed that these delegates themselves were to return with confirmation of a settlement of the schism. This attitude is remarkable, and its implications have not been mistaken by such historians of the early Church as Lightfoot, Harnack, and Lietzmann. The ancient history of the Church shows no similar letter of rebuke and reproval sent by one Christian community to another, and we judge that none would have been received except from Rome. The respect and honor paid to the letter by the Corinthians was not short-lived. Evidence found in Eusebius[4] shows that it received regular public reading at Corinth as late as nearly a century after its composition.

Of no slight importance is the information furnished by the letter on the hierarchical organization of the Church. The higher clergy are clearly designated as 'bishops and deacons' (42.4) but from Ch. 44 it is clear that the term 'bishops' (episkopoi, lit., overseers) is used synonymously with presbúteroi, i.e., to designate—as in Acts 20.17, 28 and the letters of St. Paul—the college of priests. It is clearly stated that the

---

4 Eusebius, *Historia ecclesiastica* 4.23.11.

community had no right to depose them: they derived their authority not from the congregation, but directly from the Apostles, who acted according to the instructions of Christ (42; 44). Their principal duty was the offering of the sacrifice (44.4). We must remember that in Apostolic times the function of a 'bishop' in the proper sense, and especially the power of ordination, was still exercised, without restriction to a local church, by the Apostles themselves or their delegates (Titus, Timothy), and thereafter by those 'other eminent men' whom St. Clement mentions (44.3) as the successors of the Apostles. It is from these, and not from the local college of *episkopoi-presbúteroi* that the office of the one bishop who in each local church ordains and presides over priests and deacons (so already St. Ignatius, *ad Philad.* 4; 7; *ad Trall.* 2; 3, etc.) is derived.

Students of the liturgies have a document of high importance in the lengthy prayer of thanksgiving (59.4-61.3), which sounds very much like the beginning of the ancient Eucharistic canon.

For the historian the letter contains a tantalizing assembly of allusions to facts too well known to the Corinthians to require elaboration by Clement. Details would have been welcomed of the 'multitude' of martyrdoms at Rome, including those of Sts. Peter and Paul mentioned in Chapters 5 and 6. Concerning the latter it is stated that he journeyed 'to the confines of the West,' evidence which, originating at Rome, supports the position that the Apostle traveled to Spain. Indication of the circulation of St. Paul's *Epistles to the Corinthians* is found in the instruction to the Corinthians to 'take up the letter' which 'blessed Paul the Apostle' had written them.

Corroborative evidence for the early date of the letter is found in the Scriptural quotations. Those from the Old

Testament are frequent and lengthy. Anything that may be taken as a quotation from the New Testament is not specified as such. Instead, we find a large number of phrases and sentences which may be thought of as part of the normal vocabulary of the newly founded Church, rather than as intentional quotations. The text followed in the present translation is that of Karl Bihlmeyer, *Die apostolischen Väter* (Tübingen 1924).

SELECT BIBLIOGRAPHY

Texts and Translations:

J. B. Lightfoot, *The Apostolic Fathers* . . . revised texts with short introductions and English translations . . . edited and completed by J. R. Harmer (London 1891).

K. Lake, *The Apostolic Fathers*, with English translation (Loeb Classical Library, New York 1912) 1.

K. Bihlmeyer, *Die apostolischen Väter*, Neubearbeitung der Funkschen Ausgabe (Tübingen 1924).

W. K. Lowther Clarke, *The First Epistle of Clement to the Corinthians* (London 1937).

C. T. Schaefer, *S. Clementis Romani Epistula ad Corinthios quae vocatur prima graece et latine* (Florilegium Patristicum, fasc. 44 Bonnae 1941).

J. A. Kleist, *The Epistles of St. Clement of Rome and St. Ignatius of Antioch* (Ancient Christian Writers, Westminster 1946).

Secondary Works:

O. Bardenhewer, *Geschichte der altkirchlichen Literatur* (2nd. ed. Freiburg i. Br. 1913) 1, 119 ff.

G. Edmundson, *The Church in Rome in the first century* (London, 1913. The Bampton Lectures).

A. Ehrhard, *Die altchristliche Literatur und ihre Erforschung seit 1880*, 2 vols. (Freiburg 1894/1900).

THE LETTER OF ST. CLEMENT TO THE CORINTHIANS[1] ~96

THE CHURCH OF GOD which dwells as a pilgrim in Rome to the Church of God in pilgrimage at Corinth —to you who have been called and made holy by the will of God through our Lord Jesus Christ. May you be filled with grace and peace from Almighty God through Jesus Christ.[2]

Chapter 1

1 Dear brothers, because of the sudden misfortunes and calamities which have fallen upon us, one after another,[1] we have been, we confess, somewhat tardy in turning our attention to the matters in dispute, and especially to the abominable and unholy schism, among you.[2] It is a thing alien and foreign to those who have been called by God. It was started by a handful of impetuous and self-opinionated persons. It has been inflamed to such a degree of madness that your name, once so well known and loved and revered by all, has suffered a grave reproach. 2 There was a time when everyone who lived among you thought highly of the

---

1 The title, not forming part of the original letter, varies in the manuscripts: 'To the Corinthians,' 'Epistle of Clement to the Corinthians,' 'Clement to the Corinthians.'

2 This salutation has noticeable resemblances to that of St .Paul's First Epistle to the Corinthians and to St. Peter's First Epistle, and may have been the model for that used for the *Martyrdom of Polycarp*.

---

1 This is understood to refer to the recent persecution under Domitian, A.D. 95

2 One may note that a firm stand is taken at the start.

full virtue and firmness of your faith, admired the sweet reasonableness of your Christian piety, heralded abroad your reputation for unbounded hospitality, and praised the fullness and soundness of your knowledge.[3] 3 You did all things without respect of persons and walked in accordance with the commands of God—subject to those in office and properly respectful to the presbyters of your community. You educated the minds of your young men to moderation and modesty. You exhorted girls to do their duty with a blameless, modest, and pure conscience. And you taught married women to love their husbands as they should, to be subject to them according to the rule of obedience, and to manage their homes with piety and much wisdom.

Chapter 2

1 Every one of you used to walk in humbleness of mind, without boasting, preferring to obey rather than to command, to give rather than to receive,[1] satisfied with the rations[2] served by Christ. You gave heed to His words; you were careful to keep them in your hearts; His sufferings were before your eyes. 2 Thus to all were granted a deep and radiant peace and an untiring longing to do good, and there came upon all an abundant outpouring of the Holy Spirit. 3 You were filled with holy counsel and in pious zeal and reverent confidence you stretched forth your hands to Almighty God, beseeching Him to be merciful to your involuntary shortcomings. 4 Day and night you kept up your efforts

---

3 'Knowledge' (Greek *gnosis*) means a deep understanding of the mysteries of the Christian faith. The word is much favored by St. Paul.

---

1 Cf. Acts. 20.35.

2 The Greek word *ephódia* (literally 'things for the journey,' Latin *viaticum*) was especially appropriate in military usage.

on behalf of the whole brotherhood, so that, with mercy and compassion, the full number of His chosen ones might be saved. 5 You were pure and simple and forgiving toward one another. 6 All sedition and schism of any sort was abominated by you. You wept for the failings of your neighbors and you reckoned as your own their shortcomings. 7 You were without regret for any good you had done and were ready to 'undertake any kind of honorable service.'[3] 8 Adorned with the habits of virtue and reverence, you performed all your duties in the fear of God. The commandments and ordinances of the Lord 'were written on the tablets of your heart.'[4]

Chapter 3

1 All glory and greatness was granted you,[1] and what the Scripture said was fulfilled: 'My beloved ate and drank, and was enlarged and grew fat and kicked.'[2] 2 From this came jealousy and envy,[3] quarreling and dissension, persecution and disorder, war and captivity. 3 Thus the 'unhonored' rose up against those 'in honor,'[4] those without reputation against those with a good name, the foolish against the wise, 'the young against their elders.'[5] 4 The reason why

---

3 Titus 3.1 (Msgr. Ronald Knox's translation—London 1944).
4 Prov. 7.3.

---

1 Whether the Corinthians specifically deserved all this praise or not, we have here St. Clement's ideal picture of the Christian community. With the end of this sentence the tone of commendation changes to one of rebuke.
2 Deut. 32.15.
3 The phrase 'jealousy and envy' and its equivalents will be repeated many times. St. Clement evidently regarded these vices as the explanation of the whole trouble at Corinth, as well of all past persecutions and troubles.
4 Isa. 3.5.
5 *Ibid.*

righteousness and peace are far removed[6] is because each one
abandons the fear of God, becomes blind in the things of
His faith, does not walk in the ways of His commandments,
and does not live worthy of Christ. Instead, each one pro-
ceeds according to the evil desires of his heart, yielding to
a wicked and impious jealousy, by which also 'death came
into the world.'[7]

Chapter 4

1 For it is written thus:[1] 'And it came to pass after some
days that Cain from the fruits of the earth offered a sacrifice
to God, and Abel also offered of the first born of the sheep
and their fat. 2 And God looked on Abel and his gifts, but
He did not regard Cain and his sacrifices. 3 And Cain was
greatly grieved and his countenance fell. 4 And God said to
Cain: "Why are you pained and why has your countenance
fallen? If you have offered rightly but not divided rightly,
have you not committed sin? 5 Restrain your envy; you can
repel it, and you must control it."[2] 6 And Cain said to Abel
his brother: "Let us go into the plain." And it happened
while they were in the plain that Cain rose up against Abel
his brother and killed him.' 7 You see, brothers—jealousy
and envy brought about the murder of a brother. 8 Because
of jealousy our father Jacob fled from the face of Esau his

---

6 Isa. 59.14.
7 Wisd. 2.24.

---

1 The narrative contained in the first six sections of the chapter is
partly a translation, partly a paraphrase of Gen. 4.3-8. Here, as
elsewhere, the author at will makes free use of Scriptural texts.
2 The Greek text of the passage is obscure. The translation has been
brought somewhat into line with the Hebrew, which itself is not
wholly clear.

brother.³ 9 Jealousy caused Joseph to be pursued to death,
and to become enslaved.⁴ 10 Jealousy compelled Moses to
flee from the face of Pharaoh, King of Egypt, when he was
asked by his countryman:⁵ 'Who set you up as a judge or arbi-
ter over us? Do you wish to kill me as you killed the Egyptian
yesterday?' 11 Through jealousy Aaron and Miriam were
lodged outside the camp.⁶ 12 Jealousy plunged Dathan and
Abiron alive into Hades for having rebelled against Moses
the servant of God.⁷ 13 Because of jealousy David received
ill will not alone from foreigners, but was persecuted even
by Saul, King of Israel.⁸

Chapter 5

1 But, to leave the ancient examples, let us come to the
heroes¹ nearest ourselves; let us consider the noble examples
of our own generation. 2 Through jealousy and envy the
greatest and holiest pillars² [of the Church] were persecuted,
and they endured to the death.³ 3 Let us put before our eyes
the good apostles: 4 Peter, because of unrighteous jealousy,
underwent not one or two but many sufferings, and having

---

3 Gen. 27.41. Note how the Gentile Christians spoke of Jacob as 'our
 father.'
4 E.g., Gen. 37.5.
5 Exod. 2.14.
6 Cf. Num. 12; 16.
7 Num. 61; 26.9; Deut. 11.6.
8 1 Kings 18.8-9.

---

1 The Greek word, athletés, means combatant, champion.
2 Cf. Gal. 2.9.
3 The two martyrdoms occurred in the reign of Nero, A.D. 54-68. See
 also note on 6.1 below.

thus borne testimony[4] went to his well-deserved place of glory. 5 Because of jealousy and dissension Paul pointed out the way to the reward of endurance: 6 Seven times he was put in chains; he was banished, stoned;[5] he became a herald in the East and in the West and received the noble renown of his faith. 7 He taught righteousness to the whole world, and after reaching the confines of the West,[6] and having given testimony before rulers, passed from the world and was taken up to the Holy Place, having become the outstanding model of endurance.

Chapter 6

1 Besides these men who lived such holy lives, there was a great multitude of the elect who suffered many outrages because of jealousy and became a shining example among us.[1] 2 It was because of jealousy that women were paraded as Danaids and Dircae and put to death after they had suffered horrible and cruel indignities. They kept up the race

---

4 The Greek verb *marturéo* in Christian usage implies courageous testimony to the faith, not necessarily (as in this case) sealed by death. The Latin *confiteor* was used with the same meanings. Hence the two words 'martyr' and 'confessor.' An important study is that of H. Delehaye, S. J., 'Martyr et confesseur' in *Analecta Bollandiana* 39 (1921) 20-49.

5 See St. Paul's summary of his persecutions, 2 Cor. 11.23 ff. and the appropriate references to Acts.

6 See Introduction.

---

1 These are presumably the Christians whose execution under Nero is described by Tacitus, *Annals* 15.44, where his phrase *multitudo ingens* agrees closely with the 'great multitude' of St. Clement. The phrase with which the sentence ends, 'among us,' localizes at Rome the martyrdoms of which St. Clement is here immediately speaking and, by a compelling inference, those of Sts. Peter and Paul. For the 'great multitude' of martyrs see *Roman Martyrology* 24 June.

of faith to the finish and, despite their physical weakness, won the prize they deserved. 3 It was jealousy that separated wives from their husbands and changed the saying of our father Adam, 'This is now bone of my bone and flesh of my flesh.'² 4 Jealousy and quarreling have destroyed great cities and uprooted mighty nations.

Chapter 7

1 These things, dearly beloved, we are writing, not only to warn you, but also to remind ourselves; for we are in the same arena, and the same contest lies before us. 2 For this reason let us abandon empty and silly concerns, and come to the glorious and holy rule of our tradition. 3 Let us see what is good and pleasing and acceptable in the sight of our Maker. 4 Let us fix our gaze on the blood of Christ and realize how precious it is to His Father, seeing that it was poured out for our salvation and brought the grace of conversion to the whole world. 5 Let us look back over all the generations, and learn that from generation to generation the Lord has given an opportunity of repentance¹ to all who would return to Him. 6 Noe preached penance,² and those who heeded were saved. Then Jonas announced destruction to the Ninivites and they repented of their sins,³ besought God in prayer and, estranged though they were from God, obtained salvation.

---

2 Gen. 2.23.

---

1 Wisd. 12.10.
2 Gen. 7.
3 Jonas 3; Matt. 12.41.

Chapter 8

1 The ministers of God's grace preached on repentance[1] with the help of the Holy Spirit. 2 And the Lord of all things Himself spoke of repentance, with an oath:[2] 'For as I live, saith the Lord, I desire not the death of the sinner but his repentance.' He added this kindly assurance: 3 'Repent, O house of Israel, of your wickedness. Say to the sons of my people: "If your sins reach from the earth to Heaven, and if they be redder than scarlet, and blacker than sackcloth, and you return to Me with all your heart and say, Father, I will listen to you as a holy people." ' 4 And in another place He speaks thus:[3] 'Wash and cleanse yourselves, put away wickedness out of your souls from before my eyes, cease from your wickedness, learn to do good, seek judgment, rescue the oppressed, give judgment to the fatherless and justice to the widow, and come and let us consider together, saith the Lord; and if your sins be as scarlet, I will make them white as snow, and if they be as crimson, I will whiten them as wool; and if you be willing and listen to me, you shall eat the good things of the earth, but if you be unwilling and listen not to me, a sword shall devour you, for the mouth of the Lord has spoken these things.' 5 Desiring therefore that all His beloved should share in repentance, He established it by His Almighty Will.

Chapter 9

1 And so let us obey His magnanimous and glorious will.

---

1 In view of the controversy which sprang up later (cf. *The Shepherd of Hermas*), it should be noticed that this chapter establishes the true teaching of the Church on repentance and foregiveness of sins, without any limitations of kind or number.
2 Ezech. 33.11.
3 Isa. 1.16-20.

Let us become suppliants of His mercy and kindness and prostrate ourselves and turn to His compassion. Let us abandon vain effort and quarreling and the jealousy which leads to death. 2 Let us fix our gaze on those who have perfectly served His magnificent glory. 3 Let us take Henoch, who was found righteous in obedience, and was taken up, without there being a trace of his death.[1] 4 Noe was found faithful by reason of his service; he proclaimed a new birth to the world, and through him the Lord saved the living creatures who entered in harmony into the Ark.[2]

Chapter 10

1 Abraham, who was called 'the Friend,'[1] proved himself faithful by becoming obedient to the words of Cod. 2 It was through obedience that he went out from his country, and from his kindred and from his father's house. It was by leaving a small country and a weak kindred and a small household that he hoped to inherit the promises of God. For He says to him:[2] 3 'Depart from thy country and from thy kindred and from thy father's house, to the land which I shall show thee, and I will make of thee a great nation, and I will bless thee, and I will magnify thy name, and thou shalt be blessed. And I will bless them that bless thee, and I will curse them that curse thee, and in thee shall all the families of the earth be blessed.' 4 And again, when he separated from Lot, God said to him:[3] 'Lift up thine eyes and look from the place where thou art now, to the North and to the

---

1 Gen. 5.24; Heb. 11.5.
2 Gen. 6.8; 7.1; Heb. 11.7; 2 Peter 2.5.

---

1 Isa. 41.8; James 2.23.
2 Gen. 12.1-3.
3 Gen. 13.14-16.

South and to the East and to the West; for all the land which thou seest I will give to thee and to thy seed for ever. 5 And I will make thy seed as the dust of the earth. If a man can count the dust of the earth, then can thy seed be counted also.' 6 And again He says:[4] 'God brought Abraham forth and said to him, "Look up to the heaven and count the stars if thou canst count them. So shall thy seed be." And Abraham believed God, and this was reputed to him for justice.' 7 Because of his faith and hospitality a son was given him in his old age, and it was through obedience that he offered him as a sacrifice to God on the mountain which He showed him.[5]

Chapter 11

1 Because of his hospitality and piety Lot was saved from Sodom, when the whole region round about was judged by fire and brimstone.[1] The Lord made clear that He does not abandon those who hope in Him, but that He delivers to punishment and torture those who turn away. 2 For as his wife was going out with him, becoming of a different mind and not remaining in harmony, she was turned into a sign. She became a pillar of salt and remains so to this day, so that all may know that the double-minded and the doubters of God's power come into judgment and become a warning to all generations.[2]

Chapter 12

1 Because of her faith and hospitality Rahab the harlot

---

4 Gen. 15.5,6; Rom. 4.3.
5 Gen. 18-22 embrace the incidents referred to. Cf. Heb. 11.17.

---

1 Gen. 19; 2 Peter 2.6,7.
2 Cf. Luke 17.32.

was saved.[1] 2 For when spies had been sent to Jericho by Josue the son of Nun,[2] the king of the land knew that they had come to spy on his country and sent men to capture them, so that when they were taken they might be put to death. 3 So the hospitable Rahab received them and hid them in the top of the house under stalks of flax. 4 And when the men from the king came and said: 'The men spying on our land came into thee; bring them out, for the king has so commanded,' she answered, pointing for them in the opposite direction: 'The men whom you seek did indeed come to me, but they left immediately and are continuing on their journey.' 5 And she said to the men: 'I surely know that the Lord God is giving you this land, for the fear and dread of you has fallen upon all its inhabitants. When therefore you shall have taken it, save me and my father's house.' 6 And they said to her: 'It will be just as thou hast requested us; as soon as thou knowest that we are on the way, gather all thy people under thy roof and they shall be saved; for as many as shall be found outside will be killed.' 7 And they gave her a sign, that she should hang from her house something scarlet in color, clearly indicating beforehand that through the blood of the Lord will redemption come to all who believe and hope in God. 8 You see, beloved, that not only faith but also prophecy is found in this woman.

Chapter 13

1 Let us, therefore, be humble-minded, brothers, putting away all boasting and conceit and silliness and anger, and let

---

1 This story of Rahab is partly quoted and partly summarized from Josue 1-2. Rahab is also used as an example in James 2.25 and Heb. 11.31.

2 St. Clement, following the Septuagint, has 'Jesus, son of Nave.'

us do what is written, for the Holy Spirit says:[1] 'Let not the
wise man glory in his wisdom, nor let the strong man glory
in his strength, nor the rich man in his riches, but let him that
glories glory in the Lord, to seek Him and to do judgment
and justice.' Especially should we remember the words which
the Lord Jesus spoke, when He taught clemency and long-
suffering. 2 For He spoke thus:[2] 'Be merciful, that you may
obtain mercy. Forgive, that you may be forgiven. As you do,
so shall it be done to you. As you give, so shall it be given
to you. As you judge, so shall you be judged. As you are
kind, so shall you be treated kindly. With what measure you
measure, with the same shall it be measured to you.' 3 In
this commandment and in this counsel let us strengthen
ourselves to walk obedient to His holy words, being humble-
minded, for the Holy Writ says:[3] 4 'On whom shall I have
regard except on the meek and gentle and him who trembles
at My words.'

Chapter 14

1 And so, brothers, it is right and holy for us to be obedient to God rather than to follow those who in arrogance
and insubordination are the leaders in abominable jealousy.
2 For we shall suffer no ordinary harm, but run a very great
risk, if we rashly entrust ourselves to the designs of men who
aim at strife and sedition, to alienate us from what is right.
3 Let us be kind to one another after the model of the compassion and sweetness of Him who made us. 4 For it is

---

1 Jer. 9.23-24; 1 Kings 2.10; 1 Cor. 1.31;   2 Cor. 10.17.
2 These quotations from Christ's Sermon on the Mount are probably
   derived from oral tradition rather than from the written gospels. See
   Matt. 5.7; 6.14,15; 7.1,12 and Luke 6.31, 36-38.
3 Isa. 66.2.

written:[1] 'The kindly shall remain inhabitants of the land, and the innocent shall be left upon it; but the lawbreakers shall be entirely destroyed from off it.' 5 And again He says:[2] 'I saw the wicked lifted up and exalted as the cedars of Lebanon. And I passed by, and behold, he was no more, and I sought his place, and did not find it. Conserve innocence and regard righteousness; for there is a remnant for the peaceful man.'

Chapter 15

1 And so let us cleave to those who are peaceable in piety and not to those who desire peace in hypocrisy. 2 For He says in one place:[1] 'This people honors me with their lips, but their heart is far from me.' 3 And again:[2] 'They blessed with their mouth, but they cursed in their heart.' 4 And again He says:[3] 'They loved Him with their mouth, and they lied to Him with their tongue, and their heart was not right with Him, nor were they faithful in His covenant.' 5 Therefore, 'Let the deceitful lips which speak iniquity against the just man become mute.'[4] And again,[5] 'May the Lord destroy all the lying lips, the tongues that boast, and those who say: "Let us magnify our tongue, our lips are our own, who is lord over us?" 6 Because of the misery of the poor and the groans of the needy, now I will arise, says the Lord, I will set him in safety; 7 I will deal plainly with him.'

---

1 Ps. 36.9,11,38; Prov. 2.21,22.
2 Ps. 36.35-37.

---

1 Isa: 29.13; Mark 7.6.
2 Ps. 61.5.
3 Ps. 77.36,37.
4 Ps. 30.19.
5 Ps. 11.4-6.

Chapter 16

1 For Christ belongs to the humble-minded, not to those who exalt themselves above His flock. 2 The scepter of the majesty of God, the Lord Jesus Christ, came not in the pomp of boasting or of arrogance, though He was mighty; but he was humble-minded, as the Holy Spirit spoke concerning Him. For He says:[1] 3 'Lord, who has believed our report, and to whom is the arm of the Lord revealed? We announced in his presence—he is as a child, as a root in thirsty ground. There is no beauty in him, nor comeliness, and we have seen him, and he had neither form nor beauty, but his form was without honor, deficient in comparison with the form of men; a man living in stripes and hardships, and knowing how to bear weakness, for his face was turned away, and he was despised and not blessed. 4 This is he who bears our sins and is hurt for us, and we regarded him as subject to pain and stripes and affliction. 5 But he was wounded for our iniquities, he was bruised for our sins. The chastisement of our peace was upon him, and by his bruises we are healed. 6 We all went astray like sheep; everyone went astray in his own way. 7 And the Lord delivered him up for our sins, and he did not open his mouth on account of his affliction. As a sheep he was led to the slaughter, and as a lamb dumb before its shearer he opens not his mouth. In humiliation his judgment was taken away. 8 Who shall declare his generation? For his life is taken away from the earth. 9 For the iniquities of my people he has come to death. 10 And I will give the wicked for his burial, and the rich for his death; for he did no iniquity, nor was deceit found in his mouth. And the Lord wills to purify him from his wounds. 11 If you make an offering for sin, your soul shall see a seed with long life. 12

---

1 Isa. 53.1-12.

And the Lord wills to take from the labor of his soul, to show him light and to form him in understanding, to justify a righteous man who serves many well. And he himself shall bear their sins. 13 On this account he shall inherit many, and shall share the spoils of the strong; because his soul was delivered to death, and he was counted among the wicked. 14 And he bore the sins of many, and for their sins he was delivered up.' 15 And again He says Himself:[2] 'But I am a worm and no man, the reproach of men, and the outcast of the people. 16 All who saw me laughed me to scorn, they spoke with their lips, they shook their heads [saying], "He hoped in the Lord; let Him deliver him, let Him save him, seeing that he delights in Him." ' 17 You see, beloved, what is the example given to us. For if the Lord was thus humble-minded, what shall we do who through Him have come under the yoke of His grace ?

Chapter 17

1 Let us become imitators also of those who went about 'in goatskins and sheepskins,'[1] preaching the coming of Christ. We mean Elias and Eliseus, and also Ezechiel, the prophets, and beside them the famous men of old. 2 Abraham was greatly praised and was proclaimed the 'Friend of God,' and he in his humility, fixing his gaze on the Glory of God, says:[2] 'But I am dust and ashes.' 3 Besides, it is also written thus concerning Job:[3] 'And Job was righteous and blameless, true, a worshipper of God, keeping himself from all evil.' 4 But

---

2 Ps. 21.7-9.

---

1 Heb. 11.37.
2 Gen. 18.27.
3 Job. 1.1.

he accuses himself, saying:[4] 'No one is pure from defilement, not even if his life be but for a single day.' 5 Moses was called 'faithful in all his household,'[5] and through his instrumentality God judged Egypt with their plagues and torments. But even he, when he was given great praise, did not utter proud words, but when an oracle was given him at the bush, said: 'Who am I, that Thou sendest me? I am feeble of speech and slow of tongue.'[6] 6 And again he says: 'But I am as smoke from a pot.'[7]

Chapter 18

1 What shall we say of the celebrated David, to whom God said:[1] 'I have found a man after my own heart, David the son of Jesse, in eternal mercy I have anointed him.' 2 But even he says to God:[2]

'Have mercy on me, O God, according to Thy great mercy, and according to the multitude of Thy tender mercies blot out my iniquity.

Wash me yet more from my iniquity, and cleanse me from my sin;

For I knew my iniquity, and my sin is always before me.

To Thee only have I sinned, and have done evil before Thee, that Thou mayst be justified in Thy words, and mayst overcome when thou art judged.

For, behold, I was conceived in iniquities, and in sins did my mother bear me.

---

4 Job 14.4,5.
5 Num. 12.7; Heb. 3.2.
6 Exod. 3.11; 4.10.
7 Source unknown.

---

1 Ps. 88.21; 1 Kings 13.14; Acts 13.22.
2 With the exception of the last two verses, this is Psalm 50, the *Miserere.*

For, behold, Thou hast loved truth; the dark and hidden
things of Thy wisdom Thou has made clear to me.
Thou shalt sprinkle me with hyssop, and I shall be cleansed;
Thou shalt wash me, and I shall be whiter than snow.
Thou shalt cause me to hear joy and gladness; the bones
that have been humbled shall rejoice.
Turn away Thy face from my sins, and blot out all my
iniquities.
Create a clean heart in me, O God, and renew a right
spirit within me.
Cast me not away from Thy face, and take not Thy Holy
Spirit from me.
Restore to me the joy of Thy salvation, and strengthen
me with Thy governing spirit.
I will teach the lawless ones Thy ways, and the impious
shall be converted to Thee.
Deliver me from the guilt of blood, O God, the God of
my salvation; my tongue shall rejoice in Thy justice.
Lord, Thou wilt open my mouth, and my lips will declare
Thy praise.
For if Thou hadst desired sacrifice, I would have given it;
with holocausts Thou wilt not be pleased.
A sacrifice to God is a contrite spirit; a contrite and hum-
bled heart God will not despise.'

Chapter 19

1 The humility and obedient submissiveness of so many
men of such proven reputations have made us better—and
not only us, but likewise our fathers before us and all who
have received His words in fear and truth. 2 Sharing, then,

in their many great and glorious deeds,[1] let us run toward
the goal of peace which from the beginning has been handed
down to us, let us look steadfastly toward the Father and
Creator of the whole world, and hold fast to His magnificent and surpassing gifts of peace and kindness to us. 3 Let
us see Him with our mind and with the eyes of the soul let
us look on His long-suffering purpose. Let us realize how
peacefully He acts toward His whole creation.

Chapter 20

1 The heavens move at His direction and are subject to
Him in tranquility.[1] 2 Day and night complete the course
assigned by Him without hindering each other. 3 Sun and
moon and the choir of stars revolve in harmony according
to His command in the orbits assigned to them, without
swerving the slightest. 4 The earth, flowering at His bidding
in due seasons, brings forth abundant food for men and beasts
and all the living beings on its surface, without reluctance
and without altering any of His arrangements. 5 The unsearchable places of the bottomless pit and the indescribable
regions of the lower world are subject to the same decrees.
6 The mass of the boundless sea, gathered together in one
place according to His plan, does not overrun the barriers
appointed to it, but acts as He commanded it. 7 For He
said:[2] 'Thus far shalt thou come, and thy wave shall be

---

1 For this sentence cf. Heb. 12.1.

---

1 This chapter, ending, as do others later, with its own doxology, is
an eloquent statement of the God-governed order in the universe.
For a comparable utterance from a pagan Greek see the 'Hymn to
Zeus' of Cleanthes; a good version in T. F. Higham and C. M. Bowra,
The Oxford Book of Greek Verse in Translation (Oxford 1938)
483-485. Comparable also, in their own ways, are the Canticle in
Dan. 3.57 ff. and St. Francis' 'Praise of Creatures.'
2 Job 38.11.

broken within thee.' 8 The ocean, impassable by men, and the worlds beyond it are regulated by the same decrees of the Lord. 9 The seasons of spring, summer, fall and winter give way in turn, one to the other, in peace. 10 The winds from the different quarters, each in its proper season, perform their service without hindrance. The ever-flowing springs, made for enjoyment and for health, unfailingly offer their breasts to sustain the life of man. The very smallest of the animals come together in harmony and in peace. 11 The great Creator and Lord of the universe commanded all these things to be at peace and in harmony; He does good to all, and more than superabundantly to us who have found refuge in His mercies through our Lord Jesus Christ. 12 To whom be glory and majesty forever and ever. Amen.

Chapter 21

1 Be on your guard, brothers, lest His many benefits turn into a judgment upon all of us. This will be so if we do not, by performing in concord virtuous deeds pleasing to Him, live lives worthy of Him. 2 For He says in one place:[1] 'The Spirit of the Lord is a light, searching the inward parts.' 3 Let us see how near He is, and that not one of our thoughts or the plans we make escapes Him. 4 It is right, then, that we should not be deserters from His will. 5 If we must offend, let it be foolish and senseless men who exalt themselves and boast in the arrogance of their reason, rather than God. 6 Let us fear the Lord Jesus, whose blood was given for us; let us respect our leaders; let us honor the presbyters; let us teach the young in the school of the fear of God. Let us guide our women toward what is good. 7 Let them reveal an exquisite

---

1 Prov. 20.27.

disposition to purity, let them exhibit an unfaltering will to be meek. Let them show forth the control of their tongue by their silence. Let them show their affection, not with partiality but in holiness, equally to all who fear God. 8 Let your children take part in the instruction which is in Christ, let them learn how powerful with God is humility, how strong is a pure love, how the fear of Him is beautiful and great and saves those who live in it in holiness with a pure mind. 9 For He is a searcher of thoughts and desires;[2] His breath is in us, and when He wills, He will take it away.

Chapter 22

1 Faith in Christ confirms all these things, for He Himself through the Holy Spirit thus calls us to Himself:[1]

'Come, children, hearken to Me; I will teach you the fear of the Lord.

Who is the man that desireth life; who loveth to see good days?

Keep thy tongue from evil, and thy lips from speaking guile.

Turn away from evil and do good; seek after peace and pursue it.

The eyes of the Lord are upon the just; and His ears unto their prayers.

But the countenance of the Lord is against them that do evil, to destroy the memory of them from the earth.

The just man cried out, and the Lord heard him, and delivered him out of all his troubles.

The tribulations of the just are many, but mercy will encompass those who hope in the Lord.'

---

2 Cf. Heb. 4.12.

---

1 Ps. 33.12-18,20; 31.10.

Chapter 23

1 The all-merciful and beneficent Father has compassion on them who fear Him, and with gentleness and kindness bestows His favors on those who approach Him with a simple mind. 2 So, let us not be double-minded, nor let our soul form false ideas about His extraordinary and glorious gifts. 3 Let that Scripture be far from us where He says:[1] 'Miserable are the double-minded who doubt in their soul and say: "These things have we heard even in the days of our fathers, and behold, we are grown old, and none of these things has happened to us." 4 O senseless men, compare yourselves to a tree. Take a vine: First it sheds its leaves, then there comes a bud, then a leaf, then a flower, and after that the unripe grape, then the full bunch.' You see how in a little time the fruit of the tree reaches its ripeness. 5 Truly His will shall be fulfilled swiftly and suddenly, as the Scripture testifies:[2] 'He shall come quickly and not delay; and the Lord shall come suddenly to his temple, the Holy One whom you expect.'

Chapter 24

1 Let us consider, beloved, how the Lord is continually revealing to us the resurrection that is to be. Of this He has constituted the Lord Jesus Christ the first-fruits, by raising Him from the dead.[1] 2 Let us look, beloved, at the resurrection in regard to the seasons. 3 Day and night demonstrate

---

1 This prophecy of unknown source is also quoted (in a longer and somewhat different form) in Chapter 11 of the pseudo-Clementine homily translated below (p. 72).
2 Cf. Isa. 14.1 (13.22 in Septuagint); Mal. 3.1.

---

1 1 Cor. 15.20.

a resurrection: the night sleeps and the day arises; the day departs and night returns. 4 Let us take the crops, to see how and in what manner the planting takes place. 5 'The sower went forth'[2] and cast each of the seeds into the ground, and they, falling on the ground dry and bare, decay. Then from their decay the greatness of the Lord's providence raises them up, and from one seed many grow up and bring forth fruit.

Chapter 25

1 Let us look at the strange phenomenon[1] which takes place in the East, that is, in the regions near Arabia. 2 There is a bird which is called the phoenix. This bird, the only one of its species, lives five hundred years. As the time of its dissolution in death approaches, it makes a nest of incense and myrrh and other spices, into which it enters when its time is completed, and dies. 3 Now, as its flesh decays a worm is born, which is nourished by the moisture of the dead bird and grows wings. Then, growing strong, it picks up that nest, in which are the bones of its predecessor, and carries them from the country of Arabia as far as Egypt, to the city called Heliopolis. 4 And in the daylight, in the sight of all, flying to the altar of the Sun, it places them there and so sets out on its return. 5 Then the priests look up the records of the years, and they find that it has come at the end of the five-hundredth year.

2 Matt. 13.3; Mark 4.3; Luke 8.5.

1 Among pagan authors who related the widely credited fable of the phoenix are Ovid, *Metamorphoses* 15.392-407; Pliny, *Natural History* 10.2; and Tacitus, *Annals* 6.34. A Christian poem on the phoenix ascribed to Lactantius may be read both in English and in Latin in Otto J. Kuhnmuench, S. J. *Early Christian Latin Poets* (Chicago 1929) 48-63. The most important systematic study on the phoenix is to be found in Roscher, *Ausführliches Lexikon der griechischen und römischen Mythologie* (Leipzig 1909) 3, 3450-3472.

Chapter 26

1 Do we think it something great and marvellous, then, if the Creator of the universe shall bring about a resurrection of those who served Him in holiness, in the confidence of a good faith, considering that He demonstrates the greatness of His promise by means even of a bird? 2 For He says somewhere:[1] 'And Thou shalt raise me up, and I will praise Thee,' and[2] 'I lay down and slept; I rose up for Thou art with me.' 3 And again, Job says:[3] 'And Thou shalt raise up this flesh of mine which has endured all these things.'

Chapter 27

1 With this hope, then, let our souls be bound to Him who is faithful in His promises[1] and just in His judgments. 2 He who commanded us not to lie will be far from lying Himself. For nothing is impossible to God, except to lie.[2] 3 Let faith in Him, then, be enkindled in us, and let us reflect that all things are near to Him. 4 By the word of His majesty He has set up all things, and by a word He can overturn them. 5 'Who shall say to Him, "What hast Thou done?" or who shall stand against the force of His power?'[3] When He wishes, and as He wishes, He will do all things, and none of the things decreed by Him shall fail. 6 All things are before Him, and nothing is hid from His planning.

7 'The heavens show forth the glory of God, and the firmament declareth the work of His hands.

1 Source unknown; cf. Ps. 27.7.
2 Cf. Ps. 3.5.
3 Job 19.26 (free citation).

1 Cf. Heb. 10.23; 11.11.
2 Cf. Heb. 6.18.
3 Wisd. 12.12.

Day utters speech to-day; and night proclaims knowledge tonight.

And there are no words or sounds, and their voices are not heard.'[4]

Chapter 28

1 Seeing, then, that all things are seen and heard, let us fear Him, and abandon the unclean lust of evil deeds, that we may be shielded by His mercy from the future judgments to come. 2 For where can any of us flee from His mighty hand? What world will receive any one of the deserters from Him? 3 For the Scripture[1] says in one place:[2]

'Where shall I go, and where shall I hide from Thy face?
If I go up into heaven, Thou art there:
If I go off to the ends of the earth, there is Thy right hand;
If I make my bed in the abyss, Thy spirit is there.'

4 Where, then, shall a man go off or where escape from Him who embraces all things?

Chapter 29

1 Let us come before Him, then, in sanctity of soul, lifting pure and undefiled hands to Him, loving our gentle and merciful Father who has made us His chosen portion. 2 For it is written:[1] 'When the Most High divided the nations,

---

4 Ps. 18.2-4.

---

1 Literally, 'the writing,' which was the designation of the third part of the Bible among the Jews; the first two parts being called the Law and the Prophets.
2 Ps. 138.7-9.

---

1 Deut. 32.8,9.

when He scattered the sons of Adam, He set up the boundaries of nations according to the number of angels of God. His people, Jacob, became the portion of the Lord; Israel was the allotment of His inheritance.' 3 And in another place He says:[2] 'Behold, the Lord takes to Himself a nation from the midst of nations, as a man takes the first-fruit of his threshing floor, and from that nation shall come forth the Holy of Holies.'

Chapter 30

1 Since we are a portion of the Holy One, let us do all that belongs to holiness, fleeing from evil speech, and abominable and impure embraces, from drunkenness and from rioting, and detestable lusts, foul adultery, and detestable pride. 2 'For God,' He says,[1] 'resisteth the proud but giveth grace to the humble.' 3 Let us then join with those to whom grace is given from God; let us put on concord in meekness of spirit and in self-control, keeping ourselves far from all gossip and evil speaking, being justified by works and not by words. 4 For He says:[2] 'He that speaketh much shall also hear much; or does he that speaks fair think that he is just? 5 Blessed is the man born of woman who has a short life. Be not full of words.' 6 Let our praise be with God,[3] and not from ourselves, for God hates those who praise themselves. 7 Let the testimony of our good deeds be given by others, as it was given to our fathers, who were righteous. 8 Boldness

---

2 Deut. 4.34; 14.2; Num. 18.27; Ezech. 48.12. The quotation is a medley of phrases from the Old Testament. Similar conflations will be noted below.

---

1 Prov. 3.34; James 4.6; 1 Peter 5.5.
2 Job. 11.2,3.
3 Cf. Rom. 2.29.

and arrogance and presumption belong to those who are cursed by God; gentleness and humility and meekness belong to those who are blessed by God.

Chapter 31

1 Let us, then, cling to His blessing, and let us see what are the ways of blessedness. Let us recall the events of old.[1] 2 Why was our father Abraham blessed? Was it not because he performed justice and truth through faith? 3 Isaac, knowing the future in confidence, was willingly led forth as a sacrifice. 4 Jacob went out from his own country with meekness because of his brother, and went to Laban and served him, and the twelve tribes of Israel were given to him.

Chapter 32

1 And, if anyone will examine fairly each example, he will recognize the greatness of the gifts given by God. 2 For from him[1] come the priests and the Levites who minister at the altar of God; from him comes the Lord Jesus according to the flesh;[2] from him come the kings and rulers and leaders in the line of Judah. And the other tribes are in no slight honor, since, as God promised:[3] 'Thy seed shall be as the stars of heaven.' 3 They were all glorified and magnified, not through themselves or their own works or the good deeds which they did, but through His will. 4 And we also, having been called through His will in Christ Jesus, are not justified by ourselves, or by our own wisdom or understanding or piety

---

1 See Gen. 12.2,3; 18.18; 22.7 ff.; 28 f.

---

1 I.e., from Jacob.
2 Rom. 9.5.
3 Gen. 15.5; 22.17; 26.4.

or the works we have done in holiness of heart, but through the faith, by which the Almighty God has justified all men from the beginning; to whom be glory for all ages. Amen.

Chapter 33

1 What, then, shall we do,[1] brothers? Shall we slacken from doing good and abandon charity? May the Lord never allow this to happen to us, but let us be diligent to accomplish every good work[2] with earnestness and zeal. 2 For the Creator and Lord of the universe Himself takes joy in His works. 3 For in His overwhelming might He has set up the heavens, and by His unsearchable wisdom He has put them in order. He has separated the earth from the surrounding water and placed it on the solid foundation of His own will; and He has called into existence the animals that move in it by His own arrangement. Having prepared the sea and the living creatures that are in it, He enclosed them by His own power. 4 Over all, with His holy and pure hands He formed man, the most excellent and greatest in intelligence, with the stamp of His own image. 5 For God spoke thus:[3] 'Let us make man according to our image and likeness; and God made man, male and female He made them.' 6 Having finished all these things, he praised and blessed them and said:[4] 'Increase and multiply.' 7 Let us consider that all the saints have been adorned with good works; and the Lord Himself, adorning Himself with good works, rejoiced. 8 Holding this pattern, then, let us follow out His will without hesitation; let us do the work of justice with all our strength.

---

1 Cf. Rom. 6.1.
2 Titus 3.1.
3 Gen. 1.26,27.
4 Gen. 1.28.

Chapter 34

1 The good laborer receives the bread of his labor with confidence; the lazy and careless one does not look his employer in the face. 2 We must, therefore, be zealous in doing good; for all things are from Him. 3 He warns us:[1] 'Behold the Lord comes, and his reward is before his face, to pay each man according to his work.' 4 He therefore urges us who believe in Him with all our heart not to be lazy or careless in any good work.[2] 5 Let our glorying and our confidence be in Him; let us be subject to His will. Let us consider the whole multitude of angels, how they stand and minister to His will. 6 For the Scripture says:[3] 'Ten thousand times ten thousand stood by him, and thousands of thousands ministered to him, and they cried, "Holy, Holy, Holy, Lord of hosts the whole creation is full of His glory." ' 7 We, therefore, gathering together in concord in our conscience, also should cry out earnestly as with one voice to Him, that we may become participants in His great and glorious promises. 8 For He says:[4] 'Eye has not seen, nor ear heard, nor has it entered into the heart of man, what great things the Lord has prepared for those who wait for him.'

Chapter 35

1 How blessed and wonderful are the gifts of God, beloved. 2 Life in immortality, joyousness in justice, truth in confidence, faith in trustfulness, continence in holiness. And all these things fall within our understanding. 3 And what shall we say of the things that are being prepared for those who

---

1 Isa. 40.10; 62.11; Prov. 24.12; Apoc. 22.12.
2 Titus 3.1.
3 Dan. 7.10; Isa. 6.3.
4 1 Cor. 2.9.

persevere. Only the Creator and Father of the ages, the all-holy One, knows their greatness and beauty. 4 Let us strive, therefore, to be found in the number of those who wait for Him, that we may share in the promised gifts. 5 But how shall this be, beloved? If our mind be fixed by means of faith on God; if we seek what is pleasing and acceptable to Him; if we perform what is proper to His faultless will and follow the path of truth, casting from us all injustice and wickedness, covetousness, strife, malice and deceit, gossiping and evil speaking, hatred of God, arrogance and boasting, vainglory and inhospitality. 6 For they who do these things are detestable to God, and 'not only those who do them, but also those who consent to them.'[1] For the Scripture says:[2]

'But to the sinner God hath said: Why dost thou declare my justices, and take my covenant in thy mouth?

Thou who hatest discipline and hast cast away my words behind thee.

If thou seest a thief, thou dost run with him; and with adulterers thou hast had a share.

Thy mouth has been full of evil, and thy tongue hath framed plans of deceit.

Thou didst sit to speak evil against thy brother, and hast laid a stumbling block against thy mother's son.

These things hast thou done; and I was silent.

Thou hast thought, O wicked man, that I should be like to thee.

But I will convict thee and set thee before thy face.

Understand these things, you who forget God; lest he seize you as a lion, and there shall be none to deliver you.

---

1 Rom. 1.32.
2 Ps. 49.16-23.

The sacrifice of praise shall glorify me; and therein is the way by which I will show him the salvation of God.'

Chapter 36

1 This is the way, beloved, by which we found our Saviour, Jesus Christ, the high priest[1] of our offerings, the protector and the helper of our weakness. 2 Through Him let us strain our eyes toward the heights of heaven; through Him we see mirrored His spotless and glorious countenance.[2] Through Him the eyes of our heart have been opened; through Him our foolish and darkened understanding shoots up into the light; through Him the Lord willed that we should taste immortal knowledge, 'Who, being the brightness of his majesty is so much greater than the angels as he hath inherited a more excellent name.'[3] 3 For it is so written:[4] 'Who makes his angels spirits, and his ministers a flame of fire.' 4 But regarding His Son the Lord has spoken thus:[5] 'Thou art My Son; this day I have begotten Thee. Ask of Me, and I will give Thee the gentiles for Thy inheritance, and the end of the earth for Thy possession.' And again He says to Him:[6] 'Sit on My right hand until I make Thy enemies a footstool for Thy feet.' Who then are the enemies? They who are wicked and resist His will.

---

1 Heb. 2.18; 3.1. The chapter, based largely on the most discussed book in the New Testament, is a magnificent summary of the doctrine of Christ's priesthood.
2 Cf. 2 Cor. 3.18.
3 Heb. 1.3.4.
4 Ps. 103.4; Heb. 1.7.
5 Ps. 2.7,8; Heb. 1.5.
6 Ps. 109.1; Heb. 1.13. Taken together, the quotations in this passage form evidence for the existence of 'Books of Testimonies' in which Christians collected Messianic passages from the Old Testament.

Chapter 37

1 Brothers, let us be His soldiers, therefore, in all earnestness, under His faultless commands. 2 Let us consider those who are enrolled under our rulers, how well-ordered, and how readily, how obediently they carry out commands. 3 Not all are prefects, or tribunes, or centurions, or in charge of bands of fifty, and so forth; but each one in his own rank[1] carries out the commands issued by the emperor and the officers. 4 The great cannot exist without the small, nor the small without the great; there is a certain organization, and it is of benefit to all. 5 Let us take our body.[2] The head without the feet is nothing, and so also the feet without the head are nothing. The smallest members of our body are necessary and useful to the whole body. But all conspire together and unite in a single obedience, so that the whole body may be saved.

Chapter 38

1 Therefore, let our whole body be saved in Christ Jesus, and let each be subject to his neighbor, according to the position which grace bestowed on each.[1] 2 Let not the strong neglect the weak, and let the weak respect the strong. Let the rich man supply the wants of the poor, and let the poor man give thanks to God, because He has given him someone to supply his needs. Let the wise show his wisdom not in words, but in good works. Let the humble-minded not testify to his own humility, but allow others to bear him witness. Let him who is pure in the flesh be so without boasting, knowing that

---

1 1 Cor. 15.23.
2 For the following passage cf. 1 Cor. 12.

---

1 Cf. Rom. 12.4 ff; 1 Cor. 16.17; Phil. 2.30.

it is Another who grants him this continence. 3 Let us consider, brothers, of what matter we were made; who and what we are who have come into the world; from what a tomb and what darkness our Maker and Creator brought us into the world and prepared His benefits for us before we were born. 4 We who have obtained all these things from Him ought to thank Him for all, to whom be glory forever and ever. Amen.

Chapter 39

1 Foolish, unthinking, silly, and ignorant men laugh at us and deride us, wishing to exalt themselves in their own imagination. 2 For what can mortal man do? Or what is the strength of one born on earth? 3 For it is written:[1] 'There was no shape before my eyes, but I heard breathing and a voice. 4 What then? Shall a mortal be pure before the Lord? Or shall a man be blameless in his works [before God], if He believeth not in His servants, and finds defects in His angels? 5 Even the heaven is not pure in His sight. Away, you that live in houses of clay, from which, yes, from the same clay, we ourselves were made. He struck them like a moth, and between morning and evening they ceased to exist; they perished without being able to help themselves. 6 He breathed on them, and they died, because they had not wisdom. 7 Cry out, if there is anyone to hear thee; or if thou shalt see any of the holy angels. For wrath destroyeth the foolish man, and jealousy kills him that errs. 8 I have seen the foolish take root, but shortly their dwelling was consumed. 9 Let their sons be far from safety; let them be derided in the gates of their inferiors, and there will be none to rescue them. For the just shall eat what was prepared for them, and they shall not be delivered from their ills.'

---

1 Job. 4.12-18; 15.15; 4.19-5.5.

Chapter 40

1 Since all these things are clear to us,[1] and we have looked into the depths of divine knowledge,[2] we ought in proper order to do all things which the Lord has commanded us to perform at appointed times. 2 He has commanded the offerings and ministrations to be carried out, and not carelessly or disorderly, but at fixed times and seasons. 3 He has Himself fixed according to His surpassing counsel where and by whom He deires them to be performed, in order that all things may be done in holy fashion according to His good pleasure and acceptable to His will. 4 Those who make their offerings at the appointed time, therefore, are acceptable and blessed, for they err not, following the ordinances of the Lord. 5 For the high priest has been allotted his proper ministrations, and to the priests their proper place has been assigned, and on the Levites their own duties are laid. The lay man is bound by the lay ordinances.

Chapter 41

1 Let us, brothers, each in his own order,[1] strive to pleace God with a good conscience and with reverence, not transgressing the fixed rule of each one's own ministry. 2 Not in every place, brothers, are the daily sacrifices for petitions and for sins and for trespasses offered, but only in Jerusalem. And even there the offering is not made in any place, but only before the sanctuary near the altar, after the offering has been inspected for defects by the high priest and the above-

---

1 Chapters 40 to 42 are important for the Christian understanding of a divinely established hierarchy in the Church.
2 Rom. 11.33.

---

1 1 Cor. 15.23.

mentioned ministers. 3 Those who do anything contrary to
what is due to Him will suffer the penalty of death. 4 You
see, brothers, the more knowledge we have been given, the
more we are exposed to danger.

Chapter 42

1 The Apostles received the Gospel for us from the Lord
Jesus Christ; Jesus Christ was sent from God. 2 Christ, therefore, is from God and the Apostles are from Christ. Both, accordingly, came in proper order by the will of God. 3 Receiving their orders, therefore, and being filled with confidence because of the Resurrection of the Lord Jesus Christ, and confirmed in the word of God, with full assurance of the Holy
Spirit, they went forth preaching the Gospel of the Kingdom
of God that was about to come. 4 Preaching, accordingly,
throughout the country and the cities, they appointed their
first-fruits, after testing them by the Spirit, to be bishops[1] and
deacons of those who should believe. 5 And this they did without innovation, since many years ago things had been written
concerning bishops and deacons. Thus, the Scripture says in
one place:[2] 'I will establish their bishops in justice and their
deacons in faith.'

Chapter 43

1 And what wonder is it if they, who had been entrusted
in Christ by God with such a work, appointed the persons
we have mentioned? After all, the blessed man Moses, 'a
faithful servant in all his house,'[1] recorded in the sacred

---

1 On the meaning of the word *episkopoi* in the Church of the first century see Introduction *above* p. 5f.
2 Isa. 60.17. This is a free adaptation of the text by St. Clement. The
Septuagint reads: 'I will establish your rulers in peace and your overseers (*episkópous*) in justice.'

---

1 Num. 12.7; Heb. 3.5.

books all the things commanded him. And the other prophets followed him, testifying with him to the laws laid down by him. 2 For, when jealousy arose about the priesthood[2] and the tribes quarreled as to which of them should be honored with that glorious name, he commanded the chiefs of the twelve tribes to bring him rods inscribed with the name of each tribe; and, taking them, he bound them, and sealed them with the rings of the chiefs, and put them away in the Tabernacle of Testimony on the table of God. 3 And, closing the Tabernacle, he sealed the keys as well as the doors. 4 And he said to them: 'Brethren, the tribe whose rod blossoms, this one has God chosen to be priests and to minister to Him.' 5 And, when morning came, he called together all Israel, six hundred thousand men, and showed the seals to the chiefs of the tribes, and opened the Tabernacle of Testimony, and brought out the rods; and the rod of Aaron was found not only to have blossomed, but also to be bearing fruit. 6 What do you think, beloved? Did not Moses know beforehand that this would happen? Certainly, he knew. But, that no disorder should arise in Israel, he acted thus to glorify the name of the true and only God, to whom be glory forever and ever. Amen.

Chapter 44

1 Our Apostles also knew, through our Lord Jesus Christ, that there would be contention over the bishop's office.[1] 2 So, for this cause, having received complete foreknowledge, they appointed the above-mentioned men, and afterwards gave them a permanent character, so that, as they died, other approved men should succeed to their ministry. 3 Those, therefore, who were appointed by the Apostles or afterwards by other eminent men, with the consent of the whole Church,

2 Num. 17.

1 *Episkope* means rank or office of bishop.

and who ministered blamelessly to the flock of Christ in humility, peaceably and nobly, being commended for many years by all—these men we consider are not justly deposed from their ministry. 4 It will be no small sin for us, if we depose from the episcopacy men who have blamelessly and in holiness offered up sacrifice. 5 Blessed are the presbyters who have gone before, since they reached a fruitful and perfect end; for now they need not fear that anyone shall remove them from the place assigned to them. 6 For we see that, in spite of their good conduct, you have forced some men from a ministry which they fulfilled without blame.

Chapter 45

1 Brothers, be eager and zealous for the things that pertain to salvation. 2 You have studied the Holy Scriptures, which are true and inspired by the Holy Spirit. 3 You know that nothing contrary to justice or truth has been written in them. You will not find that just men have been expelled by holy men. 4 Just men were persecuted, but by wicked men. They were imprisoned, but by impious men. They were stoned by breakers of the laws; they were killed by men who had conceived a foul and wicked jealousy. 5 Although suffering such things, they endured nobly. 6 What shall we say, brothers? Was Daniel cast into the lions' den by men who feared God?[1] 7 Or were Ananias, Azarias, and Misael shut up in the fiery furnace by men who observed the great and glorious worship of the Most High? God forbid! Who, then, were the men who did these acts? They were detestable men, filled with all wickedness, who were carried to such fury that they heaped humiliation on those who served God in holiness and purity of intention. They did not know that the Most High is the

---

1 Dan. 6.16,17; 3.19 ff.

protector and defender of those who minister with a pure conscience to His all holy Name, to whom be glory forever and ever. Amen. 8 But those who endured confidently gained an inheritance of glory and honor, and were exalted and inscribed by God in His memorial forever and ever. Amen.

Chapter 46

1 And so, brothers, we, too, must cling to models such as these. 2 For it is written:[1] 'Cling to the saints, for they who cleave to them shall become saints.' 3 And again in another place:[2] 'With the innocent man, Thou shalt be innocent; and with the elect man, Thou shalt be elect; and with the perverse man, Thou shalt be perverse.' 4 Let us cling, then, to the innocent and the just, for they are God's elect. 5 Why are there quarrels and ill will and dissensions and schism and fighting among you? 6 Do we not have one God and one Christ, and one Spirit of Grace poured out upon us? And is there not one calling in Christ?[3] 7 Why do we wrench and tear apart the members of Christ, and revolt against our own body, and reach such folly as to forget that we are members one of another? Remember the words of the Lord Jesus: 8 For He said:[4] 'Woe to that man! It were better for him if he had not been born, rather than scandalize one of My elect. It were better for him that a millstone were tied to him, and that he be cast into the sea, than that he should pervert one of My chosen ones.' 9 Your schism has perverted many, has thrown many into despair, has caused all of us to grieve; and your rebelliousness continues.

---

1 Source unknown.
2 Cf. Ps. 17.26,27.
3 Eph. 4.4-6.
4 Matt. 26.24; Luke 17.1,2; Mark 9.42.

Chapter 47

1 Take up the epistle of blessed Paul the Apostle.[1] 2 What did he first write to you at the beginning of his preachings?[2] 3 In truth, being inspired, he wrote to you concerning himself and Cephas and Apollos, because even then you were given to faction. 4 But that factiousness involved you in less guilt, for you were partisans of highly reputed Apostles, and of a man commended by them. 5 But consider now who they are who have perverted you, and have diminished the honor or your renowned reputation for brotherly love. 6 It is disgraceful, beloved, very disgraceful, and unworthy of your training in Christ, to hear that the stable and ancient Church of the Corinthians, on account of one or two persons, should revolt against its presbyters. 7 And this report has come not only to us, but also to those who dissent from us. The result is that blasphemies are brought upon the name of the Lord through your folly, and danger accrues for yourselves.

Chapter 48

1 Let us quickly remove this, then, and let us fall down before the Lord and supplicate Him with tears that He may become merciful and be reconciled to us, and restore us to the honored and holy practice of brotherly love. 2 For thus is the gate of justice opened to life, as it is written:[1] 'Open to me the gates of justice, that I may enter through them and praise the Lord. 3 This is the gate of the Lord, the righteous shall enter by it.' 4 Of the many gates that are opened, the one in justice is the one in Christ. All are blessed who enter

---

1 1 Cor. 1.10 ff.
2 Phil. 4.15.

---

1 Ps. 117.19,20.

by this gate and pursue their way in holiness and justice, performing all things without disorder.[2] 5 Let a man be faithful, let him be able to utter deep knowledge, let him be wise in discerning words, let him be energetic in deeds,[3] let him be pure. 6 For the greater he seems to be, so much the more should he be humble; and he ought to seek the common good of all and not his own.

Chapter 49

1 Let him who has chastity in Christ keep Christ's commandments.[1] 2 Who can explain the bond of the charity of God?[2] 3 Who can express the splendor of its beauty? 4 The height to which charity lifts us is inexpressible. 5 Charity unites us to God, 'Charity covers a multitude of sins';[3] charity bears all things, is long-suffering in all things. There is nothing mean in charity, nothing arrogant. Charity knows no schism, does not rebel, does all things in concord. In charity all the elect of God have been made perfect. Without charity nothing is pleasing to God. 6 In charity the Lord received us; out of the charity which He had for us, Jesus Christ our Lord gave His blood for us by the will of God, and His flesh for our flesh, and His life for our lives.

Chapter 50

1 You see, dearly beloved, how great and wonderful is charity, and that its perfection is beyond expression. 2 Who

---

2 Luke 1.75.
3 Cf. 1 Cor. 12.8,9.

---

1 The close resemblance of this whole chapter to St. Paul's 1 Cor. 13 is noticeable.
2 Cf. Col. 3.14.
3 Prov. 10.12; 1 Peter 4.8; James 5.20.

is good enough to be found in it except those whom God makes worthy? Let us pray, therefore, and beg of His mercy that we may be found in charity, without human partisanship, free from blame. 3 All the generations from Adam to this day have passed away; but those who were made perfect in charity by the grace of God live among the saints; and they shall be made manifest at the judgment of the Kingdom of Christ. 4 For it is written:[1] 'Enter into thy chambers a little while, until My wrath and anger pass, and I remember the good day and will raise you up out of your graves.' 5 Blessed were we, dearly beloved, if we fulfilled the commandments of God in the harmony of charity, that our sins were forgiven through charity. 6 For it is written:[2] 'Blessed are they whose iniquities are forgiven, and whose sins are covered. Blessed is the man whose sin the Lord will not reckon, and in whose mouth there is no deceit.' 7 This benediction came to those who were chosen by God through Jesus Christ our Lord, to whom be glory forever and ever. Amen.

Chapter 51

1 Whatsoever we have done wrong, and whatsoever we have done by suggestion of our adversary, let us hope that it may be forgiven us. Even those who were the leaders of rebellion and schism must look to the common hope. 2 For those who live in fear and charity prefer that they, rather than their neighbors, should undergo sufferings, and they more willingly suffer their own condemnation than the loss of that harmony which has been taught us well and justly. 3 It is better for a man to confess his sins than to harden his heart, as the heart of those who rebelled against Moses, the

---

1 Isa. 26.20; Ezech. 37.12.
2 Ps. 31.1,2; Rom. 4.7-9.

servant of God, was hardened[1]—and the verdict on them was plain. 4 For they went 'down into Hades alive' and 'death will gather them in.'[2] 5 Pharaoh and his army and all the leaders of Egypt, 'the chariots and their riders,' were drowned in the Red Sea and perished, for no other reason than that their foolish hearts were hardened, after the working of signs and wonders in the land of Egypt by God's servant Moses.[3]

Chapter 52

1 Brothers, the Lord of the universe has need of nothing; He requires nothing of anyone, except that confession be made to Him. 2 For David, the chosen one, says:[1] 'I will confess to the Lord, and it shall please Him more than a young bullock with horns and hoofs. Let the poor see it and be glad.' 3 And again he says:[2] 'Sacrifice to God a sacrifice of praise, and render to the All-High thy vows; and call upon Me in the day of affliction, and I will deliver thee, and thou shalt glorify Me.' 4 'For a contrite spirit is a sacrifice to God.'[3]

Chapter 53

1 For you understand, beloved, you well understand the Sacred Scriptures, and you have studied the oracles of God. So we write these things as a reminder. 2 For, when Moses went up the mountain and spent forty days and forty nights in fasting and humiliation, God said to him:[1] 'Go down from

1 Num. 16.
2 Num. 16.33; Ps. 48.15.
3 Exod. 14.23.

1 Ps. 68.31-33.
2 Ps. 49.14,15.
3 Ps. 50.19.

1 Deut. 9.12.

here quickly, for thy people, whom thou has brought out of Egypt, have committed iniquity; they have speedily gone astray from the way which thou hast commanded them; they have made molten images for themselves.' 3 And the Lord said to him:[2] 'I have spoken to thee once and twice, saying, "I have seen this people, and, behold, it is stiffnecked. Suffer Me to destroy them and I will wipe out their name from under heaven, and I will make thee a great and wonderful nation, far more numerous than this one." 4 And Moses said:[3] "No Lord; pardon the sin of this people, or blot me also out of the book of the living." ' 5 What great charity! What superb perfection! The servant speaks out to the Lord and asks that the people be forgiven or that he himself be blotted out with them.

Chapter 54

1 Who, now, among you is noble? Who is compassionate? Who is filled with charity? 2 Let him say: 'If on my account there are sedition and quarreling and schisms, I will leave; I will go wherever you wish and will do what is enjoined by the community, only let the flock of Christ have peace with its appointed presbyters.' 3 He who does this will win for himself great fame in Christ, and every place will receive him, for 'the earth is the Lord's, and the fullness of it.'[1] 4 Thus have they acted and will continue to act who fulfill their obligations as citizens of God without regret.

---

2 Deut. 9.13,14.
3 Exod. 32.31,32.

---

1 Ps. 23.1.

Chapter 55

1 And now to take examples from the pagans also: Many kings and rulers, when a period of pestilence occurred, followed the advice of oracles and gave themselves up to death, in order to rescue their subjects by their own blood. Many left their own cities, that these might be divided no more. 2 We know that many among ourselves have given themselves up to chains in order to redeem others. Many have surrendered themselves to slavery and provided food for others with the price they received for themselves. 3 Many women, fortified by the grace of God, have accomplished many heroic actions. 4 The blessed Judith,[1] when the city was besieged, asked permission of the elders to be allowed to go into the foreigners' camp. 5 By exposing herself to danger she went out for love of her country and of the people who were besieged, and the Lord delivered Holophernes into the hand of a woman. 6 To no less danger did Esther,[2] who was perfect in faith, expose herself, in order to save the twelve tribes of Israel that were about to be destroyed. For, by fasting and humiliation she begged the all-seeing Master of the ages and He, seeing the meeknss of her soul, rescued the people for whose sake she had faced danger.

Chapter 56

1 Therefore, let us also intercede for those who fall into any transgression, that meekness and humility may be granted them, so that they may yield not to us but to God's will. For in this way there will be for them a fruitful, perfect, and compassionate remembrance with God and the saints. 2 Let us receive correction, and not be angered by it, dearly beloved.

---

1 Judith 8 ff.
2 Esther 4.16.

The admonition which we give to one another is good and most beneficial, for it unites us to the will of God. 3 For the holy word speaks thus:[1] 'With chastisement did the Lord chastise me, and he delivered me not to death.' 4 'For whom the Lord loves He chastises, and scourges every son whom He receives.' 5 For it says: 'The just will chastise me with mercy and correct me, but let not the mercy of sinners anoint my head.' 6 And, again, it says: 'Happy is the man whom the Lord has corrected; and despise not the admonition of the Almighty, for He makes a man suffer pain and again restores him. 7 He struck, and His hands have healed. 8 Six times he shall deliver thee from troubles, and in the seventh time evil shall not touch thee. 9 In famine He shall deliver thee from death, and in war he shall free from the hand of the sword. 10 And He shall hide thee from the scourge of the tongue, and thou shalt not be afraid when evils come. 11 Thou shalt laugh to scorn the unjust and lawless men, and thou shalt not fear wild beasts. 12 For wild beasts shall be at peace with thee. 13 Thou shalt know that thy house shall be at peace, and the habitation of thy tent shall not fail. 14 And thou shalt know that thy seed shall be many and thy children like the grass of the field. 15 And thou shalt come to the grave like ripened corn that is harvested in its due season, or like a heap on the threshing floor which is gathered in at the appointed time.' 16 You see, beloved, how great is the protection given to those who are chastised by the Lord. For He chastises as a good father, that we may receive mercy through His holy chastisement.

Chapter 57

1 You, therefore, who laid the foundation of rebellion,

---

1 Ps. 117.18. For the Scripture which follows cf. Prov. 3.12; Heb. 22.6; Ps. 140.5; Job. 5.17-26.

submit to the presbyters, and accept chastisement for repentance, bending the knees of your heart. 2 Learn to be submissive, laying aside the boastful and proud self-confidence of your tongue, for it is better for you to be found 'little ones,' but honorable within the flock of Christ, than to seem to be pre-eminent, but to be cast out from His hope. 3 For the all-virtuous Wisdom speaks thus:[1] 'Behold I will bring forth to you the words of my spirit, and I will teach you my word. 4 Because I called and you did not obey, and I put forth my words and you paid no attention, but made my counsel useless and disobeyed my admonitions. Therefore I will also laugh at your destruction, and I will rejoice when ruin comes on you and when confusion suddenly overwhelms you and catastrophe descends like a whirlwind, or when affliction or a siege comes. 5 For it shall come to pass when you call upon me I will not hear you. The wicked shall seek me and shall not find me. For they hated knowledge and did not choose the fear of the Lord; neither would they heed my counsels but mocked my reproofs. 6 Therefore they shall eat the fruits of their own way, and shall be filled with their own impiety. 7 Because they wronged the simple, they shall be killed, and judgment shall destroy the impious. But he that hearkens to me shall dwell securely in hope, and shall be quiet without fear of any evil.'

Chapter 58

1 Let us, then, obey His all-holy and glorious name, and escape the threats which have been spoken by Wisdom long

---

1 Prov. 1.23-33. 'Wisdom' is here a collective title, used in the liturgy and elsewhere to designate the books of Proverbs, Ecclesiastes, Wisdom, and Ecclesiasticus. The Roman Missal invariably entitles readings from any of these books *Lectio libri Sapientiae* (*Reading from the Book of wisdom*).

ago against the disobedient, that we may encamp in confidence in the most sacred name of His majesty. 2 Take our advice, and there will be nothing for you to regret. For, as God lives and the Lord Jesus Christ lives and the Holy Spirit, the faith and hope of the elect, so shall he who with humility of mind, and ready gentleness, and without turning back, has performed the decrees and commandments given by God be enrolled and chosen among the number of those who are saved through Jesus Christ, through whom is the glory to Him forever and ever. Amen.

Chapter 59

1 But, if some shall disobey the words which have been spoken by Him through us,[1] let them know that they will involve themselves in no small transgression and danger. 2 But we shall be innocent of this sin, and shall beg with earnest prayer and supplication that the Creator of all may keep unharmed the number which has been counted of His elect in all the world, through His beloved child Jesus Christ, through whom He called us from darkness to light.[2] from ignorance to the full knowledge of the glory of His name. 3 [Grant us, Lord,][3] to hope in His name, the beginning of all creation; open the eyes of our heart[4] to know Thee, that Thou alone art the 'Highest in the highest' and remainest

---

1 St. Clement is not speaking to Christians of his own immediate Church. The present phrase suggests that he was fully aware of the special prerogatives of the See of Rome which he occupied.
2 Acts 26.18.
3 Most editors agree that something is missing in the Greek text at this point. 'Grant us Lord' is not in the Greek, but seems necessary for the sense.
4 Eph. 1.18. Other sources drawn on in this section are: Isa. 57.15; 13.11; Ps. 32.10; Job. 5.11; 1 Kings 2.7; Luke 1.53; Deut. 32.39; 1 Kings 2.16; 4 Kings 5.7; Num. 16.22; 27.16; Sam. 3.55 (Heb. Bible 3.31).

Holy among the holy. Thou dost humble the pride of the haughty, Thou dost destroy the conceits of nations, lifting up the humble and humbling the exalted. Thou art He who makes both rich and poor, who kills and who vivifies, the sole benefactor of spirits and God of all flesh. Thou 'lookest on the abysses,' Thou seest into the works of man; Thou art the helper of those in danger, the 'saviour of those in despair,' the Creator and observer of every spirit. Thou dost multiply nations upon earth and hast chosen from them all those who love Thee, through Jesus Christ Thy beloved child, and through Him Thou hast taught us, sanctified us, given us honor. 4 We beseech Thee, Lord, to be our helper and protector.[5] Save those of us who are in affliction, have mercy on the humble, raise the fallen, show Thyself to those who are in need, heal the sick, turn back the wanderers of Thy people, feed the hungry, ransom our prisoners, raise up the weak, comfort the faint-hearted. Let all the nations know Thee, that Thou alone art God, and that Jesus Christ is Thy Servant, and that 'we are Thy people and the sheep of Thy pasture.'

Chapter 60

1 For thou hast made manifest the eternal fabric of the world through Thy operations. Thou, Lord, didst create the world. Thou who art faithful in all generations, just in Thy judgment, wonderful in strength and majesty, wise in Thy creation, and prudent in establishing Thy works, good in the things which are seen, and compassionate to those who trust in Thee, merciful and compassionate[1]—forgive our sins and injustices, our trespasses and failings. 2 Count not every

---

5 Judith 9.11. Other sources for this section are: Ps. 118.11; 3 Kings 8.60; 4 Kings 19.19; Ezech. 36.23; Ps. 78.13.

1 Joel 2.13.

sin of Thy servants and handmaids, but cleanse us with the cleansing of Thy truth, and make our steps straight that we may walk in holiness and justice and simplicity of heart, and may do those things that are good and well-pleasing before Thee[2] and our rulers. 3 Yes, Lord, let Thy countenance shine on us for good in peace, that we may be protected by Thy strong hand and delivered from all sin by Thy uplifted arm, and deliver us from those who hate us unjustly. 4 Give concord and peace to us and to all the inhabitants of the earth, as Thou didst give it to our fathers, when they invoked Thee reverently in faith and truth, so that we may be saved, and grant that we may be obedient to Thy almighty and excellent name, and to our rulers and governors on earth.

Chapter 61

1 Thou, Lord, hast given the authority of the Kingdom to them through Thy all-powerful and unspeakable might, that we, acknowledging the glory and honor given them by Thee, may be subject to them and in no way resist Thy will. To them, Lord, give health, peace, concord, and firmness that they may administer without offense the government which Thou hast given them. 2 For Thou, heavenly Lord, King of the ages,[1] givest to the sons of men glory and honor, and authority over the things on earth. Direct their counsels, Lord, according to what is good and well-pleasing before Thee,[2] that by piously administering in peace and gentleness the authority granted them by Thee they may obtain Thy mercy. 3 Thou who alone art able to do these good things for us and other things more abundantly, we praise Thee through the

---

2 Ps. 118.133.

---

1 1 Tim. 5.17; Tob. 13.6,10.
2 Deut. 12.25,28; 13.18.

high priest and protector of our souls, Jesus Christ, through whom be glory and majesty to Thee both now and for all generations and for all ages. Amen.

Chapter 62

1 Brothers, we have written to you sufficiently concerning the things that befit our religion and are most helpful to the life of virtue for those who wish to direct their steps in piety and justice. 2 For, in regard to faith and repentance and genuine charity and self-control and discretion and patience, we have treated every point. We have reminded you that you must please Almighty God with holiness in justice and truth and long-suffering, in a life of concord. You should forget injuries in love and peace, and continue in gentleness, as our fathers aforementioned who, in their humility, were pleasing to God, the Father and Creator, and to all men. 3 And we have reminded you of these things the more willingly because we knew well that we were writing to men who are faithful and well-reputed and had studied the words of God's instruction.

Chapter 63

1 Confronted by so many and such great examples,[1] there-fore, we rightly should bow our necks and adopt an attitude of obedience, so that abandoning this foolish rebellion we may without blame reach the goal set before us. 2 For you will af-ford us joy and gladness if you obey what we have written through the Holy Spirit and get rid of the wicked passion of jealousy, according to the plea for peace and harmony which we have made in this letter. 3 We have sent trustworthy and

---

1 'It is right,' i.e., a matter of elementary justice. Note that the procedure of sending delegates along with the written letter is the same as that described in Acts 15.22 ff.

prudent men, who have lived among us irreproachably from youth to old age; and they will be witness between you and us. 4 We have done this in order that you may know our entire preoccupation has been and remains that you may quickly achieve peace.

Chapter 64

1 In conclusion, may the all-seeing God and Ruler of the spirits and Lord of all flesh,[1] who chose the Lord Jesus Christ and us through Him to be a special people,[2] grant to every soul upon whom His great and holy name has been invoked faith, fear, peace, patience, and long-suffering, self-control, purity and prudence, so that they may be well-pleasing to His name through our high priest and defender Jesus Christ, through whom be glory and majesty, power and honor, to Him, both now and for all ages. Amen.

Chapter 65

1 Send back to us quickly our delegates, Claudius Ephebus and Valerius Vito, together with Fortunatus, in peace with gladness, so that they may speedily announce the peace and harmony which we have prayed for and desired, and that we also may more speedily rejoice at your good order. 2 May the grace of our Lord Jesus Christ be with you and with all those, in every place, who have been called by God through Him; through whom be glory, honor, power, and majesty to Him, and eternal dominion from eternity to all eternity. Amen.

---

1 Num. 16.22; 27.16; Heb. 12.9.
2 Deut. 14.2.

THE SO-CALLED
SECOND LETTER
OF
ST. CLEMENT

BEING

AN ANCIENT HOMILY

BY AN ANONYMOUS AUTHOR

Translated

by

FRANCIS X. GLIMM, S.T.L.

Seminary of the Immaculate Conception

Huntington, N. Y.

INTRODUCTION

T HE WORK here translated is one that immediately follows the genuine letter of St. Clement of Rome in two Greek manuscripts[1] and in one Syriac manuscript. Like St. Clement's letter, it carries the heading 'To the Corinthians.'

The supposed existence of a second letter by this author was known to Eusebius,[2] who states, however, that he knew of no use of it made by the 'ancients.' Whether or not Eusebius had in mind the text furnished by the manuscripts cited above, it is clear that the document is not a letter, but a homily intended for public reading. Stylistic and other reasons show that the work does not belong to St. Clement. Its attribution to him depends only upon its inclusion in the manuscripts.

Opinions vary as to the probable place of origin and the occasion of the homily. Certain scholars, among them Lightfoot, conclude that it was preached at Corinth, attaching decisive importance to the allusions (7.1-4) to athletic contests, which, it is proposed, refer to the Isthmian games held at Corinth. As a homily of local origin, it could well have

---

1 The famous fifth-century Codex Alexandrinus, now at the British Museum, Royal MS IDV-VIII, and the Codex Hierosolymitanus, or Constantinopolitanus, of 1056 A.D., originally belonging to the Church of the Most Holy Sepulchre, later preserved at Constantinople and more recently transferred to Jerusalem.

2 Eubebius, *Historia ecclesiastica* 3.38.4.

61

been preserved in the archives of the Corinthian Church and have been copied at a later date with St. Clement's letter to the same Church. Lack of a title prefixed to the homily might have led to the supposition that the document was a letter and might thus have produced the epistolary heading, 'To the Corinthians.'

The second most favored opinion has the advantage of giving the homily a closer historical connection with St. Clement's letter. Harnack[3] and the others who have favored this opinion identify the work with a letter known from Eusebius to have been sent to Bishop Dionysius of Corinth by Soter, Bishop of Rome (*ca.* 170).[4] Such a document would reasonably have been preserved in the Corinthian Church archives with St. Clement's letter, which, we know from Dionysius' reply to Soter, was then being read publicly in the Corinthian Church together with the latter's epistle. The subsequent joint copying of the two texts—no doubt in a book used for public reading—would thus have been a natural eventuality. To explain how a homily could have been used as a letter, it is simply suggested that it was possibly the practice of the time for bishops to exchange homilies on subjects of general interest as letters of exhortation.

Unless Harnack's opinion be accepted, no certain dating is possible with the facts now at hand. Otherwise, the contents of the letter permit us to place it anywhere in the second or third centuries.

The interior organization of the homily is loose and its contents varied. Among its doctrinal teachings, particular notice should be taken of the clear assertion (1.1) of the

---

3 A. Harnack, *Die Chronologie der altchristlichen Literatur bis Eusebius* (Leipzig 1897) 1 438 ff.
4 Eusebius, *op. cit.* 4.23.11.

divinity of Jesus Christ and of the emphasis on the resurrection of the body as a motive for abstaining from sin (9.1-5). Chapter 8 in its entirety is a valuable and neglected source of ideas on penance.

While historians can regret that the early history of the homily is little more than conjecture, it seems not unworthy of the place of distinction it later won through its inclusion in the Codex Alexandrinus. Whatever other merit the work has, it appears to be the oldest example of Christian preaching that we possess outside of Holy Scripture.

The text followed in the present translation is that of Karl Bihlmeyer, *Die apostolischen Väter* (Tübingen 1924).

SELECT BIBLIOGRAPHY

Texts and Translations:

J. B. Lightfoot, *The Apostolic Fathers* . . . revised texts with short introductions and English translations . . . edited and completed by J. R. Harmer (London 1891).

K. Lake, *The Apostolic Fathers,* with an English translation (Loeb Classical Library, New York 1912) 1.

T. W. Crafer, *The Second Epistle of Clement to the Corinthians* (S.P.C.K. Texts for Students No. 22, London 1921).

An English translation of the So-Called Second Epistle of Clement to the Corinthians (S.P.C.K. Texts for Students No. 22A, London 1922).

Secondary Works:

F. X. Funk, *Kirchengeschichtliche Abhandlungen und Untersuchungen III,* 1907, 261, 75.

A. Harnack, *Die Chronologie der altchristlichen Literatur bis Eusebius* (Leipzig 1897) 1.

Th. Wehofer, 'Untersuchungen zur altchristlichen Epistolographie' (*Sitzungsberichte der Wiener Akademie,* Philol. hist. Kl. 143, 1900, Nr. 17).

THE SO-CALLED SECOND EPISTLE OF
ST. CLEMENT TO THE CORINTHIANS

Chapter 1

BROTHERS, we must think of Jesus Christ as of God—
as the 'judge of the living and the dead.'[1] And we
must not think lightly of our Savior. 2 For, in thinking lightly of Him, we also hope to receive but little. And we
sin, those of us who listen as if to an unimportant matter, not
knowing whence, by whom, and to what place we have been
called, and how much suffering Jesus Christ endured for our
sakes. 3 What return, then, shall we make to Him, or what
fruit worthy of that which He has given us? How much devotion do we owe Him! 4 He has lavished the light upon us; He
has spoken to us as a father to his sons; He has saved us when
we were perishing. 5 What praise, then, shall we give to Him,
or what payment in return for what we have received? 6
Blinded in our understanding, we bowed down to sticks and
stones and gold and silver and brass, the works of men; and
our whole life was nothing else but death. While we were
covered with darkness and our sight was obscured by this mist,
by His will we recovered our sight, putting off the cloud which
invested us. 7 For He had mercy on us and, out of pity, saved
us, seeing in us much waywardness and destruction and no
hope of salvation except such as might come from Him.
8 For He called us when we were not, and out of nothing
willed us to be.

Chapter 2

1 'Rejoice, O thou barren, thou bearest not; sing forth and

---

1 Acts 10.42.

shout, thou that dost not travail; for many are the children of the desolate, more than heirs that hath a husband.'[1] By saying 'Rejoice, O thou barren, that bearest not' He meant us, for our Church was barren before being given children. 2 And by saying 'Shout, thou that dost travail' He means this: to offer up our prayers in simplicity to God and not grow weary like women in labor. 3 And by saying 'Many are the children of the desolate, more than heirs that hath a husband' He meant that our people seemed to be abandoned by God, but now, having believed, we have become more numerous than those who seemed to have God. 4 And another Scripture says:[2] 'I came not to call the just, but sinners.' This means that all who are perishing must be saved. 6 For it is a great and wonderful thing to sustain, not the things that are standing, but those that are falling. 7 So, also, Christ willed to save the things that were perishing,[3] and He saved many men, when He had come and called us who were, even now, perishing.

Chapter 3

1 Since, then, He has bestowed such mercy on us, first that we the living do not sacrifice to gods who are dead nor worship them, but through Him know the Father of Truth—what is true knowledge concerning Him except not to deny Him through whom we knew the Father? 2 He Himself says:[1] He who confessed me before men, I will confess him

---

1 Isa. 54.1, quoted also by St. Paul, Gal. 4.27.
2 Matt. 9.13; Mark 2.17; Luke 5.32. This may be the earliest instance in which the New Testament is quoted as 'Scripture' (Greek *graphé*). Below, at 6.8 and 14.2, the same word designates Old Testament books; at 14.1 the reference is either to St. Matthew or to Jeremias.
3 Cf. Matt. 18.11; Luke 19.0.

---

1 Matt. 10.32; Luke 12.8.

before my Father.' 3 This, then, is our reward, if we confess Him through whom we were saved. 4 But how do we confess Him? By doing what He says, and not disobeying His commandments, and honoring Him not only with our lips but 'with all our heart and all our mind.'[2] 5 And He says also in Isaias:[3] 'This people honors me with their lips, but their heart is far from me.'

Chapter 4

1 Let us not merely call Him Lord, then, for this will not save us. 2 For He says:[1] 'Not everyone who says to me Lord, Lord, shall be saved, but he who works justice.' 3 So, then, brothers, let us confess Him in our works by loving one another, by not committing adultery, nor speaking against one another, by not being envious, but by being self-controlled, kindly, good; and we ought to sympathize with one another and not be avaricious. By these works we confess Him, and not by the contrary. 4 And we must not fear men rather than God. 5 For this reason, provided you do these things, the Lord said:[2] 'If ye be gathered together with Me in My bosom and do not carry out My commandments, I will cast you off and will say to you: Depart from me; I know not whence you come, you workers of iniquity.'

Chapter 5

1 Therefore, brothers, leaving behind life as strangers in this world, let us do the will of Him who called us, and let us not be afraid to go forth from this world. 2 For the Lord

---

2 Mark 12.30; cf. Luke 10.27 and Matt. 22.37.
3 Isa. 29.13; cf. Matt. 15.8 and Mark 7.6.

---

1 Cf. Matt. 7.21 and (less close) Luke 6.46; also Rom. 2.13.
2 The source of this quotation is unknown; it may come from the lost 'Gospel of the Egyptians.'

said:[1] 'You shall be as lambs in the midst of wolves.' 3 And
Peter answered and said to Him: 'What if the wolves should
tear the lambs?' 4 Jesus said to Peter: 'The lambs should not
fear the wolves after they are dead. And so with you—fear
not those who kill you and can do nothing more to you; but
fear Him who after your death has power over soul and
body, to cast them into hell fire.' 5 And understand, brothers,
that the lingering of our flesh in this world is short and passing, but the promise of Christ is great and wonderful and
is a repose in the kingdom to come and in eternal life. 6 What,
then, shall we do to secure these things, except to conduct
ourselves in holiness and justice and regard these things of
the world as foreign to us and not desire them? 7 For it is
by desiring to possess these things that we fall from the path
of justice.

Chapter 6

1 The Lord says:[1] 'No servant can serve two masters.' If
we desire to serve both God and Mammon, it is no good to
us. 2 'For what is the advantage if a man gain the whole
world and lose his soul?'[2] 3 This world and the future world
are two enemies. 4 This world talks of adultery and corruption and love of money and deceit, but that world says farewell to these things. 5 We cannot, then, be friends of both,
but we must say farewell to this to possess the other. 6 We
think that it is better to despise the things which are here, for
they are small and passing and perishable, and to love the

---

1 Here again the source of the quotation (sects. 2-4) is unknown,
possibly an apocryphal gospel. The chief ideas are found in the
canonical gospels: Luke 10.3 and Matt. 10.16; Matt. 10.28 and
Luke 12.4,5.

---

1 Luke 16.13; Matt. 6.24.
2 Matt. 16.26; Mark 8.36; Luke 9.25.

things which are there, things good and imperishable. 7 For if we do the will of Christ, we shall find repose; but if not, nothing shall save us from eternal punishment, if we neglect His commandments. 8 And the Scripture also says, in Ezechiel, that 'although Noa and Job and Daniel arise, they shall not rescue their children in the captivity.'[3] But if even such just men cannot rescue their children by their own just actions, with what confidence shall we enter into the palace of God, if we do not keep our baptism pure and unspotted? Or who shall be our patron if we are not found to have holy and just works?

Chapter 7

1 So then, my brothers, let us strive, knowing that the contest is close at hand[1] and that many make voyages for corruptible contests, but not all are crowned—only those who have labored much and striven well. 2 Let us strive, then, that we may all be crowned. 3 Let us run the straight course, then, the incorruptible contest, and let many of us sail to it, and strive, that we also may receive the crown; and, if we cannot all be crowned, let us at least come near to the crown. 4 We must remember that he who takes part in a corruptible contest, if he be found dealing dishonestly, is flogged, taken away, and thrown off the course. 5 What do you think? What shall he suffer who cheats in the contest for immortality? 6 For, concerning those who have not kept the seal,[2]

---

3 Cf. Ezech. 14.14,18,20.

---

1 The figures of speech drawn in sects. 1-5 from athletic contests are like those in St. Paul, 1 Cor. 9.25-26. Some hold this passage (with 20.2 below) as evidence that the homily was preached at Corinth, where the famous Isthmian games were held. See Introduction.
2 Possibly baptismal vows are meant; cf. above, 6.9.

He says: 'Their worm shall not die, and their fire shall not be extinguished, and they shall be a spectacle to all flesh.'[3]

Chapter 8

1 While we are yet on earth, let us repent. 2 For we are as clay for the hand of the workman. Just as the potter, if he makes a vessel and it bends or breaks in his hands, shapes it over again, but if he has gone so far as to put it into the fiery oven, can do nothing to help it any more; so let us also, while we are still in this world, repent with our whole heart of the evil things we have done in the flesh, that we may be saved by the Lord while we have time for repentance. 3 For, after leaving the world, we cannot there confess or repent any more. 4 So then, brothers, by doing the will of the Father and preserving the flesh pure and keeping the commandments of the Lord, we shall obtain eternal life. 5 For the Lord says in the Gospel.[1] 'If you do not keep what is small, who will give you what is great? For I say to you, that he who is faithful in that which is least is faithful also in that which is great.' 6 He means, therefore, this: Keep the flesh pure and the seal[2] undefiled that we may receive eternal life.

Chapter 9

1 And let not any one of you say that this flesh is not judged and does not rise again. 2 Understand: In what state were you saved, in what did you recover your sight, except in this flesh? 3 We must, therefore, guard the flesh as a temple of God. 4 Just as you were called in the flesh, so shall you come in the flesh. 5 If Christ the Lord, who saved us, being spirit

---

3 Isa. 66.24; Mark 9.44.

---

1 Luke 16.10-12.
2 See note on 7.2 above.

at first, became flesh and so called us, so also shall we receive our reward in this flesh. 6 Let us, then, love one another, that we may all arrive at the Kingdom of God. 7 While we have time to be healed, let us give ourselves to God our Healer, giving Him some recompense. 8 What recompense? Repentance from a sincere heart. 9 For He has foreknowledge of all things and knows what is in our hearts. 10 Let us, then, give Him everlasting praise, not only from our mouth, but also from our heart, that He may receive us as sons. 11 For the Lord said:[1] 'Those who do the will of my Father are my brethren.'

Chapter 10

1 Therefore, my brothers, let us do the will of the Father who called us, that we may live, and let us rather seek virtue and abandon vice as the forerunner of our sins, and let us flee from ungodliness, lest evil things come upon us. 2 For, if we are zealous to do good, peace will follow us. 3 On this account it is not possible for men to find peace,[1] when they bring in human fears and prefer the pleasures of the present to the promises of the future. 4 For they know not what great torture the pleasures of the present bring and how great is the joy of the promised future. 5 And if only they themselves did these things, it could be endured; but, as it is, they continue teaching evil to innocent souls, not knowing that they will incur a double condemnation, themselves and their hearers.

---

1 Matt. 12.50; Mark 3.35; Luke 8.21.

---

1 The text appears to be corrupt here. The word 'peace' has been added to complete the sense. Something also may have been lost before the following clause.

Chapter 11

1 With a pure heart, then, let us serve God, and we shall be just; but if, through our not trusting the promises of God, we do not serve Him, we shall be miserable. 2 For the prophetic word says:[1] 'Miserable are the double-minded, who hesitate in their heart and say: All these things we have heard even in our fathers' time, but we have waited from day to day and have seen none of them. 3 O foolish men, compare yourselves to a tree. Take a vine; first it sheds its leaves, then there comes a bud, after this a sour berry, then the bunch of ripe grapes. 4 So also my people had upsets and afflictions, but afterwards it shall receive good things.' 5 Therefore, my brothers, let us not be double-minded, but let us be patient in hope, that we may also gain our reward. 6 'For He is faithful who promised'[2] to pay to each the wages of his works. 7 If, then, we perform justice before God, we shall enter into His kingdom and receive the promises which 'ear has not heard, nor eye seen, nor has it entered into the heart of men.'[3]

Chapter 12

1 Let us, then, wait for the Kingdom of God, from hour to hour, in love and justice, since we know not the day of God's manifestation. 2 For the Lord Himself, when asked by someone when His Kingdom would come, said:[1] 'When the two shall be one, and the outside as the inside, and the male

---

1 This same 'prophecy' is quoted as 'Scripture' in the authentic letter of Clement, Ch. 23, 3f. (p. 29). The source is unknown, but it shows an interesting literary connection between this work and *The Letter to the Corinthians*.
2 Heb. 10.13.
3 1 Cor. 2.9.

---

1 The unknown source of this quotation may be an apocryphal gospel.

with the female neither male nor female.' 3 Now, the 'two
are one' when we speak truth to each other, and there is one
soul in two bodies without dissimulation. 4 And 'the outside
as the inside' means this: the inside is the soul and the outside
the body. Therefore, just as your body is visible, so let your
soul be apparent in your good works. 5 And 'the male with
the female neither male nor female' means that a brother
seeing a sister has no thought of her as female, nor she of
him as male. 6 'If you do this,' He says, 'the Kingdom of
my Father shall come.'

Chapter 13

1 Accordingly, brothers, let us now at last repent and be
watchful for the good, for we are full of great folly and evil;
let us cleanse from ourselves our previous sins, and by repentance from our very heart gain salvation. Let us not be
pleasers of men, nor seek to please ourselves alone, but rather
by our justice those also who are outside, that the Name be
not blasphemed because of us. 2 For the Lord says:[1] 'My
name is continually blasphemed among all the Gentiles,' and
again: 'Woe to him on whose account my name is blasphemed.'[2] How is it blasphemed? By your not doing what I
desire. 3 For when the Gentiles hear from our mouth the
oracles of God, they wonder at their beauty and grandeur;
afterwards, when they find out that our works are unworthy
of the words we speak, they turn from this to blasphemy,
saying that it is a myth and a delusion. 4 For, when they
hear from us that God says:[3] 'It is no credit to you, if you

---

1 Isa. 52.5.
2 Cf. Matt. 18.7.
3 Luke 6.32,35; Matt. 5.44. Cf. *Didache* 1.3.

love them that love you, but it is a credit to you if you love
your enemies and those who hate you'—when they hear this,
they wonder at its surpassing goodness; but when they see
that not only do we not love those who hate us but not even
those who love us, they laugh scornfully at us, and so the
Name is blasphemed.

Chapter 14

1 Thus, brothers, by doing the will of God our Father, we
shall belong to the first Church, the spiritual one established
before the sun and the moon; but if we do not the will of
the Lord, we shall verify the Scripture which says:[1] 'My house
has become a den of thieves.' Let us choose, therefore, to
belong to the Church of life, that we may be saved. 2 I do
not think that you are ignorant that the living Church is 'the
body of Christ.'[2] For the Scripture says:[3] 'God made man
male and female'; the male is Christ and the female is the
Church. The sacred books, moreover, and the Apostles say
that the Church is not of the present time, but existed from
the beginning. For she was spiritual, as also our Jesus, and
He was revealed in the last days to save us.[4] 3 And the
Church, being spiritual, was revealed in the flesh of Christ,
showing us that if any of us guard her in the flesh and do
not corrupt her, he shall receive her again in the Holy Spirit.
For this flesh is an antitype of the Spirit; no one, accordingly,
who has corrupted the antitype shall receive the reality. So,
then, brothers, it means this: Guard the flesh, so that you may
share in the Spirit. 4 But if we say that the flesh is the Church

---

1 Matt. 21.13; Jer. 7.11.
2 Eph. 1.23.
3 Gen. 1.27.
4 1 Peter 1.20.

and the Spirit is Christ, then he who has abused the flesh has abused the Church. Such a one, accordingly, will not share in the Spirit, which is Christ. 5 The flesh is able to share in this great life and immortality, provided the Holy Spirit is joined to it. No one can declare or tell 'the things which the Lord has prepared'[5] for His chosen ones.

Chapter 15

1 It is no negligible advice, I think, that I have given you concerning self-control, and by following it a man will not regret, but will save both himself and me who advised him. For the reward is not small for having converted a straying and perishing soul to salvation. 2 For we have this return to make to God who created us, if both he who speaks and he who hears, speak and hear with faith and charity. 3 Let us, then, remain just and holy in the things which we have believed, that we may pray in confidence to God, who says:[1] 'While thou art still speaking, I will say: Behold, here I am.' 4 For this saying is the sign of great promise; for the Lord says that He is more ready to give than a man is to ask. 5 Being sharers of such great kindness, then, let us not begrudge ourselves the obtaining of such benefits. For, as these words contain a great joy for those who follow them, so they hold a great judgment for the disobedient.

Chapter 16

1 So, brothers, having received no slight opportunity to repent, let us, when there is yet time, turn to God who called us, while we still have One who awaits us. For if we bid farewell to these pleasures and overcome our soul by refusing

---

5 1 Cor. 2.9.

---

1 Isa. 58.9.

to carry out its evil desires we shall share in the mercy of Jesus. 3 But you know that 'the day' of judgment 'is now coming, kindled as a furnace,'[1] and 'the powers of heaven shall dissolve';[2] and the whole earth shall be as lead melting in the fire, and then shall the secret and public deeds of men be made known. 4 Almsgiving, therefore, is good as penance for sin; fasting is better than prayer, but almsgiving is better than both; and 'charity covers a multitude of sins,'[3] but prayer from a good conscience delivers from death. Blessed is every man who is found full of these things; for almsgiving relieves the burden of sin.

Chapter 17

1 Let us, then, repent wholeheartedly, that no one of us may perish by the way. For, if we have commandments to do this also, to snatch men away from idols and to instruct them, how much more necessary is it that a soul which already knows God should not be lost? 2 So let us help one another and guide those who are weak in goodness, that we may all be saved; and let us convert and encourage one another. 3 And let us not merely seem to pay attention and to believe now, while being admonished by the presbyters,[1] but also, when we have gone home, let us remember the commandments of the Lord and let us not be carried away by worldly lusts; but let us try to come here more frequently and to advance in the commandments of the Lord, that 'keeping the same mind'[2] we may be gathered together unto life. 4 For

---

1 Mal. 4.1.
2 Isa. 34.4.
3 1 Peter 4.8; cf. Prov. 10.12.

1 One of the indications that the present text is essentially a homily and not a letter, as once was believed. See Introduction.
2 Rom. 12.16.

the Lord said:[3] 'I come to gather together all the nations, tribes, and languages.' By this He means the day of His appearing. when He will come and redeem us, each according to his works. 5 And the believers 'shall see his glory[4] and might and shall be astounded when they look upon the sovereignty of the world given to Jesus and shall say: 'Woe to us, for it was thou, and we knew it not and did not believe, and were disobedient to the presbyters who preached to us about salvation.' And 'their worms shall not die and their fire shall not be quenched, and they shall be a spectacle to all flesh.'[5] 6 He means that day of judgment when they shall see those who were ungodly among us and contradicted the commandments of Jesus Christ. 7 But the just, who have done good and endured tortures and hated the pleasures of the soul, when they see how those who have sinned and denied Jesus by their words or their deeds are punished by terrible torture in unquenchable fire, shall give 'glory to their God,'[6] saying: 'There shall be hope for him who has served God with all his heart.'

Chapter 18

1 Let us also be of those who give thanks, who have served God, and not of the ungodly who are judged. 2 For I myself also am altogether sinful and have not escaped temptation, but, being still surrounded by the devices of the devil, I strive to pursue justice, so that I may have the strength at least to approach it, fearing the judgment to come.

---

3 Isa. 66.18.
4 Ibid.
5 Isa. 66.24; Mark 9.44.
6 Apoc. 11.13.

Chapter 19

1 Therefore, brothers and sisters, [following] the God of truth, I am reading to you an exhortation to heed what is written, that you may both save yourselves and him who is reading to you.[1] As a reward, I ask you to repent with your whole heart, giving yourselves salvation and life. By doing this, we shall set a goal for all the young who wish to work in the cause of piety and goodness of God. 2 And let us not be annoyed or displeased, fools that we are, when anyone corrects us and turns us from justice to justice. For sometimes we do evil unknowingly because of the double-mindedness and unbelief within our breasts, and we are 'darkened in our understanding'[2] by vain desires. 3 Let us, then, do justice that we may be saved in the end. Blessed are those who obey these instructions; although for a short time they suffer in this world, they shall reap the immortal fruit of the resurrection. 4 Let not the godly man grieve, then, if he be distressed in these present times. A time of blessedness awaits him; he shall live again above with the fathers and rejoice in an eternity without sorrow.

Chapter 20

1 But do not let it disturb your mind that we see the unjust

---

1 This may refer to the office of Reader (*lector*), which was definitely one of the minor orders at Rome in the time of Pope Cornelius (Eusebius, *Historia ecclesiastica* 6. 43.11). On the hypothesis that the present text is basically a homily sent in letter-form by Pope Soter at Rome to the Church at Corinth (see Introduction), it is not unreasonable that Chapters 1-18 (with 20.5 possibly appended) represent the text of the communication received from Rome, Chapters 19-20 (possibly less 20.5) being an addition made by the *lector* appointed at Corinth to read the communication.
2 Eph. 4.18.

wealthy and the servants of God in straitened circumstances. 2 Let us, then, have faith, brothers and sisters. We are contending in the contest of the living God and are being trained by the present life that we may obtain the crown in the life to come. 3 No one of the just has reaped fruit quickly, but waits for it. 4 For if God should pay out the reward of the just quickly, it would be immediately apparent that our training was in commerce and not in godliness, for we should seem to be just when we were pursuing not piety but gain. And for this cause the divine judgment punishes an unjust spirit and loads it with chains.[1] 5 To the one God, invisible,[2] Father of Truth, who sent us the Savior and Prince of Immortality, through whom also He manifested to us Truth and the life of heaven, to Him be glory for all ages. Amen.

---

1 In the above rendering the two verbs translated in the present tense appear in the Greek as past (aorist). Such so-called 'gnomic' use of the aorist is not uncommon in Classical Greek, and reasonably certain examples are found in the New Testament (James 1.24; 1 Peter 1.24 and James 1.11 are complicated by direct or indirect quotation from the Hebrew). If this interpretation is disallowed, the sentence would seem to refer to Satan: '. . . the divine judgment punished the Unjust Spirit, and loaded him with chains.'

2 1 Tim. 1.17.

THE LETTERS
OF
ST. IGNATIUS
OF ANTIOCH

Translated

by

† GERALD G. WALSH, S.J., M.A. (Oxon), Ph.D., ST.D.
Fordham University

IMPRIMI POTEST:

F. A. MCQUADE, S.J., PRAEP. PROV.

Neo Eboraci
die 8 Sept., 1946

INTRODUCTION

THE SEVEN LETTERS, which are here translated from the Greek text as established by critical researches of modern scholars,[1] are among the most precious treasures of early Christian literature. They reveal a rounded, living, lovable personality—a saint of gigantic spiritual stature; a passionate lover of the Cross and of the Church of Jesus Christ; a man of both ardor and order, with a heart large enough to hold tender human affections along with zealous pastoral solicitude, and a mind broad enough to range from the mysteries of angelology to practical matters of ecclesiastical and moral discipline; a genius too tumultuous for the petty proprieties of grammar and rhetoric, who rushes headlong from one bursting idea to another without bothering about the structure of his periods or paragraphs.

Yet, of the life of St. Ignatius of Antioch we know practically nothing beyond the meager allusions in the Letters themselves. It has been conjectured that he was born about the time of the passion and resurrection of our Lord. There is a legend—perhaps suggested merely by the name Theophorus ('God-borne' or 'God-bearing')—that he was a child carried in the arms of our Lord, as related by St. Mark.[2] On the other hand, there may be a hint in the expression

---

1 J. B. Lightfoot, *The Apostolic Fathers.* Edited and completed by J. R. Harmer (London 1891) : Kirsopp Lake, *The Apostolic Fathers* (Loeb Classical Library, New York 1912) 1; K. Bihlmeyer, *Die apostolischen Väter* (Tübingen 1924). Besides the translations by Lake and Lightfoot, there is a more recent one, J. H. Strawley, *The Epistles of Saint Ignatius* (S.P.C.K., London 1935).
2 Mark 9.36,37.

éktroma,[3] 'one born out of due time,' that he was a convert
to Christianity late in life.[4] There is reason to suppose that
he came into direct contact with more than one of the Apostles. The historian Eusebius,[5] who is careful in such matters,
tells us that Ignatius was the third bishop of Antioch—suc-
ceeding Evodius, the successor of St. Peter. Some details of
the martyrdom are given in a document of somewhat doubtful historical accuracy published by Ruinart in 1689.[6] The
saint seems to have been thrown to the beasts in the Flavian
amphitheatre in Rome in the second half of the reign of the
Emperor Trajan (98-117 A.D.) What bones were left were
religiously collected and returned for burial outside the Gate
of Daphne at Antioch. They were finally, in 637, transferred
to the Church of San Clemente in Rome.

It is possible, from the Letters, to establish part of the
saint's itinerary on his way from Antioch to Rome. He reports
that he was in the custody of guards 'on land and at sea.'[7]
This suggests that he sailed from Seleucia, the port of Antioch,
to Attilia in Pamphilia. We learn, too, that he passed through
Philadelphia on his way to Smyrna, where he rested to receive
delegations of Christians from the communities of Ephesus,
Magnesia and Tralles. From Smyrna, where Polycarp was
bishop, Ignatius proceeded to Troas. It is further clear, from
a letter written by Polycarp to the community at Philippi, that
Ignatius passed through this latter city.[8]

It was Polycarp who first mentioned a collection of letters

3 Letter to the Romans 9.
4 Cf. Trallians 13 and Smyrnaeans 11.
5 *Historia ecclesiastica* 3.36.
6 A critical edition of the so-called *Martyrium Colbertinum* will be
found in Funk-Diekamp, *Patres Apostolici* (1913) 2. 324ff.
7 Letter to the Romans 5.
8 For Polycarp's letter see below pp. 129ff., and particularly Chapters
9 and 13.

written by Ignatius. One of Polycarp's disciples, Irenaeus,[9] shows his familiarity with at least one of the Letters by quoting a phrase from the Letter to the Romans. The historian Eusebius is the first to indicate that there were seven letters in the collection with which he was familiar.[10]

In later centuries the original seven letters were expanded by interpolations; and additional letters, not written by Ignatius, were ascribed to him. On the other hand, copyists or translators were content to make a series of excerpts from a selection of the seven letters.[11] The result was that the authenticity of the Letters was long in debate and has only been settled by a determined effort of modern critical scholarship.

The dogmatic significance of the Letters will be obvious to every reader. Even when allowance is made for the normal development of doctrine and discipline during the last eighteen hundred years, St. Ignatius' firm handling of the mysteries of the Trinity, Incarnation, Redemption, and Eucharist, his insistence on the hierarchy of bishops, priests and deacons and the primacy of the see of Rome, his clear conception of the Church as Catholic, in the sense of one and universal, his allusions to the practice of Christian virginity, to the religious character of marriage, and to other such matters set up a standard by which all who are eager to adhere to the tradition of Apostolic Christianity may measure the degree of their conformity with this early witness.

---

9 *Adversus haereses* 5.28.4. This passage and several other witnesses to St. Ignatius and his Letters will be found collected in Migne, *Patrologia Graeca* 5.9-32.

10 *Historia ecclesiastica* 3.36.

11 An abbreviated Syriac form of the Letters to Polycarp, to the Ephesians and to the Romans, was published by W. Cureton, *The Ancient Syriac Version of the Epistles of S. Ignatius* (London 1945). See, too, Cureton's *Corpus Ignatianum* (London 1845). Altaner, *Patrologia* (Rome 1940) 59f., gives more references to the Syriac and Latin versions.

THE LETTERS OF ST. IGNATIUS OF ANTIOCH

I

To The Ephesians

IGNATIUS THEOPHORUS greets the Church of Ephesus in Asia, congratulating you as you deserve and wishing you perfect joy in Jesus Christ—you who have grown in spiritual stature through the fullness of God the Father, and have been predestined from eternity to eternal abiding and unchanging glory, and have been united and chosen through a true passion by the will of the Father and of Jesus Christ, our God.

(1) I have welcomed in God your well beloved name, which is yours by reason of your natural [sense and]¹ goodness in accord with faith and charity in Jesus Christ, our Savior. Imitators of God as you are, with hearts warmed in the blood of God, you have done perfectly the work that fell to you to do; for you were eager to visit me when you heard that I was on my way from Syria, in chains because of our common name and hope, and longing, with the help of your prayers, to face the wild beasts in Rome and not to fail and so become a disciple. And so in God's name I received your whole community in the person of Onesimus, your bishop, in the flesh, a man whose charity is beyond all power to say. I beg of you to love him in Jesus Christ and to be like him to a man. May He be blessed who gave you the grace to have and to deserve to have such a bishop.

---

1 The words in square brackets represent an addition to the Greek text suggested by Lightfoot. The words appear in an early Syriac version.

(2) A word about Burrhus, my fellow worker and your deacon by the will of God, a man blessed in every way. It is my prayer that he may continue with me to your honor and that of your bishop. Crocus, too, who is worthy of God and of yourselves, I have received as an exemplar of the love you bear me. He has been a great comfort to me in every way. May the Father of Jesus Christ reward him with His grace—and not only him but Onesimus, Burrhus, Euplus and Fronto; for in them I saw the love of all of you. If only I deserve it, may I have joy in you always. And so it is right for you to glorify Jesus Christ in every way, who has given you glory so that you may be made perfect in a single obedience to your bishop and the priests and be made holy in every way.

(3) I do not give you orders as though I were a person of importance, for I have not yet been made perfect in Jesus Christ, even though I am a prisoner for His name. But, at last, I am beginning to be His disciple and speak to you as His disciples, too. For I have need of being trained[2] by you in faith, counsel, endurance and long-suffering. Still, love will not let me be silent in your regard, and so I make bold to beg you to be in harmony with God's mind. For Jesus Christ, the life that cannot be taken from us, is the mind of the Father, and the bishops appointed to ends of the earth[3] are of one mind with Jesus Christ.

(4) Hence, it is right for you to concur, as you do, with

---

2 Literally, 'anointed,' that is, rubbed with embrocation as trainers do with athletes.
3 'Of one mind with . . .' Literally, 'in the mind of . . .' The theme of the unity of Christ with the Father, of the bishops with Christ, and of the faithful with the bishops is one that is very dear to the heart of Ignatius. The 'ends of the earth' meant for Ignatius in the beginning of the second century the Churches as far east as Mesopotamia and as far west as Gaul.

the name of the bishop. For your priests, who are worthy of the name and worthy of God, like the strings of a lyre, are in harmony with the bishops. Hence it is that in the harmony of your minds and hearts Jesus Christ is hymned. Make of yourselves a choir, so that with one voice and one mind, taking the key-note of God, you may sing in unison with one voice through Jesus Christ to the Father, and He may hear you and recognize you, in your good works, as members of His son. It is good for you, therefore, to be in perfect[4] unity that you may at all times be partakers of God.

(5) And if I, in a short time, have achieved such spiritual and not merely human communion with your bishop, all the more do I congratulate you who have become one with him, as the Church is one with Jesus Christ and as Jesus Christ is one with the Father, so that all things may be in harmony. Let no man be deceived. If a person is not inside the sanctuary[5] he is deprived of the Bread [of God]. For if the prayer of one or two men[6] has so much force, how much greater is that of the bishop and of the whole Church. Any one, therefore, who fails to assemble with the others has already shown his pride and set himself apart. For it is written: 'God resists the proud.'[7] Let us be careful, therefore, not to oppose the bishop, so that we may be obedient to God.

(6) And let a man respect the bishop all the more if he sees him to be a man of few words. For, whoever is sent by the Master to run His house, we ought to receive him as we would receive the Master himself. It is obvious, therefore, that we ought to regard the bishop as we would the Lord Himself. I should tell you that Onesimus himself is full of

4 Literally, 'blameless.'
5 Literally, 'the place of sacrifice.'
6 Cf. Matt. 18.18-20.
7 Prov. 3.34.

praise for your orderly, religious behavior, because all of you are living according to truth and because among you no heresy finds a home. Indeed, you do not so much as listen to anyone unless his speech is of Jesus Christ in truth.

(7) There are some who, in guile and wickedness, have a way of bearing the Name about while behaving in a way unworthy of God. Such men you must shun as you would wild beasts; for they are mad dogs that bite when you are not on your guard. Of these you must beware, for these men are hard to heal. There is one Doctor active in both body and soul, begotten and yet unbegotten, God in man, true life in death, son of Mary and Son of God, first able to suffer and then unable to suffer, Jesus Christ, our Lord.

(8) Let no one, therefore, deceive you as, in fact, being wholly given to God, you are not deceived. For, so long as no passion within you has an established power to torment you, you are certainly living according to God. As a cheap sacrifice[8] in your stead I offer myself for you Ephesians, for your Church which will be remembered in every age. Carnal men can no more do the works of the spirit than those who walk in the spirit do the things of the flesh; nor can faith do the things of infidelity nor infidelity the things of faith. Since you do all things in Jesus Christ, even those things are spiritual which you do according to the flesh.

(9) I have learned that some strangers[9] holding bad doctrine have passed your way, but that you have not allowed

---

8 The word here used is *peripsema*. It is the word used by St. Paul in 1 Cor. 4.13. It is used again by Ignatius in Ch. 18 of this Letter. Literally, *peripsema* means 'offscouring'; but it is sometimes applied to the 'scum,' the 'jail birds,' who were offered in sacrifice to appease the wrath of the gods in times of affliction. St. Ignatius wants to imply that his life is being offered up for the Church and, at the same time, that it is a life of no value.
9 Literally, 'persons from yonder.'

them to sow their seed among you and have stopped your ears lest you should receive what they sowed. Like the stones of a temple, cut for a building of God the Father, you have been lifted up to the top by the crane of Jesus Christ, which is the Cross, and the rope of the Holy Spirit. For your faith has drawn you up and charity has been the road leading to God. You are all fellow pilgrims,[10] carrying with you God and His temple; you are bearers of Christ and of holy offerings, decked out in the commandments of Jesus Christ. And with this letter I am able to take part in your festivity, to be of your company, to share in the joy that comes from setting your heart not on what is merely human in life, but on God.

(10) And so do not cease to pray for all other men, for there is hope of their conversion and of their finding God. Give them the chance to be instructed, at least by the way you behave. When they are angry with you, be meek; answer their words of pride by your humility, their blasphemies by your prayers, their error by your steadfastness in faith, their bullying by your gentleness. Let us not be in a hurry to give them tit for tat, but, by our sweet reasonableness, show that we are their brothers. Let us rather be eager to imitate the Lord, striving to be the first in bearing wrongs, in suffering loss, in being despised, so that no weed of the evil one may be found among you; but abide in Jesus Christ in perfect purity and temperance of body and soul.

(11) The last days are at hand. For the rest, let us live in reverence and fear of the patience of God, lest it turn in

---

10 The rapid change of metaphors, from seed and soil to stones and building and now to pilgrims with their festal clothes and carved offerings, is typical of St. Ignatius' tumultuous style. For an illustration of such a pagan procession see Lightfoot, *Ignatius and Polycarp* 2.17. See, too, Acts 19.24 for silver shrines made by Demetrius of Ephesus for the pilgrims to the temple of Artemis.

judgment against us. Either let us fear the wrath which is to come or else let us love the grace we have—one or the other, so long as we are found in Jesus Christ unto true life. Let nothing appeal to you apart from Him, by whose help I bear my chains about with me like spiritual pearls; and in these, with your prayers—in which I trust always to have a share—may I rise again, so that I may be found in the company of the Christian Ephesians who have always been at one with the Apostles through the power of Jesus Christ.

(12) I know who I am and to whom I am writing. I am a condemned man; you have received mercy. I am in danger; you are safe. You are the road for those on the way to die for God. You have shared in the sacraments[11] with Paul who was made a saint, who died a martyr, who deserved to be blessed—in whose footsteps may I be found when I reach God; in whose every letter[12] there is a mention of you in Christ Jesus.

(13) Be zealous, therefore, to assemble more frequently to render thanks[13] and praise to God. For, when you meet together frequently, the powers of Satan are destroyed and danger from him is dissolved in the harmony of your faith. There is nothing better than peace in which an end is put to the warfare of things in heaven and on earth.

(14) You are aware of all these truths if you have perfect faith and love for Jesus Christ—the beginning and end of life; for faith is the beginning and the end is love and God is the two of them brought into unity. After these comes whatever else makes up a Christian gentleman. No one

---

11 Literally, 'you are initiated into the mysteries along with Paul.'
12 This may mean 'throughout the whole of one of those letters,' namely, the Epistle to the Ephesians.
13 The verb *eucharistein* may well have here the more special sense of 'to celebrate the Eucharist.'

commits sin who professes the faith, and no one hates who is possessed of charity. A tree is shown by its fruit,[14] and in the same way those who profess to belong to Christ will be seen by what they do. For what is needed is not mere present profession,[15] but perseverance to the end in the power of faith.

(15) It is better to say nothing and be [a Christian] than to speak and not to be [one]. It is good to teach, if one practices what he preaches. There is one Teacher who spoke—and the thing was done;[16] and even the things He did without speaking are worthy of the Father. Anyone who is really possessed of the word of Jesus can listen to His silence[17] and so be perfect; so that he may act through his words and be known by his silence. Nothing is hidden from the Lord and even the things we hide are near Him. Let us do all that we do, therefore, as though He were dwelling within us—we as His temple and He within as our God. And so, indeed, it is, and will be clearly seen by us from the love we justly bear Him.

[margin, handwritten: Literal indwelling of Christ]

(16) Make no mistake, brethren; the corrupters of families will not inherit the kingdom of God. If, then, those are dead who do these things according to the flesh, how much worse if, with bad doctrine, one should corrupt the faith of God for which Jesus Christ was crucified. Such a man, for becoming contaminated, will depart into unquenchable fire; and so will any one who listens to him.

(17) It was for this reason that the Lord received the

---

14 Cf. Matt. 12.33; Luke 5.44.
15 This may mean: 'At present the Work (i.e., of preaching and practicing the Christian religion) is no mere matter of profession.' Cf. Acts 15.38; Phil. 2.30; John 4.34; 6.29; 17.4.
16 Cf. Ps. 32.9.
17 I.e., can learn the lessons of His hidden life at Nazareth, of His silence during the passion.

ointment on his head[18]—that he might breathe the odor of incorruptibility into the Church. Be not anointed with the bad odor of the doctrine of the prince of this world, lest he lead you away captive from the life proposed to you. Why do we not all become wise by accepting the knowledge of God which is Jesus Christ? Why do we perish in our folly by being ignorant of the grace which the Lord has truly sent us?

(18) I offer up my life as a poor substitute[19] for the Cross, which is a stumbling block to those who have no faith, but to us salvation and eternal life. Where is the wise man? Where is the philosopher?[20] Where is the boasting of the so-called men of prudence? For our God Jesus Christ was, according to God's dispensation, the fruit of Mary's womb, of the seed of David; He was born and baptized in order that He might make the water holy by His passion.

(19) The maidenhood of Mary and her child-bearing and also the death of the Lord were hidden from the prince of this world—three resounding mysteries wrought in the silence of God. How, then, did He appear in time? A star, brighter than all other stars, shone in the sky, and its brightness was ineffable and the novelty of it caused astonishment. And the rest of the stars, along with the sun and the moon, formed a choir about the star; but the light of the star by itself outshone all the rest. It was a puzzle to know the origin of this novelty unlike anything else. Thereupon all magic was dissolved, every bond of malice disappeared, ignorance was destroyed, the ancient kingdom was ruined, when God ap-

---

18 Cf. John 12.3.
19 The same word *peripsema* occurs here as in Ch. 8. Literally 'my spirit (or life) is a cheap sacrifice in comparison with the Cross.'
20 Cf. 1 Cor. 1.20,23,24.

peared in the form of man to give us newness of eternal life. What had been prepared in God now had a beginning. And, because of the plan for the abolition of death, all things were disturbed.

(20) If, through your prayers, Jesus Christ should make me worthy and if it should be His will, and still more if the Lord should reveal it to me, in a second letter which I intend to write to you, I shall explain more fully what I have merely touched upon—the dispensation of becoming the new man Jesus Christ, who is of the race of David according to the passion and resurrection. Come together in common, one and all without exception in charity, in one faith and in one Jesus Christ, who is of the race of David according to the flesh, the son of man and Son of God, so that with undivided mind you may obey the bishop and the priests, and break one Bread[21] which is the medicine of immortality and the antidote against death, enabling us to live for ever in Jesus Christ.

(21) I am offering up my life[22] for you and for those whom, to the honor of God, you sent to Smyrna; and from here I write to you, thanking the Lord and loving Polycarp as I love you. Remember me as Jesus Christ remembers you. Pray for the Church which is in Syria, from which I, the last of the faithful there, am being led away a prisoner to Rome; for so I was deemed worthy to be found to God's glory. Farewell in God the Father and in Jesus Christ our common hope.

---

21 A clear reference to Holy Communion. Cf. Acts 2.46; 20.7; 1 Cor. 10.16,17; John 6.53,54.
22 The word *antipsychon* which is used here and again in the Letter to the Smyrnaeans, Ch. 10, and in the Letter to Polycarp, Chs. 2 and 6, seems to have something of the force of *peripsema*. The central idea is that St. Ignatius is dying physically in order that his brothers may live supernaturally. Cf. the counsel in 1 John 3.16.

II

To the Magnesians

IGNATIUS THEOPHORUS to the Church in Magnesia near the Maeander that is blessed with the grace of God the Father through Jesus Christ our Savior. I salute you and wish you every joy in God the Father and in Jesus Christ.

(1) I have heard of the perfect order of your love toward God; and so it is with great joy and in the faith of Jesus Christ that I have decided to address you. Honored as I have been with a name so dear to God,[1] I sing, in the chains I bear about with me, the praise of the Churches. And I pray that the Churches may have unity in the flesh and spirit of Jesus Christ, who is our everlasting life—a union in faith and charity that is to be preferred to all else and, especially, union with Jesus and the Father, through whom we shall reach God if only we bear with and escape from the wanton attacks of the prince of this world.

(2) It was possible[2] for me to see you in the persons of your devout bishop Damas and the worthy priests, Bassus and Apollonius, and my fellow worker, the deacon Zotion. May I continue to have joy in him, since he is obedient to the bishop, as to the grace of God, and to the priests, as to the law of Jesus Christ.

(3) It ill becomes you to treat your bishop too familiarly because of his youth. You should show him all reverence out of respect for the authority of God the Father. This, I understand, the holy priests do. They take no advantage of his

---

1 He may mean the name *Theophorus*, which is Greek for 'God bearer' or 'God-borne,' according to the accent.
2 In the Greek text St. Ignatius begins with 'Since it was possible . . . and leaves the sentence unfinished.

youthful appearance, but they yield to him as to one who is wise in God—not, of course, merely to him, but to the Father of Jesus Christ, who is the bishop over all. To the honor of Him who loves you, you must obey without any insincerity; for in this case one does not so much deceive a bishop who can be seen as try to outwit one who is invisible—in which case one must reckon not with a man, but with God who knows our hidden thoughts.

(4) It is not enough to be Christians in name; it behooves us to be such in fact. So, too, there are those who invoke the name of the bishop while their actions are without any regard for him. Such men, it seems to me, are lacking in good conscience, for they do not assemble regularly as enjoined.

No valid authority

(5) Seeing that all things have an end, two things are proposed to our choice—life and death; and each of us is to go to his appropriate place. As there are two currencies, the one of God, and the other of the world, each stamped in its own way, so the unbelieving have the stamp of the world; those who, in charity, believe have the stamp of God the Father through Jesus Christ. And, unless it is our choice to die, through Him, unto His passion, His life is not in us.

Marks of salvation

(6) In the persons I have mentioned I have seen in faith, and have loved, your whole community; and so I exhort you to be careful to do all things in the harmony of God, the bishop having the primacy after the model of God and the priests after the model of the council of the Apostles, and the deacons (who are so dear to me) having entrusted to them the ministry of Jesus Christ—who from eternity was with the Father and at last appeared to us. Let all reverence one another in conformity with God's will. Let no man regard his neighbor with the eyes of the flesh, but in Jesus Christ love one another at all times. Let there be nothing among

you to divide you; but be at one with the bishop and with
those who are over you, thus affording a model and lesson
of immortal life.

(7) Just as the Lord, being one with the Father, did
nothing, either in His own person or through the Apostles,
without the Father, so you should do nothing without the
bishop and the council of priests. Nor should you try to make
a thing out to be reasonable, merely because it seems so to
you personally; but let there be in common a single prayer,
one petition, one mind, one hope, in love, in the unmixed[3]
joy which is Jesus Christ who is the best of all. Hasten all of
you together as to one temple of God, to one altar, to Jesus
Christ alone, who came forth from one Father in whom He
is and to whom He has returned.

(8) Do not be led astray either by new doctrines or old
fables which are now useless, for, to go on observing Jewish
rites[4] is to deny that we have received grace. Remember that
the holiest prophets lived according to Jesus Christ, and for
this reason they were persecuted; they were inspired by His
grace so that unbelievers might be fully assured that there is
one God, who has manifested Himself in Jesus Christ His Son,
who is His Word proceeding[5] from silence, and who in all
things was pleasing to Him who sent Him.

(9) How, then, shall we be able to live apart from Him,
seeing that the prophets were His disciples in the Spirit and

---

3 Literally, 'joy without blame.'
4 One of the main difficulties that St. Ignatius had to contend with
   was the 'Judaizing' tendency of early Christians who emphasized
   the Law more than Grace. He tried to insist on what St. Paul says in
   Gal. 2.21: 'If we can be justified through the law, then Christ's death
   was needless.'
5 The Greek text, as we now have it, says 'not proceeding.' However,
   the Armenian version, made from an early Syriac translation, says
   'proceeding.' This suits the context better.

expected Him as their Master, and that many who were brought up in the old order have come to the newness of hope? They no longer observe the Jewish Sabbaths, but keep holy the Lord's day, on which, through Him and through His death, our life arose; and by this mystery—though some deny Him—we have received our faith, and therefore we persevere in the hope of being found to be the disciples of Jesus Christ, our only Master; and because of this mystery He whom the prophets rightly waited for came and raised them from the dead.

(10) And, therefore, let us not be ungrateful for His loving kindness; for, were He to act toward us as we do toward Him, we should perish. So, let us become His disciples; let us learn to live the life that Christianity calls for. No one with any other name than this can belong to God. Put away, therefore, the bad leaven which is old and stale, and be converted into the new leaven which is Jesus Christ. Be salted in Him, lest any of you lose your savor, for by your savor will you be judged. It is out of place to preach Jesus Christ and to practice Judaism. For Christianity did not believe in Judaism, but Judaism in Christianity; it was in this that men of every tongue believed and were gathered together in God.

(11) Do not think that I have heard that any among you, my beloved, are practicing Judaism; but I say these things, small as I am in comparison with yourselves, to forewarn you against falling into the snares of an empty doctrine. I hope, rather, that you may be fully convinced of the birth and passion and the resurrection that took place during the period of the governorship of Pontius Pilate. These things were really and truly[6] done by Jesus Christ, our hope; and

---

6 Here, as in many other parts of these Letters, Ignatius has in mind the danger of the heresy of Docetism, according to which our Lord merely *seemed* to have lived and suffered in a human way.

from this hope may God forbid that any of you should be turned aside.

(12) If only I am worthy, I hope I may have joy in you in every way. It is true that I am in bonds, but in comparison with any of you who are at liberty I am no one. I know that you are not vain, for you have Jesus Christ within you; and when I praise you I know that you reprove yourselves more than ever—for, it is written: 'The just man is his own accuser.'[7]

(13) Be eager, therefore, to be confirmed in the commandments of our Lord and His Apostles, so that 'whatever you do may prosper'[8] in body and spirit, in faith and charity, in the Son and Father and Spirit, in the beginning and in the end, along with your most reverend bishop and the priests —the spiritual wreath that so fitly crowns him—and the deacons, who are men of God. Be obedient to your bishop and to one another, as Jesus Christ in His human nature was subject to the Father and as the Apostles were to Christ and the Father. In this way there will be union of body and spirit.

(14) I have exhorted you briefly, because I know that you are full of God. Remember me in your prayers, so that I may reach God, and also the Church in Syria, of which, however unworthily, I am a member. I need your united prayer and love in God, if the Church in Syria is to have the grace of being bedewed by your fervent prayer.

(15) From Smyrna, where I am writing to you, the Ephesians salute you. They are with me, like yourselves, for

---

7 This is a quotation from the Septuagint Greek version of Prov. 18.17.
8 According to the Septuagint translation of Ps. 1.3.

the glory of God, and have been an unfailing consolation to me; so, too, Polycarp, the bishop of the people of Smyrna, and all the other Churches, too, salute you in honor of Jesus Christ. Trusting that you may remain in the harmony of God, possessed of the spirit of union which is Jesus Christ, farewell.

III

To the Trallians

GNATIUS THEOPHORUS to the holy Church which is in Tralles in Asia. Beloved as you are by God, the Father of Jesus Christ, elect and worthy of God, outwardly and inwardly at peace through the passion of Jesus Christ, in whom we have hope through our resurrection unto Him, I salute you in the fullness of God, as the Apostles used to do, and I wish you every joy.

(1) By the will of God and of Jesus Christ your bishop, Polybius, has visited me here in Smyrna. He tells me that by nature more than by habit you are faultless in disposition and resolute in patience. In spite of the bonds I bear for Jesus Christ, he filled me with such consolation that in him I was able to behold your whole community. Accepting your spiritual benevolence through him, I thanked God to find, as I had heard, that you are imitators of God.

(2) For it seems to me that, when you are obedient to the bishop as you would be to Jesus Christ, you are living, not in a human way, but according to Jesus Christ, who died for us that by faith in His death you might escape death. You must continue, then, to do nothing apart from the bishop. Be obedient, too, to the priests as to the apostles of Jesus Christ, our hope—in whom we shall be found, if only we live in Him. And, as ministers of the mysteries of Jesus Christ, the deacons should please all in every way they can; for they are not merely ministers of food and drink, but the servants of the Church of God. They must avoid all reproach as they would beware of fire.

(3) In the same way all should respect the deacons as

they would Jesus Christ, just as they respect the bishop as representing the Father and the priests as the council of God and the college of the Apostles. Apart from these there is nothing that can be called a Church. In such matters I am sure you feel as I do, for I have received a sample of your love in the person of your bishop who is here with me. His demeanor is a great lesson; his meekness is his power. I am sure that even the infidels esteem him. Because I love you I treat you gently; but on his behalf I could write more sharply. However, prisoner as I am, I have not felt myself in a position to command you as though I were an Apostle.

(4) By the grace of God I am not lacking in wisdom; but I measure my words, lest my boasting should be fatal. I must, in fact, be more afraid than ever of paying attention to those who flatter me. Their words only serve to scourge me. I long to suffer, but I do not know if I am worthy. To most people my ardor[1] is not apparent, but for my part it is becoming irresistible.[2] My prayer is for humility, by which the prince of this world is overcome.

(5) It is not that I am unable to write to you of heavenly realities, but I am afraid that, children as you are, I might do you harm. Please share my convictions, else you may be choked by what you cannot swallow. For myself, I do not pretend to be a disciple merely because I am in chains and can contemplate such mysteries as the ordered hierarchy of angels and principalities and the visible and invisible worlds. Much must be lacking to us, if we are not to lose God.

(6) I exhort you, then, to leave alone the foreign fodder of heresy and keep entirely to Christian food. It is not I, but the love of Jesus Christ, that speaks. For the heretics mingle

1 Some translate éris as though it meant the 'envy of Satan.'
2 Literally, 'it makes war on me.'

poison wih Jesus Christ, as men might administer a deadly drug in sweet wine, without giving a hint of their wickedness, so that without thought or fear of the fatal sweetness a man drinks his own death.

(7) Against such men be on your guard. This will be possible if you are not proud and if you keep close to Jesus Christ and the bishop and the ordinances of the Apostles. Anyone who is within the sanctuary is pure and anyone who is outside is impure, that is to say, no one who acts apart from the bishop and the priests and the deacons has a clear conscience.

(8) Not that I have heard of anything of this sort among you; but I keep watch over you as ones I love, foreseeing, as I do, the snares of the devil. And so, put on the armor of forbearance and refresh yourselves in faith, that is, in the body of the Lord, and in love, that is, in the blood of Jesus Christ. Let no one be down on his neighbor. Let not the folly of a few give occasion to the pagans to calumniate your pious community. 'Woe unto him through whom my name is calumniated before others without cause.'[3]

(9) And so, be deaf when anyone speaks to you apart from Jesus Christ, who was of the race of David, the son of Mary, who was truly born and ate and drank, who was truly persecuted under Pontius Pilate and was really crucified and died in the sight of those 'in heaven and on earth and under the earth.'[4] Moreover He was truly raised from the dead by the power of His Father; in like manner His Father, through Jesus Christ, will raise up those of us who believe in Him. Apart from Him we have no true life.

---

3 Isa. 52.5, freely translated. Cf. the same quotation in the Letter of Polycarp to the Philippians, Ch. 10.
4 Phil. 2.10.

(10) If, as some say who are godless in the sense that they are without faith, He merely seemed to suffer—it is they themselves who merely seem to exist—why am I in chains? And why do I pray that I may be thrown to the wild beasts? I die, then, to no purpose. I do but bear false witness against the Lord.

(11) Avoid, therefore, the evil sprouts that bring forth deadly fruit. Merely to taste this fruit is to meet a sudden death. Such are not the plants of the Father. If they were, they would appear as branches of the Cross and their fruit would be immortal. It is by the Cross, by His passion, that He invites you who are His members. The Head cannot be born without the members, since it was God, that is, He Himself, who promised to keep them together.

(12) I am writing these greetings from Smyrna. With them goes those of the others of God's Churches who are with me. They have been of comfort to me in many ways, both physical and spiritual. My bonds—which I bear about with me for the cause of Jesus Christ and as a petition that I may reach God—are my exhortations to you. Persevere in harmony with one another and in common prayer together. All of you without exception, and particularly the priests, must help to keep up the bishop's spirit out of reverence for the Father and Jesus Christ and the Apostles. I beg you to give heed in charity to what I say, so that my letter may not be taken in evidence against you. Pray for me, for by the mercy of God I stand in need of your charity, if I am to be worthy of the end I am eager to meet and am not to be found reprobate.

(13) The Smyrnaeans and Ephesians greet you in love. Remember in your prayers the Church in Syria of which— unworthy as I am, for I am the least among them—I am

a member. Farewell in Jesus Christ. Be obedient to your bishop—and to the priests as well—as to the commandment [of God]. With undivided heart let each and all of you love one another. My life is offered for you, both now and when I shall be with God. I am not yet out of danger, but the Father, through Jesus Christ, can be counted on to answer both your prayer and mine. May we be found with Him without blame.

To the Romans

IGNATIUS THEOPHORUS to the Church on which the majesty of the most high Father and of Jesus Christ, His only Son, has had mercy; to the Church beloved and enlightened by the faith and charity of Jesus Christ, our God, through the will of Him who has willed all things that exist—the Church in the place of the country[1] of the Romans which holds the primacy. I salute you in the name of Jesus Christ, the Son of the Father. You are a Church worthy of God, worthy of honor, felicitation and praise, worthy of attaining to God, a Church without blemish, which holds the primacy of the community of love,[2] obedient to Christ's law, bearing the Father's name. To you who are united, outwardly

[handwritten marginal note: i.e., territorial primacy]

---

1 The reading *en tópo choriou*, 'in the place of the country,' makes very poor sense. It was suggested by P. S. Phillimore in an article in the *Journal of Theological Studies* 19 (1919) 276 that we should read *Christoû for choriou*. In this case the meaning would be 'the Church of the Romans that holds the primacy in the place of Christ.' This should be compared with the expression in the Letter to the Magnesians 6 which means either 'the bishop having the primacy in the place (*tópo*) of God' or 'having the primacy according to the pattern (*typo*) of God.' the reading with *tópos* has the authority of our present Greek text and of the Latin translation. The reading with *typo* is suggested by the Syriac and Armenian versions.

2 It has been well argued by F. X. Funk that the word *agápe*, 'love' has often the meaning in St. Ignatius of 'the community.' The Greek verb *prokáthemai*, 'I preside over,' is always found followed, as in Plato (*Laws* 758 D), by some such word as 'city' and never by a merely abstract noun like 'love.' Whether St. Ignatius has in mind a pre-eminence of authority or of charity, the context seems to imply that he means a universal and not merely a local pre-eminence. It will be noted that, unlike the other Letters in this series, the one to the Roman Church contains no hint of doctrinal or disciplinary disunion.

and inwardly, in the whole of His commandment and filled with grace, in union with God and with every alien stain filtered away, I wish every innocent joy in Jesus Christ, our God.

(1) In answer to my prayer and beyond all I asked for, I have at last seen the faces I have longed to see.[3] In chains as I am for Jesus Christ, I hope to salute you, if only it be His will to grant me grace to reach my goal. I shall know that the beginning is providential[4] if, in the end, without hindrance, I am to obtain the inheritance. But I am afraid of your love; it may do me wrong. It is easy for you to have your way, but if you do not yield to me, it will be hard for me to reach God.

(2) I would have you think of pleasing God—as indeed you do—rather than men. For at no later time shall I have an opportunity like this of reaching God; nor can you ever have any better deed ascribed to you—if only you remain silent. If only you will say nothing in my behalf, I shall be a word of God. But, if our love is for my body, I shall be once more a mere voice.[5] You can do me no greater kindness than to suffer me to be sacrificed to God while the place of sacrifice is still prepared. Thus forming yourselves into a chorus of love, you may sing to the Father in Jesus Christ

---

3 This may mean simply 'your holy faces.' *Axiótheos* means 'worthy of God, holy' and *axiothéos* means 'worth seeing.' The Armenian version takes the meaning 'worth seeing.'

4 Literally, 'well ordained.'

5 St. Ignatius seems to have in mind the difference between the 'word,' *lógos*, that was made flesh (John 1.14), and the 'voice,' *phoné*, of one crying in the wilderness (John 1.23). The choice for St. Ignatius was between dying, and so making his life meaningful, in some sense like the *Lógos*, the 'only begotten Son, who abides in the bosom of the Father' and who 'has himself brought us a clear message'; or of being spared and so finding his life without meaning, like an unintelligble cry. Cf. what is said below in 3, 'for our God, Jesus Christ, is manifest the more now that He is hidden in God.'

that God gave the bishop of Syria the grace of being transferred from the rising to the setting sun.[6] It is good to set,
leaving the world for God, and so to rise in Him.

(3) Never have you envied anyone. You have been others'
teachers. I trust that what you have taught and prescribed
to others may now be applied by yourselves.[7] Beg only that
I may have inward and outward strength, not only in word
but in will, that I may be a Christian not merely in name but
in fact. For, if I am one in fact, then I may be called one
and be faithful long after I have vanished from the world.
Nothing merely visible is good, for our God, Jesus Christ, is
manifest the more now that He is hidden in God. Christianity
is not the work of persuasion, but, whenever it is hated by
the world, it is a work of power.

(4) I am writing to all the Churches to tell them all that
I am, with all my heart, to die for God—if only you do not
prevent it. I beseech you not to indulge your benevolence
at the wrong time. Please let me be thrown to the wild beasts;
through them I can reach God. I am God's wheat; I am
ground by the teeth of the wild beasts that I may end as
the pure bread of Christ. If anything, coax the beasts on to
become my sepulcher and to leave nothing of my body un-
devoured so that, when I am dead, I may be no bother to
anyone. I shall be really a disciple of Jesus Christ if and
when the world can no longer see so much as my body. Make
petition, then, to the Lord for me, so that by these means I
may be made a sacrifice to God. I do not command you, as
Peter and Paul did. They were Apostles; I am a condemned

---

6 That is, from the East to the West.
7 St. Ignatius means that the Church of Rome, so far from begrudg-
ing anyone the grace of martyrdom, has exhorted others to follow the
example of the martyrs. Cf. the Letter of Clement of Rome to the
Corinthians.

man. They were free men; I am still a slave. Still, if I suffer, I shall be emancipated by Jesus Christ and, in my resurrection, shall be free. But now in chains I am learning to have no wishes of my own.

(5) I am already battling with beasts on my journey from Syria to Rome. On land and at sea, by night and by day, I am in chains with ten leopards around me—or at least with a band of guards who grow more brutal the better they are treated. However, the wrongs they do me make me a better disciple. 'But that is not where my justification lies.'[8] May I find my joy in the beasts that have been made ready for me. My prayer is that they will be prompt in dealing with me. I shall coax them to devour me without delay and not be afraid to touch me, as has happened in some cases. And if, when I am ready, they hold back, I shall provoke them to attack me. Pardon me, but I know what is good for me. I am now beginning to be a disciple; may nothing visible or invisible prevent[9] me from reaching Jesus Christ. Fire and cross and battling with wild beasts, [their clawing and tearing,[10]] the breaking of bones and mangling of members, the grinding of my whole body, the wicked torments of the devil —let them all assail me, so long as I get to Jesus Christ.

(6) Neither the kingdoms of this world nor the bounds of the universe can have any use for me. I would rather die for Jesus Christ than rule the last reaches of the earth. My search is for Him who died for us; my love is for Him who rose for our salvation. The pangs of new birth are upon me. Forgive me, brethren. Do nothing to prevent this new life.

'What you have to do, do quickly.'

---

8 1 Cor. 4.4.

9 Literally, *zelósai* means 'envy' or 'be jealous of' as in Gal. 4.17.

10 The words in square brackets are supplied from the version in the *Martyrium* of St. Ignatius.

Do not desire that I shall perish. Do not hand over to the world a man whose heart is fixed on God. Do not entice me with material things. Allow me to receive the pure light. When I reach it, I shall be fully a man. Allow me to be a follower of the passion of my God. Let those who hold Him in their hearts understand what urges me, realize what I am choosing, and share my feelings.

(7) The prince of this world is eager to tear me to pieces, to weaken my will that is fixed on God. Let none of you who are watching the battle abet him. Come in, rather on my side, for it is the side of God. Do not let your lips be for Jesus Christ and your heart for the world. Let envy have no place among you. And even, when I am come, if I should beseech you, pay no attention to what I say; believe, rather, what I am writing to you now. For alive as I am at this moment of writing, my longing is for death. Desire[11] within me has been nailed to the cross and no flame of material longing is left. Only the living water speaks within me saying: Hasten to the Father. I have no taste for the food that perishes nor for the pleasures of this life. I want the Bread of God which is the Flesh of Christ, who was of the seed of David; and for drink I desire His blood which is love that cannot be destroyed.

(8) I desire no longer to live a purely human life; and this desire can be fulfilled if you consent. Make this your choice, if you yourselves would be chosen. I make my petition in a few words. Please believe me; Jesus Christ will make it clear to you that I speak the truth, for He was the mouth without deceit through which the Father truly spoke. Beg for me that, through the Holy Spirit, I may not fail. I have

---

11 The word *éros* which is here used may mean 'my Love' or 'my Beloved,' that is, Jesus Christ.

not written to you after the manner of men, but according to the mind of God. If I die, it will prove you loved me; if I am rejected, it will be because you hated me.

(9) Remember in your prayers that Church of Syria, which now, in place of me, has God for its pastor. Jesus Christ, along with your love, will be its only bishop. For myself, I am ashamed to be called one of them, for I am not worthy, being the last among them and, as it were, born out of due time.[12] If I reach God, I shall be some one only by His mercy. My spirit salutes you—and with it the love of the Churches which welcomed me in the name of Jesus Christ. They treated me as more than a passing pilgrim; for even the communities that did not lie along the route I was taking conducted me from city to city.

(10) I am writing this letter to you from Smyrna by the hands of the Ephesians, who deserve all praise. Among many others who are with me there is my dear friend Crocus. I trust you have come to know those who went ahead of me from Syria to Rome for the glory of God. Please tell them that I am not far away. All of them are worthy of God and of yourselves. You will do well to help them in every way. The date of this writing is the ninth day before the calends of September.[13] Farewell, and persevere to the end in Jesus Christ.

---

12 *Ektroma.* St. Paul uses the word of himself in 1 Cor. 15.8. Some have seen in the expression a hint that St. Ignatius was converted late in life.
13 August 24.

V

To the Philadelphians

GNATIUS THEOPHORUS to the Church of God the Father and of Jesus Christ in Philadelphia in Asia.[1] You have felt God's mercy and are firmly established in union with God and with unduring joy in the passion of our Lord, through abundant mercy you have been given full assurance of His resurrection. I greet you in the blood of Jesus Christ. Your Church is to me a cause of unending and unbroken joy. It will be even more so, if all continue to be at one with the bishop and with his priests and with the deacons, who have been appointed according to the mind of Jesus Christ. All these are men after His own will and He has confirmed them in stability through His Holy Spirit.

(1) I know that your bishop has been given his ministry for the common good, not by any effort of his own or of others nor out of vain glory, but through the love of God the Father and of the Lord Jesus Christ. I am full of admiration for the sweet reasonableness of a man who can do more by his silence than others by speaking. He has been attuned to the commandments like a harp with its strings. And so my soul blesses his determination which is fixed on God. I know how virtuous and perfect it is, how unperturbable and calm, how modeled his life is on the sweet reasonableness of God.

(2) You are children of truth; shun schisms and heresies. Follow, as sheep do, wherever the shepherd leads. There are many wolves plausible enough to ensnare the pilgrims of God[2]

---

1 Unlike the preceding Letters which were written from Smyrna, this and the following Letters were written from Troas.
2 Literally, 'the runners in God's race.' Cf. Gal. 5.7; 1 Cor. 9.24.

by evil pleasure. However, the harmony among you will leave
no place for them.

(3) Keep away from the poisonous weeds which grow
where Jesus Christ does not till the soil, for they are not of
the planting of the Father. Not that I have found any division among you—except the filtering away of impure elements.
For, all who belong to God and Jesus Christ are with the
bishop. And those, too, will belong to God who have returned,
repentant, to the unity of the Church so as to live in accordance with Jesus Christ. Make no mistake, brethren. No one
who follows another into schism inherits the Kingdom of
God.[3] No one who follows heretical doctrine is on the side of
the passion.

(4) Be zealous, then, in the observance of one Eucharist.[4]
For there is one flesh of our Lord, Jesus Christ, and one
chalice that brings union in His blood. There is one altar,[5]
as there is one bishop with the priests and deacons, who are
my fellow workers. And so, whatever you do, let it be done
in the name of God.

(5) Dear brothers, my love for you is full and overflowing, and with immense joy I give you whatever assurance I
can; and yet not I, but Jesus Christ for whom I am in chains
—for I am more and more afraid that I am far from perfection. However, your prayer to God will make me perfect, so
that I may gain the inheritance that God's mercy has assigned
me, if only I take refuge in the Gospel as in the body of
Jesus and in the Apostles as the priests of the Church. Let us
likewise love the prophets, for it was they who foretold the

---

3 Cf. 1 Cor. 6.9.
4 Mass in the *Didache*, Chs. 9 and 14 and in the Letter of Clement of
Rome, Chs. 40-44.
5 The word here used, *thysiastérion*, means 'a place for sacrifice.'

Gospel and hoped in Him and looked for His coming. By their faith and union with Jesus Christ they were saved. They are worthy of love and admiration for their holiness. They were approved by Jesus Christ and numbered with us in the good news of our common hope.

(6) Still, if anyone preaches a Judaizing system to you, do not listen to him. It is better to listen to Christianity preached by one who is circumcized than to Judaism preached by one who is not. Both alike, if they fail to preach Jesus Christ, are for me tombstones and graves inscribed merely with the names of men. Beware of the tricks and traps of the prince of this world, else you will succumb to his wiles and grow languid in love. Assemble together, all of you in oneness of heart. I thank God that my conscience is clear, for there is not one among you who can claim, covertly or openly, that I have been burdensome to him in any matter, great or small. I pray that nothing that I have said may be taken in evidence against any to whom I have spoken.

(7) There may be some who outwardly sought to deceive me, but the spirit, which is from God, is not deceived. He knows whence it comes and whither it goes;[6] and He makes clear what is hidden. I cried out in your midst and I spoke with a loud voice—the voice of God: Give heed to the bishop, the priests and the deacons. When I said this, there were those who suspected that I knew ahead of time of the schism of some among you. But He is my witness, for whom I am in chains, that I knew of this from no human lips. It was the Spirit that proclaimed these words: Apart from the

---

6 Cf. John 3.8; 8.14. Here, as in so many other instances, the language of St. Ignatius is parallel to rather than identical with the expressions of the Gospels and Epistles. This indicates that, at the time, the oral teachings of the Church was as authoritative as the written word of the Scriptures.

bishop let nothing be done. Guard your flesh as a temple of God. Love unity. Shun schisms. Be imitators of Jesus Christ, as He is of His Father.

(8) As for me, I played my part, like a mediator appointed to bring about unity. For, wherever there is division or anger, God has no place. Now God forgives all who repent, so long as their repentance turns to union with God and to communion with the bishop. I have faith in the grace of Jesus Christ; He will break all your bonds. I beseech you to do all in the light of Christ's teaching and nothing in a party spirit. There are some whom I heard to say: Unless I find it in the documents,[7] I do not believe in what is preached. When I said: It is the written word, they replied: That is what is in question. For me, Jesus Christ is the written word, His cross and death and resurrection and faith through Him make up the untampered documents. Through these, with the help of your prayers, I desire to be justified.

(9) The priests[8] were good; but still better is the High Priest to whom the Holy of Holies was committed, to whom alone the mysteries[9] of God were committed. He is the door[10] of the Father through which Abraham and Isaac and Jacob and the prophets, the Apostles and the Church all enter. All these enter into the unity of God.[11] But what distinguishes the

---

7 It is not certain whether we should read *archeiois* or *archaiois*, 'archives' or 'ancient writings.' In either case the historical fact of the death and resurrection of our Lord is put above any merely written record, whether of prophecy or of narration.

8 The reference is to the priests of the Old Testament. The High Priest, of course, is Jesus Christ, as in St. Paul's Epistle to the Hebrews.

9 Literally, 'secret things.'

10 A reference to John 10.9. Cf. the Letter of Clement of Rome 48; also the Shepherd of Hermas, Parable 9.4,12,15.

11 That is, 'enter into the unity of Divine Revelation'; or perhaps; 'help in uniting men with God.'

Gospel is that it contains the coming of the Savior, Our Lord Jesus Christ, His passion, His resurrection. The preaching of the beloved prophets had Him in view. The Gospel is the perfection of Eternal Life. Taken together, all these things are good so long as your faith is alive with chastity.

(10) The news has reached me that, thanks to your prayer and the sympathy you showed in Christ Jesus, the Church of Antioch in Syria is enjoying peace. I feel that you ought, as a Church of God, to choose a deacon to go there as an ambassador of God, for the glory of the Name and to congratulate them when they assemble together. Blessed in Jesus Christ is the man who is to be found worthy of this ministry. All praise to you, too, who send him. You can do this for the Name of God if only you choose to; just as the Churches which are near neighbors sent deacons or priests and, some of them, bishops.

(11) The deacon, Philo of Cilicia, a man of good name who is now ministering to me in the word of God, and Rhaius Agathopus, an outstanding person of Syria who gave up his present occupations[12] to follow me, join in speaking highly of you. I give thanks to God for your kindness in receiving them with the kindness which the Lord shows to you. But may the grace of Jesus Christ forgive those who treated them with scant respect. The love[13] of the brethren in Troas salutes you. I am writing from here by the hand of Burrhus, who was sent by the Ephesians and Smyrnaeans to accompany me as a token of respect. The Lord Jesus Christ will reward them who hope in Him in body, soul and spirit, in faith, and love and concord. Farewell in Christ Jesus, our common hope.

---

12 *Bios*, 'life,' in the sense of 'the normal life of ordinary men.'
13 *Agápe* here, as in the beginning of the Letter to the Romans, may mean 'the community of love,' 'the Christian community.'

VI

To the Smyrnaeans

IGNATIUS THEOPHORUS to the Church of God the
Father and of the beloved Jesus Christ which is at
Smyrna in Asia. I wish you every joy in an unblemished spirit and the word of God. Your Church has been
mercifully blessed with every gift and is lacking in none; it has
been filled with faith and charity; it is most worthy of God
and fruitful in holiness.[1]

(1) I give glory to Jesus Christ, the God who has imbued
you with such wisdom. I am well aware that you have been
made perfect in unwavering faith, like men nailed, in body and
spirit, to the Cross of our Lord, Jesus Christ, and confirmed
in love by the blood of Christ. In regard to our Lord, you are
thoroughly convinced that He was of the race of David according to the flesh, and the Son of God by His Will and
power; that He was truly born of the Virgin and baptized
by John in order that all due observance might be fulfilled[2]
by Him; that in His body He was truly nailed to the Cross
for our sake under Pontius Pilate and Herod, the tetrarch—
of His most blessed passion we are the fruit[3]—so that, through
His resurrection, He might raise, for all ages, in the one body
of His Church, a standard[4] for the saints and the faithful,
whether among Jews or Gentiles.

---

1 Literally, 'bearer of sacred vessels.' As so often, St. Ignatius uses
the vocabulary of pagan religion to convey a Christian meaning.
The 'sacred vessels' for a Christian community are the graces and
virtues of the saints and other faithful.
2 Cf. Matt. 3.15.
3 Reading *karpoi* instead of *karpou*.
4 As though the standard of the Cross were a fulfillment of the standard of Yahweh for the rallying of the chosen people alluded to in
Isa. 5.26; 49.22; 62.10. Cf., too, John 12.32: 'Yes, if only I am
lifted up from the earth, I will attract all men to myself.'

(2) For He suffered all these things for us, that we might be saved. And He suffered truly, and just as truly raised Himself from the dead. He did not suffer merely in appearance, as some of the unbelievers say—they themselves being merely in appearance; for it will be their fate, in accordance with their faith, to be bodiless and ghost-like.[5]

(3) As for me, I know that even after His resurrection He was in the flesh, and I believe this to be true. For, when He came to those who were with Peter, He said to them: 'Take hold on me and handle me and see that I am not a spirit without a body.'[6] And, as soon as they touched Him and felt His flesh and pulse,[7] they believed. It is for this reason that they despised death and even showed themselves superior to death. After His resurrection He ate and drank with them like anyone else with a body, although in His spirit He was one with the Father.

(4) Although I know you believe these things to be so, dearly beloved, I warn you. I am forearming you against wild beasts in the shape of men. If possible, you should not so much as meet them, let alone welcome them. However, you must pray for them, so that, difficult as this is, they may somehow repent. This is possible for Jesus Christ, who is our true life. If the things He did were done by our Lord merely in appearance, then I am in chains merely in appearance. And why, then, did I give myself up to death, to fire, to the sword,

---

5 By denying the reality of our Lord's human body, the Docetists implicitly denied the hope of any resurrection of the body.

6 The words, according to Luke 24.39, were: 'Look at my hands and my feet . . . touch me and look; a spirit has not flesh and bones, as you see that I have.'

7 The Armenian version has 'blood,' but St. Ignatius may have in mind John 20.20-22: 'And with that, he showed them his hands and his side . . . With that, he *breathed* on them, and said to them, Receive the Holy *Spirit*.'

to the wild beasts? The fact is, near the sword, near to God; among the beasts, along with God—provided only that, in the name of Jesus Christ, I suffer along with Him. I endure all, for He who is perfect man is my strength.

(5) There are some who deny Him, because they do not know Him; or, rather, they are denied by Him, because they are more in favor of death than of truth.[8] These men have been persuaded neither by the prophecies, nor the law of Moses, nor, at least so far, by the Gospel, nor by the sufferings of any one of us in particular; for they think of us as they think of Him. In any case, what is the use of a man thinking well of me, if he speaks ill of my Lord by denying that He had a body. Any one who denies this denies Him altogether— and is himself dead.[9] I do not think it right for me to set down the names of such men, so long as they are unbelievers. Indeed, I trust that I shall not so much as call them to mind until they return to faith in the passion which is our resurrection.

(6) Let no man be deceived. Judgment will be meted out even to heavenly beings, to the glorious angels and to principalities, visible or invisible, if they do not believe in the blood of Christ. He that can take, let him take it.[10] Let no one's position puff him up; for faith and charity are all in all, and nothing is to be preferred to them. Consider how contrary to the mind of God are the heterodox in regard to the grace of God which has come to us. They have no regard for charity, none for the widow, the orphan, the oppressed, none for the man in prison, the hungry or the thirsty. They

---

8 By denying the truth of the resurrection, the Docetists denied the hope of our immortality.
9 Literally, a 'corpse-bearer.' By the denial of immortality the living body of a Docetist was already practically a corpse.
10 Matt. 19.12.

abstain from the Eucharist and from prayer because they do *real presence* not admit that the Eucharist is the flesh of our Savior Jesus Christ, the flesh which suffered for our sins and which the Father, in His graciousness, raised from the dead.

(7) And so denying the gift of God, these men perish in their disputatiousness. It were better for them to love and so to rise again. It is well for you to keep away from such persons and not even to speak of them in private or in public. It is better to keep to the prophets and especially to the Gospel in which the passion is presented and the resurrection is an accomplished fact.

(8) Shun schisms, as the source of troubles. Let all follow the bishop as Jesus Christ did the Father, and the priests, as you would the Apostles. Reverence the deacons as you would the command of God. Apart from the bishop, let no one perform any of the functions that pertain to the Church. Let that Eucharist be held valid which is offered by the bishop or *Episcopal authorization* by one to whom the bishop has committed this charge. Wherever the bishop appears, there let the people be; as wherever Jesus Christ is, there is the Catholic Church.[11] It is not lawful to baptize or give communion[12] without the consent of the bishop. On the other hand, whatever has his approval is pleasing to God. Thus, whatever you do will be safe and valid.

---

11 The expression *katholiké ekklesía* here appears for the first time in Christian literature. Later, as in the *Catecheses* of St. Cyril of Jerusalem, *katholiké* meant both 'universal' and 'orthodox.' Here the word seems to mean only 'universal.'

12 Literally, 'to hold a love-feast' or 'community meal.' The precise relation of the agape to the Eucharistic Communion is not clear. There is a hint in 1 Cor. 11.20 that the community meal preceded Holy Communion. In the famous letter of Pliny to Trajan, written near the time of the martyrdom of St. Ignatius, there is a hint that the *sacramentum* preceded the taking of food which, Pliny thought, was 'ordinary and harmless.'

(9) It will be well for us from now on to return to sobriety, to set our minds on God while still there is time. It is good to acknowledge God and the bishop. A man who honors the bishop is certainly honored by God. A man who acts without the knowledge of the bishop is serving the devil. And so, may all, by grace, abound among you as you deserve. You have been a consolation to me in every way. May Jesus Christ be the same to you. Whether I was with you or away, you loved me. May God repay you. You will be with Him one day, if you will but bear all things for his sake.

(10) It was good of you to welcome Philo and Rhaius Agathopus as deacons of God, for they followed me for the sake of God. They give thanks to the Lord for you in return for the manifold consolation you gave them. Nothing you gave is lost to you. I offer up my life for you and also my bonds, which you did not despise—nor were you ashamed of them. Neither will Jesus Christ, who is fidelity itself, be ashamed of you.

(11) Your prayer has reached as far as the Church in Antioch of Syria, to which, however unworthily—for I am the least among them—I belong. I come from there in chains which are pleasing to God, and I salute you all. By the divine will it has been vouchsafed to me that, through your prayer, I might reach God. This is not through any merit of mine, but by the grace of God; and I pray that the final grace may be given me. If you would have your work perfect in heaven and on earth, you should have your Church appoint for the honor of God an ambassador of God to go to Syria to congratulate them for being in peace after returning to their proper size and after having had restored to them their corporate character.[13] It seemed to me a deed that is worthy

---

13 The Church of Antioch had been diminished and disorganized by persecution.

of you to send some one from among you with a letter, so that he might join with them in giving glory for the calm which has come upon them from God and for the fact that, with your prayers, they have reached the harbor. Your perfection calls on you for perfect resolutions. If only you are ready to do good, God will be ready to help you to do it.

(12) The love[14] of the brethren who are at Troas salutes you. I am writing from here by the hand of Burrhus, whom you and your brethren from Ephesus sent to accompany me. Burrhus has consoled me in ever so many ways. He is a model in God's ministry, and I could wish that every one would imitate him. God's graciousness will repay him for all his kindness. I salute your saintly bishop and your venerable priests and my fellow laborers, the deacons. I salute each and all of you in the name of Jesus Christ, and in His flesh and blood, in His passion and resurrection in body and spirit, in oneness with God and with you. Grace be to you and mercy, peace and patience at all times.

(13) I salute the families of my brethren, with their wives and children and the virgins who are called widows.[15] I bid you farewell in the power of the Father. Philo, who is with me, sends his greetings. I salute the family of Gavia, and I pray that she may be rooted in faith and charity in body and spirit. I salute Alce, a name that is dear to me, and Daphnus who has no equal, and Eutecnus, and all and each by name. Farewell in the grace of God.

---

14 Or, perhaps, 'the community.'
15 The support of poor widows was carefully organized in the early Church. It is not clear that there was any 'religious order' of consecrated virgins or widows in the time of St. Ignatius.

VII

To Polycarp

IGNATIUS THEOPHORUS to Polycarp, the Bishop of the Church of the Smyrnaeans—or, should I say, to one who is under the bishopric of God the Father and Jesus Christ?—I wish you every joy.

(1) I was glad enough to learn that your mind is grounded in God as on an immovable rock, but I rejoice exceedingly to have been able to see your face. May its candor be a joy to me in God. I exhort you by the grace with which you are clothed to press forward in the race, and exhort all others, so that they may be saved. Live up to the demands of your office by unceasing care in your practical and spiritual[1] duties. Be preoccupied about unity, for nothing is better than this. Help others along, as the Lord helps you. Bear with all out of love, as indeed you do. Find time for unceasing prayer. Ask for more wisdom than you have. Keep your spirit awake and on the watch. Copy the ways of God in speaking to each as an individual person. Like an athlete in perfect condition, give a hand to all who are sick. Where there is more work, there is much reward.

(2) There is no thanks for liking good pupils. The real task is by mildness to bring to obedience the ones who plague you. Not every wound is healed by the same salve. Where the pains are sharp, give relief with embrocation. In all things be wise as the serpent and at all times be as simple as the dove.[2] You are made of flesh and spirit so that you may be

---

1 Literally, 'of flesh and spirit.'
2 Cf. Matt. 10.16.

124

able to persuade what you can see to come to you;[3] as for the invisible realities, pray that they may be revealed to you. In this way nothing will be lacking, and you will abound in every gift. The age is in need of you, if it is to reach God—as pilots need the winds and as a storm-tossed sailor needs port. Be temperate, like an athlete of God; the prize is immortality and eternal life. Of this you have no doubt. I offer up all for you, both myself and my bonds which you loved.[4]

(3) There are some who seem plausible enough, but who teach heretical doctrine. Do not let them disturb you. Stand firm like an anvil under the hammer. A great boxer will take a beating and yet win through. We ought to put up with anything especially for the sake of God, so that He will put up with us. Become more zealous even than you are. Understand the age in which we live.[5] Look for Him who is beyond all time, the Eternal, the Invisible who became visible for our sake, the Impalpable, the Impassible who suffered for our sake, who endured every outrage for our sake.

(4) Do not let the widows be neglected. After God, you should be their guardian. Let nothing be done without your consent; and continue, as at present, to do nothing yourself without the consent of God. Do not weaken. Let your assemblies be more frequent. Seek out all by name, and do not overlook the slaves, whether men or women. At the same time, they should not be puffed up, but rather better workers for the glory of God, so that they may be given by God an even

---

3 The general idea seems to be that the 'world' can be humored into obedience to God if the ministers of the Gospel become, like St. Paul, all things to all men.

4 It is not unlikely that the faithful kissed the chains of the martyr on his way to death.

5 Cf. Luke 12.56: 'Poor fools, you know well enough how to interpret the face of land and sky; can you interpret the times you live in?'

better freedom. Lest they become slaves of their own desires, they should not long to obtain freedom at the public cost.

(5) Avoid anything like magic, but do not fail to speak to the people about such things. Tell my sisters to love the Lord and to be satisfied with their husbands in flesh and spirit. In the same way tell my brothers in the name of Jesus Christ to love their wives as the Lord does the Church.[6] If anyone is able to persevere in chastity to the honor of the flesh of the Lord, let him do so in all humility. If he is boastful about it, he is lost; if he should be more esteemed than the bishop,[7] his purity is gone. When men and women marry, the union should be made with the consent of the bishop, so that the marriage may be according to the Lord and not merely out of lust. Let all be done to the glory of God.

(6) Pay attention to the bishop, if you would have God pay attention to you. I offer myself up for those who obey the bishop, priests and deacons. May it be my lot to be with them in God. Toil and train together, run and suffer together, rest and rise at the same time, as God's stewards, assistants and servants. Please the leader under whom you serve, for from him you receive your pay. May none of you turn out a deserter. Let your baptism be ever your shield, your faith a helmet, your charity a spear, your patience a panoply. Let your works be deposits, so that you may receive the sum that is due to you. In humility be patient with one another, as God is with you. May I rejoice in you always.

(7) I have been told that, through your prayers, the Church in Antioch of Syria has found peace; and so I have become very comforted and without a care in God—or shall be, if only through suffering I come to God, so that, by the

---

6 Cf. Eph. 5.25.
7 The meaning may be: If the vow of chastity is revealed to any other than the bishop, the parade of virtue is another kind of immodesty.

help of your prayers, I may be reckoned a disciple. Polycarp, you have been abundantly blessed by God and it behooves you to call a religious council to elect some one who is particularly loved and who is tireless and fit to be named a messenger of God. Let him be appointed to go to Syria so as to glorify your tireless love, to the glory of God. A Christian is not his own master, since all his time belongs to God. When you have done this work, it will be God's and yours. I trust in His grace that you are ready to do good in the service of God. I have exhorted you in so short a letter, because I know your eagerness for the truth.

(8) It has been impossible for me to write to all the Churches, since I must set sail at once from Troas for Neapolis, as God's will enjoins. And so, may I ask you, as one knowing the mind of God, to write to the neighboring Churches and have them do the same. Let those who can send messengers, and let the others send letters by your messengers, so that you may have the glory, as you deserve, of a work that will never be forgotten.

I greet all of you by name, not forgetting the wife of Epitropus[8] with all who serve her and her children. I greet Attalus whom I love, and the one who is to be thought fit to go to Syria. Grace will be with him forever and with Polycarp who sends him. I bid you a long farewell in our God, Jesus Christ. Persevere, through Him, in communion with God and under his guidance. I salute Alce, a name very dear to me. Farewell in the Lord.

---

8 Epitropus may not be a proper name but may mean simply the procurator, the *epitropos strategós,* an official title which appears on inscriptions found at Smyrna.

THE LETTER
OF
ST. POLYCARP
TO THE PHILIPPIANS

Translated

by

FRANCIS X. GLIMM, S.T.L.

Seminary of the Immaculate Conception

Huntington, N. Y.

INTRODUCTION

OLYCARP WAS a well-known and venerable figure of the first half of the second century. From Tertullian, Irenaeus, and Eusebius we learn that he had listened at Ephesus to St. John the Apostle, who had appointed him bishop of nearby Smyrna.[1] Here he was host to Ignatius of Antioch, from whom he received at least one letter.[2] This and other letters of St. Ignatius he forwarded to the Philippians at their request, as well as the letter here translated. At a later time he journeyed to Rome to consult with Pope Anicetus on the matter of the controversy over the date of Easter. Of numerous letters known to have been written by St. Polycarp, only the *Letter to the Philippians* has been preserved. St. Polycarp was a man of more than eighty[3] when a violent persecution broke out in Smyrna and finally engulfed him (A.D. 156). An authentic account of his heroic and Christian end is given in the *Martyrdom* which in this volume immediately follows the present letter. A *Life* of St. Polycarp ascribed to a certain Pionius is altogether legendary.

A recent study[4] has made it appear probable that what the manuscripts have handed down as the single letter of St. Polycarp to the Philippians is really composed of two letters

1 Tertullian, *De praescriptione haereticorum* 32.2; Irenaeus, *Adv. haer.* 3.3,4; Eusebius, *Historia ecclesiastica* 5.20.5 ff.
2 See Ch. 13. The letter in question is presumably the extant letter of St. Ignatius, translated elsewhere in this volume (pp. 124 ff.).
3 In the *Martyrdom of St. Polycarp* 9 (see p. 155ff. below), the saint is quoted at the point of death, as saying that he had served Christ for eighty-six years.
4 That of P. N. Harrison. See Select Bibliography.

to these same persons. The letter earlier in time would comprise Chapters 13 and 14 of the traditional text.[5] This would have been a short note to the Philippians, written while St. Ignatius was still on his way to Rome for trial or, at least, before St. Polycarp had received any news of his death (*ca.* 110). There would have accompanied this note the various letters of St. Ignatius mentioned above. St. Polycarp's concern for the bishop of Antioch is shown by his request that the community of Philippi (which was nearer to Rome than Smyrna was) should tell him anything they might learn of the fate of St. Ignatius and of those with him.

Chapters 1 to 12 form the second letter supposed by the recent analysis of the text. This letter would be surely of later date since, in Chapter 9, St. Ignatius is now considered as dead. St. Polycarp is here replying to a request for counsel made to him by the Philippians (1.1). The exact nature of this request to St. Polycarp, then the most venerable ecclesiastic in the East, is not clear; it is suggested that the Philippians were seeking advice as to the proper steps to take against the Marcionite heresy.[6] If such were the situation, a date around 135 could be fairly conjectured.

Chapter 14 has the ring of a postscript, naming the bearer of the letter, a certain Crescens, and commending to the Philippians both Crescens and his sister. It might belong to either the earlier or the latter letter.

It is the earlier letter which presents the figure in his full stature as bishop, successor of the Apostles. The writer, to be sure, affirms his inability to rival 'the blessed and glorious Paul,' reminding the Philippians of the oral and written teach-

---

5 Possibly Ch. 14 belongs instead to the latter letter. See below.
6 For St. Polycarp's frank defiance of Marcion see *Martyrdom* 22.4 and p. 163, below.

ing given them by the Apostle (3.1-3;11.1.). In his own letter St. Polycarp twice employs phrases taken from that of St. Paul.[7] The doctrinal content of St. Polycarp's letter, while varied, hardly requires analysis. As shedding light on the organization of the Church at Philippi, we may note the mention of 'presbyters and deacons' (5.3). It is to them that submission is to be given; St. Polycarp nowhere speaks of a bishop. Repeated warnings are given against avarice and greed.[8] Of these instances one in particular stands out as noteworthy—a passage (Ch. 11) dealing with the presbyter Valens and his wife, 'the Ananias and Saphira of the Philippian community.'[9] The Philippians are to take warning from their example, but are to seek charitably for their return to the Church.

St. Polycarp's complete letter is preserved only in a Latin version, the Greek text ending with Chapter 9.[10]

The text followed in the present translation is that of Bihlmeyer, *Die apostolischen Väter* (Tübingen 1924).

---

7 See 9.2; 12.3, below.
8 2.2; 4.1,3; 6.1; 11.
9 Lightfoot, *Apostolic Fathers* 166.
10 See note on Ch. 9, below.

SELECT BIBLIOGRAPHY

Texts and Translations:

J. B. Lightfoot, *The Apostolic Fathers.* Part II: S. Ignatius, S. Polycarp. Revised Texts . . . (London 1885)

K. Bihlmeyer, *Die Apostolischen Väter,* Neubearbeitung der Funkschen Ausgabe (Tübingen 1924).

P. N. Harrison. *Polycarp's Two Epistles to the Philippians* (London 1936). This is an exhaustive study with an extensive bibliography.

THE LETTER TO THE PHILIPPIANS OF SAINT POLYCARP, BISHOP OF SMYRNA AND HOLY MARTYR

POLYCARP AND the Presbyters who are with him to the Church of God dwelling at Philippi; may mercy and peace be richly increased in you from God Almighty and Jesus Christ our Saviour.

Chapter 1

1 I greatly rejoice with you in our Lord Jesus Christ for having followed the pattern of true charity and for having escorted, as far as you could, those who were chained in saintly bonds; for they are the jewels of those who have been truly chosen by God and our Lord. 2 And I rejoice because the firm root of your faith, famous in times past, still flourishes and bears fruit unto our Lord Jesus Christ, who for our sins endured to face even death. 'Whom God had raised up, having broken the pangs of Hell.'[1] 3 In Him, 'though you see him not, you believe with unspeakable glorious joy,'[2] to which joy many desire to come, knowing that 'by grace you are saved, not through works,' but by the will of God through Jesus Christ.[3]

---

1 Acts 2.24. This is the earliest recorded quotation of the Acts of the Apostles.
2 1 Pet. 1.8.
3 Eph. 2.8.

Chapter 2

1 'Wherefore, girding up your loins, serve God in fear'[1] and in truth; abandon empty vanity and the waywardness of the crowd, 'believing in Him who raised our Lord Jesus Christ from the dead and gave Him glory,'[2] and a throne at His right hand. 'To Him are subject all things in Heaven and on earth,' Him every breath serves and He will come as 'the judge of the living and of the dead and His blood God will require from them who disobey Him.'[3] 2 Now 'He who raised him' from the dead 'will also raise us,'[4] if we do His will and advance in His commandments and love what He loved, abstaining from all injustice, covetousness, love of money, slander, false witness, 'not rendering evil for evil, nor abuse for abuse'[5] or blow for blow, or curse for curse. 3 No! Remember what the Lord said when he taught: 'Judge not, that you may not be judged. Forgive, and you shall be forgiven. Be merciful, that you may obtain mercy. With what measure you measure, it shall be measured to you in return.'[6] And again: 'Blessed are the poor, and they who are persecuted for justice' sake, for theirs is the Kingdom of God.'[7]

Chapter 3

1 Brethren, I write you this concerning righteousness, not on my own initiative, but because you first invited me. 2 For neither I, nor anyone like me, is able to rival the wisdom of

---

1 1 Pet. 1.3.
2 1 Pet. 1.21.
3 Acts 10.42.
4 2 Cor. 4.14.
5 1 Pet. 3.9.
6 Matt. 7.1-2; Luke 6.36-38.
7 Matt. 5.3,10.

the blessed and glorious Paul, who, when living among you, carefully and steadfastly taught the word of truth face to face with his contemporaries and, when he was absent, wrote you letters. By the careful perusal of his letters you will be able to strengthen yourselves in the faith given to you, 3 'which is the mother of us all,'[1] with hope following and charity leading, charity toward God and Christ and our neighbor. For, if a person remain with these, he has fulfilled the commandment of righteousness; for he who has charity is far from all sin.

Chapter 4

1 Now the beginning of all difficulties is love of money.[1] Since we know then that 'we have brought nothing into this world, and can take nothing out of it either,'[2] let us arm ourselves with the armor of righteousness and learn first to advance in the commandment of the Lord. 2 Then let us teach our wives to remain in the faith taught them and in charity and purity to cherish their husbands in all truth, loving all others impartially in complete chastity, and to bring up their children in the fear of God. 3 Teach the widows to be prudent in the faith of the Lord, and to pray without ceasing for all, to keep far from all calumny, slander, false witness, love of money and every evil, knowing that they are an altar of God, that He inspects all things, and that not one of their calculations or thoughts or 'the hidden things of the heart'[3] escapes Him.

---

1 Gal. 4.26.

---

1 Slight variant from 1 Tim. 6.10: 'evils' in 1 Tim. which omits 'all.'
2 Slight variant from 1 Tim. 6.7.
3 1 Cor. 14.25.

Chapter 5

1 Knowing, then, that 'God is not mocked,'[1] we ought to walk in a manner worthy of His commandment and glory. 2 Similarly, deacons must be blameless in the presence of His justice, like servants[2] of God and Christ, not of men; not slanderers, not double-tongued, not money-lovers, temperate in all things, compassionate, careful, walking according to the truth of the Lord, who became the servant of all.[3] If we be pleasing to Him in this world, we shall receive the future world in accordance with His promises to raise us up from the dead, and, if we act in a manner worthy of Him, 'we shall also reign with Him,'[4] provided we believe. 3 The young men, also, must likewise be blameless in all things, cherishing purity above everything else and curbing themselves from every evil.[5] For it is good to be cut off from the lusts in the world, because 'all lust wars against the Spirit,'[6] and 'neither fornicators nor the effeminate nor sodomites shall inherit the Kingdom of God,'[7] nor those who do unnatural things. Therefore, it is necessary to refrain from all this and to be subject to the presbyters and deacons as to God and Christ. The virgins must walk in a blameless and pure conscience.

Chapter 6

1 And the presbyters also must be sympathetic, merciful to all, guiding back the wanderers,[1] visiting all the sick, neg-

---

1 Gal. 6.7.
2 Play on the Greek word for deacon, i.e., waiter or servant.
3 Mark 9.33.
4 2 Tim. 2.12.
5 1 Pet. 2.11.
6 Gal. 5.17.
7 1 Cor. 6.9-10.

---

1 Ezech. 34.4.

lecting neither widow nor orphan nor pauper, but 'always providing what is good before God and men.'[2] They must refrain from all anger, from respect of persons, from unfair judgment, and keep far from all love of money; be not quick to believe anything against any man, not hasty in judgment, knowing that we are all under the debt of sin. 2 If, then, we beseech the Lord to forgive us, we should also forgive; for we stand before the eyes of the Lord God, and we 'must all stand before the judgment-seat of Christ,' and 'each must give an account of himself.'[3] 3 Accordingly, let us so serve Him with fear and all reverence, as He has commanded and as did the Apostles who evangelized us, and the prophets who fortold of the coming of our Lord; being zealous for what is good, refraining from offenses and false brethren, and from those who carry the name of the Lord in hypocrisy, to mislead foolish men.

Chapter 7

1 'For everyone who does not confess that Jesus Christ has come in the flesh is an antichrist';[1] and whoever does not confess the witness of the Cross is of the devil; and whoever perverts the sayings of the Lord to his own evil desires and says there is neither resurrection nor judgment, that one is the first-born of Satan. 2 Therefore, let us abandon the vanities of the crowd and their false teachings; let us return to the word which was delivered to us from the beginning. Let us be watchful in prayers[2] and perverse in fasting, beseeching the all-seeing God in petitions 'not to lead us into tempta-

---

2 2 Cor. 8.21.
3 Rom. 14.10,12.

---

1 1 John 4.2-3.
2 1 Pet. 4.7.

tion,'[3] as the Lord said: 'The spirit indeed is willing, but the flesh is weak.'[4]

Chapter 8

1 Without interruption, therefore, let us persevere by our hope and by the guarantee of our righteousness,[1] which is Jesus Christ, who 'bore our sins in His own body on the tree, who did no sin, nor was deceit found in His mouth';[2] but for our sake, that we might live in Him, He endured all things. 2 Let us, then, become imitators of His patient endurance, and, if we suffer for His name, let us praise Him. For He gave us this example in His own person, and we have believed this.

Chapter 9

1 I exhort you all, then, to obey the word of justice and to practice all endurance as you saw with your own eyes in the blessed Ignatius and Zosimus and Rufus. This you saw also in others from your own group and in Paul himself and the other Apostles. 2 Be convinced that all these 'ran not in vain,'[1] but in faith and in righteousness, and that they are with the Lord, with whom they also suffered in the place which they have deserved. For they 'loved not the present world,'[2] but Him who died for them and who was raised up by God for our sakes.[3]

---

3 Matt. 6.13.
4 Matt. 26.41.

---

1 Mark 14.38.
2 1 Pet. 2.22,24.

---

1 Phil. 2.16.
2 1 Tim. 4.10.
3 The Greek manuscripts end here. The remaining chapters are found in an ancient Latin translation. Their authenticity is supported by citations in Syriac and by the quotations of Ch. 13 almost in its entirety in the *Ecclesiastical History* of Eusebius.

Chapter 10

1 Stand fast, therefore, in this conduct[1] and follow the example of the Lord, 'firm and unchangeable in faith, lovers of the brotherhood, loving each other, united in truth,'[2] helping each other with the mildness of the Lord, despising no man.[3] 2 When you can do good,[4] do not put it off, 'for almsgiving frees from death.'[5] You must all be subject to one another[6] and keep your conduct free from reproach among pagans, so that from your good works[7] you may receive praise and the Lord may not be blasphemed on account of you. 3 But woe to him on whose account the name of the Lord is blasphemed.[8] Teach sobriety, therefore, to all, and practice it yourselves, also.

Chapter 11

1 I have been deeply grieved for Valens, who was once made a presbyter among you, that he so little understands the dignity which was given to him. I warn you, therefore, to abstain from avarice and to be chaste and truthful. Keep away from all evil. 2 If any man cannot control himself in these things, how can he recommend it to another? If a man does not abstain from avarice, he will be defiled by idolatry, and will be judged as one of the pagans, who 'know not the judgment of the Lord.'[1] Or do we forget 'that the saints

---

1 1 Cor. 15.58.
2 1 Pet. 2.17.
3 Rom. 12.10.
4 Prov. 3.28.
5 Tob. 4.11.
6 Eph. 5.21.
7 1 Pet. 2.12.
8 S. Ignatius, *ad Trall.* 8.

---

1 Jer. 5.4.

shall judge the world,'[2] as Paul teaches? 3 However, I have not found nor heard anything of the kind among you, among whom blessed Paul toiled, who were yourselves his epistles[3] in the beginning. For he boasts about you in all the Churches,[4] which alone knew the Lord in those times when we had not yet known Him. 4 I am exceedingly sorry, therefore, for Valens and his wife; may the Lord grant them a true repentance. Therefore, be temperate yourslves in this regard, and do not consider such persons enemies,[5] but invite them back as sinful and erring members, that you may heal the whole body of you. By doing this you edify one another.

Chapter 12

1 I am sure that you are well-trained in the Sacred Scriptures, and that nothing is hid from you; but this is not granted to me. Now, as it is said in these Scriptures: 'Be angry and sin not,'[1] and 'Let not the sun go down upon your wrath.'[2] Blessed is he who remembers this; and I believe that this is so with you. 2 Now, may God and the Father of our Lord Jesus Christ, and the 'eternal High-Priest' Himself, Jesus Christ, build you up in faith and truth and in all kindness, free from anger, patient, long-suffering in endurance and chastity. May He give you, too, a share and participation among His saints, and to us along with you, as well as to all under Heaven who shall believe in our Lord and God Jesus Christ and in His Father, who raised Him up from the dead.[3]

2 1 Cor. 6.2.
3 2 Cor. 3.2.
4 1 Thess. 1.4.
5 2 Thess. 3.15.

1 Ps. 4.5.
2 Eph. 4.26.
3 Gal. 1.1.

3 'Pray for all the saints.'[4] 'Pray also for the emperors,'[5] and authorities, and rulers, and 'for those who persecute and hate you'[6] and for 'the enemies of the Cross,'[7] that the result of your effort[8] may be manifest to all men, that you may be perfect in Him.

Chapter 13

1 You wrote to me, both yourselves and Ignatius, that, if anyone was going to Syria, he should also carry letters from you. I will do this if I get a proper opportunity, either myself or the person whom I shall send as a messenger for you also. The letter of Ignatius sent to us by himself and all the others we have here we send you, as you requested; these are subjoined to this epistle, and from them you will greatly profit. For in them there are faith and endurance and all the edification pertaining to our Lord. And let us know whatever you learn concerning Ignatius and those who are with him.

Chapter 14

I have written this to you by Crescens, whom I recommended to you recently and whom I again commend. For he has behaved blamelessly among us, and I believe likewise among you. You will receive a recommendation of his sister, also, when she shall come to you. Farewell. Good-by to you in the Lord Jesus Christ in grace, and to all who are with you. Amen.

---

4 Eph. 6.18.
5 1 Tim. 2.1.
6 Matt. 5.44.
7 Phil. 3.18.
8 I.e., *fructus*.

THE MARTYRDOM

OF

ST. POLYCARP

Translated

by

FRANCIS X. GLIMM, S.T.L.

Seminary of the Immaculate Conception

Huntington, N. Y.

INTRODUCTION

 MONG THE narratives which have been handed down
purporting to describe the passion and death of the
Christian martyrs, some have little value either as
history or literature; others may be attractively or forcefully
written, yet contain so much unauthentic elaboration that
their historical worth is small; still others do not suffer in
literary merit from being authentic, first-hand accounts of
the events they relate. It is in this third class that scholars
have generally agreed to place the *Martyrdom of St. Polycarp*,
which has, moreover, the added distinction of being among
the oldest of the formal Acts of the Martyrs—if not indeed
the very oldest—that we possess.

Of the little that can be related with certainty concerning
the life of St. Polycarp, Bishop of Smyrna in the first half
of the second century, most has been set out above in the
Introduction of his *Letter to the Philippians*.[1] To that outline
the narrative contained in the present document serves as a
happily detailed and circumstantial supplement, narrating his
martyr's death on (probably) February 22, 156.[2] The work
is so clearly and simply written that it tells its own story and
conveys its own high example of heroism without the need of

1 See above, pp. 129 f.
2 The year 155 has also been argued for. See the *Martyrdom* 21, for
day and the month. The *Roman Martyrology* enters the name of
St. Polycarp at 26 January.

147

comment or explanatory detail.[3] Yet it will not be out of place to append a brief statement of the reasons which lead to an early dating of the document and a summary discussion of its literary form.

The *Martyrdom*, as we now have it, consists of two parts:[4] (1) a letter from the Christians of Smyrna addressed to Churches everywhere and especially to that at Philomelium (Chapters 1-20); (2) a group of three supplements: (a) a chronological appendix (21), (b) a commendatory postscript (22.1), (c) a history of the transmission of the document (22.2-4).

The early date and genuineness of the body of the document, the letter of the Smyrnaeans, is virtually guaranteed by the use made of it by Eusebius,[5] who transcribes or paraphrases the greater part, holding it, moreover, to be the oldest written record of a martyrdom that he knew. Striking parallels between the Smyrnaean letter and dated documents of A.D. 165 and 177 suggest that the letter was widely disseminated well before the time of Eusebius. We may note here that the Smyrnaean letter is not only addressed to 'all the congregations of the Holy and Catholic Church in every place,' but contains a request (20.1) that steps be taken to secure its extended circulation.

The evidence of Eusebius unfortunately cannot be employed to establish the date and genuineness of the three sup-

---

3 Following suggestions of Lightfoot, *Essays* 220-223, the reader may profitably note the details of St. Polycarp's martyrdom which reproduce or parallel the Passion of our Lord. The letter itself (1.1; 19.1) shows that the Smyrnaeans were themselves aware of these resemblances.

4 This analysis and various arguments based on it are drawn from Lightfoot, *Apostolic Fathers* 185-187.

5 Eusebius, *Historia ecclesiastica* 4.15.

plements, since his quotations and paraphrases do not extend even to the very end of the main part of the document. Of the three supplements, the chronological appendix appears to be a genuine addition made by the author of the Smyrnaean letter. The commendatory postscript, though lacking in several witnesses to the text, could well have been added by the Church at Philomelium in carrying out the Smyrnaeans' request to dispatch copies of the basic letter. The history of the transmission, which appears in an expanded form in the best Greek manuscript (that of Moscow[6]), ends in all the manuscripts with a note (23.4) professing to be written by a certain Pionius, who is represented as having been enabled to find a copy of the document through a revelation of St. Polycarp himself. The miraculous element here suggested reappears in a *Life of St. Polycarp* which passes under the name of Pionius, and this writer is probably the author as well of the third supplement to the letter of the Smyrnaeans.[7] This 'Pionius' relates that upon St. Polycarp's appointment as bishop a dove hovered about his head. In the Smyrnaean letter (16.1) various witnesses to the text state that at one point in the martyrdom, when the saint's body had been pierced by a dagger, there came out 'a dove and much blood.' The evidence of Eusebius shows that the original letter contains no mention of a dove, and if the received text is sound, the strange appearance of the dove is probably due to a reworking of the Smyrnaean letter by 'Pionius.' Such reworking on his part cannot, however, have been very extensive, since so much of the letter is verified by Eusebius, who antedates 'Pionius' and reflects an uncontaminated text.

---

6 Synodal Library MS 160 (159).

7 This writer is not to be identified with a certain Smyrnaean priest of the same name, whose martyrdom, of about 250, is entered in the *Roman Martyrology* at 1 February.

As evidence for the text, we have sources that come from many parts of the ancient Christian world: the passage in Eusebius, the Greek manuscripts of the document itself, two independent Latin versions, and versions in Syriac and Coptic. The earnest wish of the Smyrnaeans that their report of the heroism of St. Polycarp be given wide dissemination did not fail of fulfillment.

The text used as the basis of the present translation is that of Bihlmeyer, *Die apostolischen Väter* (Tübingen 1924).

SELECT BIBLIOGRAPHY

Texts and Translations:

J. B. Lightfoot, *The Apostolic Fathers* . . . revised texts with short introductions and English translations . . . edited and completed by J. R. Harmer (London 1891).

K. Lake, *The Apostolic Fathers* (Loeb Classical Library, New York 1912) 1.

K. Bihlmeyer, *Die apostolischen Väter*, Neubearbeitung der Funkschen Ausgabe (Tübingen 1924).

Secondary Works:

H. Delehaye, S. J., *Les passions des martyrs et les genres littéraires* (Brussels 1921) 11 ff.; 37 ff.

J. B. Lightfoot, *Essays on the Work Entitled Supernatural Religion* (London 1889).

W. Ruening, *Zur Erklärung des Polycarp-Martyriums* (Giessen 1917). See the remarks of Père Delehaye in *Analecta Bollandiana* (1920) 200 ff.

THE MARTYRDOM OF ST. POLYCARP

HE CHURCH OF GOD dwelling as a pilgrim at Smyrna to the Church of God in pilgrimage at Philomelium and to all the congregations of the Holy and Catholic Church in every place. May the mercy and peace and love of God the Father and of our Lord Jesus Christ be multiplied.

Chapter 1

1 We write to you, brethren, the details concerning the martyrs and blessed Polycarp, who, by his martyrdom, as by a seal, put an end to the persecution. For almost all the recent events occurred that the Lord might show us a martyrdom on the Gospel model. For, like the Lord, he waited to be betrayed, that we might become his imitators, not regarding ourselves alone, but also our neighbors.[1] For it is a sign of real and steadfast love not to desire to save oneself alone, but to save also all the brethren.

Chapter 2

1 Those martyrdoms are blessed and noble, then, which take place according to the will of God, for we must be careful to ascribe to God the power over all occurrences. For everyone surely marvels at their nobility and patience and love of the Lord. 2 For, when they were so torn by whips that the structure of their flesh was visible even to the inner veins and arteries, they endured, so that even the bystanders pitied

---

1 Phil. 2.4.

them and wept; while some of them attained such a degree
of heroism that they neither groaned nor cried, thus showing
all of us that at the time of their torture the noble martyrs
of Christ were absent from the flesh, or rather that the Lord
stood by and spoke to them. 3 Because they kept in mind the
grace of Christ, they despised the tortures of the world, thus
purchasing eternal life at the price of a single hour. And the
fire of their savage torturers was cool to them; for they kept
before their eyes the escape from eternal and unquenchable
fir, and with the eyes of their heart they looked up to the good
things which are stored up for those who have persevered,
'which neither ear hath heard nor eye hath seen, nor hath it
entered into the heart of man.'[1] This they were shown by
the Lord, for they were no longer men, but already angels.
4 In the same way, also, those condemned to the beasts endured terrible tortures. With sharp shells spread out under
them they were beaten with a variety of other kinds of torments, to see, if possible, whether the tempter might bring
them to a denial by continued torture. For the devil schemed
in many ways against them.

Chapter 3

1 But, thanks to God, against none did the tempter prevail.
For, the most noble Germanicus gave them strength in their
fear by his own endurance, and his fight against the wild
beasts was outstanding. For, as the Proconsul tried to persuade him with the plea that he have pity on his youth, he
forcibly dragged the beast upon himself, in the desire to be
released the quicker from this unjust and lawless life. 2 So,
after this, the whole crowd, amazed at the nobility of the

---

1 Isa. 64.4; 1 Cor. 2.9.

God-loving and God-fearing race of Christians, shouted out: 'Down with the atheists; let Polycarp be found.'

Chapter 4

1 However, there was one, Quintus by name, a Phrygian recently arrived from Phrygia, who at the sight of the beasts became a coward. He was the one who had forced himself and some others to come forward voluntarily. The Proconsul persuaded him with many pleas to take the oath and to offer sacrifice. For this reason, therefore, brethren, we do not approve those who give themselves up, because the Gospel does not teach us this.

Chapter 5

1 Now, when the most admirable Polycarp first heard of this, he was not disturbed, but desired to stay in the city. However, the majority persuaded him to leave quietly, so he went out secretly to a farm not a great distance from the city and, remaining with a few friends, night and day he did nothing but pray for all his people and for all the Churches throughout the world, as was his custom at all times. 2 And, as he prayed, he fell into an ecstasy three days before his arrest, and he saw the pillow under him burning with fire, and, turning to those who were with him he said: 'I must be burned alive.'

Chapter 6

1 And, as the searchers continued after him, he went to another farm, where the searchers immediately stopped. But, not finding him, they seized two slave boys, of whom one turned informer after being tortured. 2 For, it was not really

possible for him to remain hidden, since those who betrayed him were of his own household. Then the police captain called Herod—that is the very name he had—hastened to bring him to the stadium so that, becoming a partaker of Christ, he might fulfill his special destiny, and his betrayers should suffer the punishment of Judas.

Chapter 7

1 So they brought the little boy along and on Friday, about supper time, the police and horsemen with their usual arms came out as if against a bandit.[1] And late in the evening they converged on Polycarp and found him resting in an upper room. Though it was still in his power to get away to another locality, he did not wish to, saying: 'The will of God be done.'[2] 2 Accordingly, when he heard they were there, he went down and conversed with them. However, the bystanders marveled at his age and his firmness, and wondered why there was such urgency to arrest such an old man. At once he had a table set for them to eat and drink at that hour, as much as they wished, while for himself he requested to be given an hour to pray without interference. 3 They agreed. So he stood and prayed, so filled with the grace of God that for two hours he could not hold his peace, to the admiration of the listeners. Many even regretted that they had proceeded against such a venerable old man.

Chapter 8

1 When finally he concluded his prayer, after remembering all who had at any time come his way—small folk and

---

1 Matt. 26.55.
2 Acts 21.14.

great folk, distinguished and undistinguished, and the whole
Catholic Church throughout the world—the time for departure came. So they placed him on an ass, and brought him
into the city on a great Sabbath. 2 The captain of police,
Herod, and his father Nicetas met him, and took him into
their own carriage and seated at his side, tried to persuade
him, saying: 'But what harm is there in saying, "Caesar is
Lord," and in offering incense, and so forth, to be saved?
At first he did not answer, but, when they persisted, he said:
'I am not going to do what you advise me.' 3 On failing to
convince him, they spoke threateningly to him and made him
descend so quickly that he bruised his shin as he got down
from the carriage. Without even turning around, as though
he had suffered nothing, he continued on his way eagerly
and speedily, and was led into the stadium. The uproar in
the stadium was such that nobody could be heard at all.

Chapter 9

1 Upon Polycarp's entrance into the arena there came a
voice from heaven, 'Be brave, Polycarp, and act like a man.'
No one saw the speaker, but our people who were present
heard the voice. 2 Finally, when he was brought forward, the
Proconsul asked him if he were Polycarp; when he admitted
it, he tried to persuade him to a denial of the faith, saying:
'Have regard for your age,' and other suggestions such as they
usually make: 'Swear by the genius of Caesar; change your
mind and say, "Away with the atheists!"' Then Polycarp,
with solemn countenance, gazed on the whole crowd of
lawless pagans in the stadium, waved his hand at them,
groaned, looked up to heaven, and said: 'Away with the
atheists!' 3 As the Proconsul urged him and said: 'Take the
oath and I release you; revile Christ,' Polycarp said: 'Eighty-

six years[1] have I served Him, and He has done me no wrong. How can I blaspheme my King who has saved me?'

Chapter 10

1 As he further insisted and said: 'Swear by the genius of Caesar,' Polycarp replied: 'If you vainly imagine that I will swear by the genius [fortune] of Caesar, as you say, and pretend not to know who I am, let me tell you plainly: I am a Christian. But if you desire to learn the teaching of Christianity, grant a day and a hearing. 2 The Proconsul said: 'Persuade the people.' But Polycarp said: 'So far as you are concerned, I should have judged you to be worthy of a discussion; for we have been taught to give honor, as is proper, to rulers and authorities appointed by God, provided it does not harm us; but I do not esteem these people worthy of making a defense before them.'

Chapter 11

1 The Proconsul said: 'I have wild animals; to them will I throw you, unless you change your mind.' But he said: 'Call them, for change of mind from better to worse is a change not allowed us; but it is good to change from wickedness to justice.' 2 Again he said to him: 'If you scorn the wild beasts, I will have you burned by fire, unless you repent.' But Polycarp said: 'You threaten the fire that burns for an hour and in a little while is quenched; for you do not know the fire of the future judgment and of eternal punishment, the fire reserved for the wicked. But why do you delay? Come, do as you wish.'

---

1 Hence, Polycarp was baptized as an infant.

Chapter 12

1 While making these and other remarks besides, he was filled with courage and joy. His countenance was filled with grace, so that not only did it not droop in anxiety at the remarks addressed to him, but the Proconsul, on the contrary, in amazement sent his own herald into the middle of the arena to announce three times: 'Polycarp has confessed himself to be a Christian.' 2 After this proclamation by the herald, the whole mob of pagans and Jews living in Smyrna shouted out with uncontrollable anger and in a loud voice: 'This is the teacher of Asia, the father of the Christians, the destroyer of our gods, who has taught many not to sacrifice and not to adore.' With these cries and shouts they demanded of Philip the Asiarch that he let loose a lion on Polycarp. However, he said that this was not legal, since he had closed the 'Sports.' 3 Then they decided to shout out unanimously to have Polycarp burned alive. For the vision revealed to him on the pillow had to be fulfilled (when he saw it burning as he prayed, and he turned and spoke prophetically to the faithful with him, 'I must be burned alive').

Chapter 13

1 This happened with indescribable speed. The crowds gathered and collected wood and faggots from the shops and baths, the Jews in particular, as is usual with them, lending zealous assistance in this. 2 But, when the pyre was ready, he took off his upper garments, loosened his belt, and tried to take his shoes off, also, a thing he did not do in the past, because the faithful were always eager each to be the first to touch his flesh. For he had been treated with every regard on account of his holy life even before his grey hair appeared. 3 Immediately, the instruments prepared for the fire were

laid around him; and, as they were ready also to nail him, he said: 'Leave me as I am, for He who gives me power to endure the fire will grant me also to remain in the flames unmoved, even without the security which nails give you.'

Chapter 14

1 Accordingly, they did not nail him, but tied him. So he put his hands behind his back and was bound like a ram marked for sacrifice out of a great flock, a holocaust prepared and acceptable to God. As he looked up to heaven, he said: 'Lord God Almighty, Father of Thy beloved and blessed Son Jesus Christ, through whom we have received knowledge of Thee, God of the angels and powers, of the whole creation and of the whole race of the righteous who live in Thy sight, 2 I bless Thee, for having made me worthy of this day and hour; I bless Thee, because I may have a part, along with the martyrs, in the chalice of Thy Christ, "unto resurrection in eternal life." [1] resurrection both of soul and body in the incorruptibility of the Holy Spirit. May I be received today as a rich and acceptable sacrifice, among those who are in Thy presence, as Thou hast prepared and foretold and fulfilled, God who art faithful and true. For this and for all benefits I praise Thee, I bless Thee, I glorify Thee, through the eternal and heavenly Hight Priest, Jesus Christ, Thy beloved Son, through whom be to Thee with Him and the Holy Spirit glory, now and for all the ages to come. Amen.'

Chapter 15

1 When he had uttered the Amen and finished his prayer, the men in charge of the fire lighted it. As a great flame

---

1 John 5.29.

flashed out, we saw a miracle, that is, those of us to whom it was granted to see. Yes! And we were preserved to report to others what happened. 2 For the fire took the shape of an arch, like a ship's sail filled with wind, and stood around the body of the martyr; and he was there in the midst, not like flesh burning, but like bread being baked, or gold and silver being purified in a furnace. And we also perceived a fragrant odor such as the scent of incense or the scent of some other costly spices.

Chapter 16

1 Finally, the lawless men, seing that his body could not be consumed by fire, ordered an executioner to approach and stab him with a dagger. When he had done this, there came out much blood,[1] so that the fire was extinguished, and the whole crowd marveled that there was such a difference between the unbelievers and the elect. 2 For the most glorious Polycarp certainly was one of the elect, an apostolic and prophetic teacher among our contemporaries and bishop of the Catholic Church in Smyrna; and every word which proceeded from his lips has been fulfilled and will be fulfilled.

Chapter 17

1 But the jealous and envious evil one, the adversary of the race of the just, saw the greatness of his martyrdom and his irreproachable life from the beginning; he saw also that he was crowned with a crown of immortality and had won an inestimable prize. So he took measures that his poor body should not be taken away by us, although many desired to

---

1 A disputed passage, where various witnesses to the text give 'a dove and much blood.'

do this and to touch[1] his holy flesh. 2 So he put up Nicetas the father of Herod, and the brother of Alce, to request the Governor not to surrender his body, 'Lest,' it was said, 'they might abandon the crucified one and begin to worship this man.' They said this at the suggestion and instigation of the Jews who also watched as we were going to take the body from the fire. For they did not know that we can never abandon the innocent Christ who suffered on behalf of sinners for the salvation of those in this world who have been saved, and we cannot worship any other. 3 For we worship Him as the Son of God, while we love the martyrs as disciples and imitators of the Lord, for their insuperable affection for their own King and Teacher. With them may we also be made companions and fellow disciples.

Chapter 18

1 On seeing the quarrel stirred up by the Jews, the centurion put the body in the middle, as was their custom, and burned it. 2 And so, afterwards, we took up his bones, more valuable than precious stones and finer than gold, and put them in a proper place. 3 There, as far as we were able, the Lord will permit us to meet together in gladness and joy and to celebrate the birthday of his martyrdom, both in memory of those who fought the fight and for the training and preparation of those who will fight.

Chapter 19

1 These are the details concerning the Blessed Polycarp, who suffered martyrdom in Smyrna, together with eleven others from Philadelphia. But he alone is especially com-

---

1 The Greek is much more graphic; it means 'have fellowship with.'

memorated by everybody, and he is spoken of in every place, even by the heathen. For he proved himself not only a famous teacher, but also a notable martyr, whose martyrdom all desire to imitate, since it was on the model of the Gospel of Christ. 2 Having overcome the unjust ruler[1] by his endurance and thus having gained the crown of immortality, he rejoices with the Apostles and all the just saints and is glorifying God, the Father Almighty, and blessing our Lord Jesus Christ, the Savior of our souls and helmsman of our bodies, the Shepherd of the Catholic Church throughout the world.

Chapter 20

1 You requested, it is true, that the details should be explained to you at length, but, for the present, we have set down a summary by our brother Marcianus. So when you have this information, send the letter to the brethren further on, that they also may glorify the Lord, who makes a choice from His own servants. 2 Now, to Him who is able to bring us all by His grace and goodness to His eternal kingdom, through His only-begotten Son, Jesus Christ, be glory, honor, power and greatness for ever. Greet all the saints. They who are with us greet you, and Evarestus who wrote the letter and his whole house.

Chapter 21

1 The Blessed Polycarp was martyred on the second day of the first part of the month Xanthicus, the seventh day before the calends of March,[1] a great Sabbath, at the eighth

---

1 I.e., the devil.

---

1 I.e., February 23. Xandicus (or Xanthicus) is a month in the Macedonian calendar. The expression 'great Sabbath.' here and at 8.1, may designate the Passover; so Lightfoot, *Essays* 221, though he adds that this interpretation has been questioned. In 156 A. D., however February 22, not 23, was a Sabbath.

hour. He was arrested by Herod, when Philip of Tralles was high priest and Statius Quadratus proconsul. But Jesus Christ rules forever; to Him be the glory, honor, majesty, eternal dominion, from generation to generation. Amen.

Chapter 22

1 God grant you health, brethren, as you march in the word according to the Gospel of Jesus Christ. With Him be glory to God and the Holy Spirit for the salvation of His holy elect. Even as the blessed Polycarp suffered martyrdom, may it be allowed us in his footsteps to be found in the Kingdom of Jesus Christ.

2 Gaius copied this from the account of Irenaeus, a disciple of Polycarp. And he lived with Irenaeus.

3 And I, Socrates, wrote it out in Corinth from the copies of Gaius. Grace be to you all.

4 And I, Pionius, after search for it, wrote it out again from the former copies, because the blessed Polycarp showed it to me in a vision, as I will explain in the following. I have collected it now when it is almost worn out by age, that the Lord Jesus Christ may gather me also with His elect into His heavenly kingdom. To Him be the glory with the Father and the Holy Spirit forever and ever. Amen.

[Instead of the three preceding paragraphs (22.2-4) the Moscow manuscript shows the following:]

2 Gaius copied these things from among the papers of Irenaeus, and he also had lived with Irenaeus, who had been a disciple of the holy Polycarp. 3 For this Irenaeus, being at Rome at the time of the martyrdom of the bishop Polycarp, was a teacher of many. Of him there are many

excellent and correct[1] writings extant, in which he mentions Polycarp, saying that he was his teacher. He ably refuted every heresy, and handed on the ecclesiastical and catholic rule just as he had received it from the saint.[2] 4 And he also says this: When Marcion, after whom the Marcionites are named, once met Saint Polycarp and said to him, 'Recognize us, Polycarp,' his answer was: 'I recognize you, yes, I recognize the eldest son of Satan.' 5 And this is also recorded in the writing of Irenaeus, that on the very day and hour that Polycarp was martyred in Smyrna and Irenaeus was in the city of Rome, he heard a voice as of a trumpet saying: 'Polycarp is martyred.'

6 From these papers of Irenaeus, then, as stated above, Gaius made a copy, and from the copy of Gaius, Isocrates[3] made one in Corinth.

7 And I, Pionius, again wrote it out from the copies of Isocrates, after search for it according to a revelation of the holy Polycarp. I gathered it together when it was almost worn out by age, that the Lord Jesus Christ may gather me also with His elect into His heavenly kingdom. To Him be the glory with the Father and the Son and the Holy Spirit forever and ever. Amen.

---

1 I.e., orthodox.
2 Catholic rule (canon): the complete faith.
3 Or Socrates, as in Chapter 22.

THE DIDACHE
OR
TEACHING
OF
THE TWELVE APOSTLES

Translated

by

FRANCIS X. GLIMM, S.T.L.

Seminary of the Immaculate Conception

Huntington, N. Y.

INTRODUCTION

IN 1873 Philotheus Bryennios, later Greek Orthodox Archbishop of Nicomedia, discovered at Constantinople a manuscript of A.D. 1056 containing, among other works, the complete text of the *Letter of Barnabas* and of the two letters attributed to St. Clement, and a small work entitled the *Didache (Teaching) of the Twelve Apostles*. A second and probably older title in this manuscript, *Teaching of the Lord to the Gentiles by the Twelve Apostles,* indicates that the *Didache* was intended for Gentile Christians. Because the manuscript is the property of the Patriarch of Jerusalem it is known as the Codex Hierosolymitanus. However, it is also referred to as Codex Constantinopolitanus from the place of discovery.

Bryennios did not publish the *Didache* for ten years. He meanwhile recognized it for a long lost work, highly venerated and much used up to the fourth century. Its contents served as a source of many later works of liturgical and canonical character: the *Didascalia,* the so-called *Egyptian Church Order,* Book 7 of the *Apostolic Constitutions,* etc. Eusebius had known a *Didache* and had classed it among the apocryphal Scriptures. Clement of Alexandria, Lactantius and Rufinus seem to have used the *Didache*. St. Athanasius recommended it by name as a good book of elementary instruction.[1]

The *Didache* is generally regarded as being the most important literary discovery in patrology made in the nineteenth

---

1 Relevant bibliographical literature with regard to the influence of the *Didache* on later writers is found in K. Bihlmeyer, *Die apostolischen Väter* (Tübingen 1924) XIII.

century. Within the first ten years of its publication several hundred books and articles were written about it,[2] and since then its critical bibliography has steadily grown. The reason for this is that, with few exceptions, critics believed that the *Didache* was the oldest Christian document outside the New Testament. Everything else had to be tested in the light of the *Didache*.

Recent criticism has somewhat reduced both the age and the importance of the *Didache*. The earlier studies tended to place it between A.D. 70 and 90, i.e., prior to St. Clement's *Letter to the Corinthians*. Some puzzling indications of an abundant use of the New Testament, however, subsequently suggested a more conservative dating, A.D. 90 to 120. But a closer comparison of the New Testament quotations and allusions in the *Didache* with those of Barnabas, St. Ignatius of Antioch, and St. Clement make it necessary to put it after all of them. Although there is no real unanimity of opinion at present as to the date of the *Didache,* it may be considered, with probability, to fall within the period A.D. 120 to 180. While Altaner regards it as composed before the rise of the Montanist heresy, Vokes sees in it evidence of moderate Montanism, which would put it toward the end of the second century. Again, as to place of origin, evidence is meager and no agreement has been reached. From two indecisive references to lack of water (7.2) and to mountains (9.4) Egypt and Syria respectively are suggested. But if the work is Montanistic, as Vokes proposed, Asia Minor must also be considered as a possibility.

Some slight analysis may help the reader to understand the puzzling character of this document. There is no attempt

---

2 In *The Ante-Nicene Fathers* (ed. by A. Roberts and G. Donaldson, 1887) 10. 83 ff., more than 200 items are listed.

at purely dogmatic teaching. At the same time an acknowl-
edgment of the Trinity is taken for granted in the baptismal
formula (7), and the work as a whole, as it now stands,
shows an acceptance of basic Christology. The *Didache* is
a composite document of at least two independent pieces,
which may be considered to have been composed separately.
The first section (1-6) comprises a document known as the
'Two Ways.' This ancient work, chiefly known through its
inclusion in the *Didache* and the *Letter of Barnabas* (18-20),
is a presentation of the moral life as a choice between the
way of God and the way of the devil. It is essentially a series
of ethical pronouncements on the virtues and vices supported
by appropriate Scriptural quotations. At first glance the New
Testament appears to have nearly equal importance with the
Old as a source of the Scriptural evidence adduced. If, however, we except a single passage (1.3-2.1), which may well be
an addition to the 'Two Ways,' the Scripture quoted or
alluded to is essentially of Old Testament origin. From this
and other evidence it can be plausibly argued that the 'Two
Ways' was originally a Jewish document intended to teach
morality to Gentile proselytes.

The second part of the *Didache* (7-16) has an entirely
different tone and purpose. It is divided, according to subject-
matter into a liturgical and a canonical (or disciplinary)
section. In the liturgical section, the Jewish prescriptions on
forbidden meats are recommended, but not made obligatory.
A fast is ordered on Wednesdays and Fridays. In Chapters 9
and 10 are preserved the most ancient Eucharistic[3] prayers
for the use of the community (although the service intended
may be not the Eucharist proper, but the Christian banquet
known as the *agápe*). Confession of sins is prescribed (14)
before the liturgy on Sunday, which (called the 'Lord's Day')
has already become the regular day of worship. A special

3 See p. 179, note 2.

place in the community is given (11-13) to certain inspired teachers called 'prophets,' which is considered by Vokes as an indication of Montanist influence. The heads of the community are designated as 'bishops and deacons,' the same names which are so frequently found coupled in the Epistles of St. Paul and in St. Clement's *Letter to the Corinthians*.

The text followed in the present translation is that of Theodore Klauser, *Doctrina duodecim Apostolorum; Barnabae Epistula* (Florilegium Patristicum, Fasc. 1 Bonn. 1940).

SELECT BIBLIOGRAPHY

Texts and Translations:

C. Bigg, *The Doctrine of the Twelve Apostles;* translated into English by the late Charles Bigg, with a new introduction and revised notes by Arthur John Maclean (London 1922).

K. Bihlmeyer, *Die apostolischen Väter*, Neubearbeitung der Funkschen Ausgabe (Tübingen 1924).

F. X. Funk, *Doctrina duodecim apostolorum* (Tübingen 1887).

T. Klauser, *Doctrina duodecim Apostolorum; Barnabae epistula* (Florilegium Patristicum, Fasc. 1, Bonn. 1940).

R. Knopf, *Die Lehre der Zwölf Apostel.* Die zwei Klemensbriefe (in Lietzmanns Handbuch zum Neuen Testament, Ergänzungsbd.: Die Apostolischen Väter 1 Tübingen 1920).

K. Lake, *The Apostolic Fathers* (Loeb Classical Library, New York 1912) 1.

J. B. Lightfoot, *The Apostolic Fathers* . . . revised texts with short introductions and English translations . . . edited and completed by J. R. Harmer (London 1891).

H. Lietzmann, *Die Didache* mit kritischem Apparat; 4th edition. (Kleine Texte, Berlin, 1936). Includes the ancient Latin version of the first six chapters.

Secondary Works:

B. Altaner, *Patrologia*, 3rd Italian edition (Rome 1944).

E. J. Goodspeed, 'The Didache, Barnabas, and the Doctrina,' *Anglican Theological Review*, 27 (1945), 228-247.

A. Harnack, *Die Apostellehre und die jüdischen zwei Wege* (Leipzig 1896).

J. A. Robinson, 'The Problem of the Didache,' *Journal of Theological Studies*, 13, (1912) 339-56. (cf. Harnack, Theol. Lit.-Ztg. 37, 1912, 528-30).

F. E. Vokes, *The riddle of the Didache. Fact or fiction, heresy or Catholicism?* (London 1938).

THE DIDACHE: TEACHING OF THE
TWELVE APOSTLES

Chapter 1

1 There are two ways, one of life and one of death; and great is the difference between the two ways.[1]

2 This is the way of life: 'First you shall love God who made you, secondly, your neighbor as yourself;[2] and whatever you would not like done to you, do not do to another.'[3]

3 The teaching of these words is as follows:[4] ['Bless those who curse you, and pray for your enemies, and fast for those who persecute you. For what is the merit of loving those who love you? Do not even the pagans do this? But, 'love those who hate you,'[5] and you will not have an enemy. 4 'Abstain from carnal desires.'[6] 'If anyone strikes you on the right cheek, turn the other to him,' and you will be perfect.[7] 'If anyone

---

1 Matt. 7.13 f.
2 Matt. 22.37-39. 6.5; Lev. 19.18.
3 Matt. 7.12. This *negative* form of the 'Golden Rule' is found in some Jewish and early Christian writers.
4 The following section, from 1.3 to 2.1 is considered by most editors to be the interpolation of some Christian writer into the supposed Jewish original of the 'Two Ways.' It contains the only unquestionable quotations from the New Testament to be found within the first six chapters, and it is lacking in both the ancient Latin translation of the 'Two Ways' and in the corresponding section of Barnabas (Barn. 19).
5 Matt. 5.44-46; Luke 6.27 f..32.
6 1 Pet. 2.11.
7 Matt. 5.39, 18.

force you to go one mile with him, go two.'[8] 'If anyone
takes your cloak, give him also your tunic.'[9] If anyone takes
what is yours, do not demand it back,[10] for you have no
power.[11]

5 Give to everyone who asks, and ask nothing in return;[12]
for the Father wishes that a share of His own gifts be given
to all. Blessed is the man who gives according to the commandment, for he is without blame. Woe to the man who
takes. However, if the one who takes is in need, he is without
blame. But should he not be in need, he shall give an account
of the why and the wherefore of his taking it. And he will be
put in prison and examined strictly about what he did, and
'shall not go out from there until he has paid the last cent.'[13]
6 But in this matter the saying also holds: 'Let your alms
sweat in your hands until you know to whom you are giving.'[14]

Chapter 2

1 The second commandment of the Teaching is] 2 You
shall not commit murder. You shall not commit adultery.
You shall not corrupt boys. You shall not commit fornication.
You shall not steal. You shall not practice magic. You shall
not practice sorcery. You shall not kill an unborn child or
murder a newborn infant. And you shall not desire the goods

---

8 Matt. 5.41. This refers to the right of officials in the Persian and
 Roman Empires to 'commandeer' a person's services for official
 business.
9 Matt. 5.40.
10 Luke 6.30.
11 This last phrase is not part of the Scriptural quotation, and its meaning is doubtful. Lake suggests 'not even if thou canst.'
12 Luke 6.30.
13 Matt. 5.26.
14 This is not a Scriptural quotation, and, as it seems to be contrary
 to the spirit of what precedes, may have been added by some copyist.

of your neighbor.[1] 3 You shall not swear falsely or bear false witness; nor shall you slander, or bring up past injuries. 4 You shall not be double-minded or double-tongued, for duplicity is the snare of death.[2] 5 Let your speech not be false or vain, but carried out in action. 6 You shall not be greedy or extortionate; nor shall you be a hypocrite, or malicious, or proud. You shall not take evil counsel against your neighbor. 7 You shall not hate any man; but some you shall admonish,[3] and pray for others, and still others you shall love more than your own life.[4]

Chapter 3

1 My son, flee from all wickedness and from everything like it. 2 Do not become angry, for anger leads to murder. Do not become jealous, or quarrelsome, or irritable, for from all these murders come. 3 My child, do not give way to evil desire, for it leads to fornication. And do not use obscene language, or let your eye wander, for from all these come adulteries. 4 My child, do not be an observer of omens, for this leads to idolatry; or engage in witchcraft, astrology, or ritual ablutions. Do not even desire to see these things (or hear them), for from all these idolatry is born. 5 My child, do not be a liar,. because a lie leads to theft; be not greedy of money or empty glory, for from all this comes thefts. 6 My child, do not be a grumbler, because it leads to blasphemy, do not be proud or malicious, for from all these arise blasphemies.

7 But be meek, for 'the meek shall inherit the land.'[1] 8 Be

---

1 Exod. 20.13-17; Deut. 5.17-21; compare Matt. 19.18. 'Second' commandment here means the second half of the Ten Commandments.
2 Prov. 21.6.
3 Jude 22 f.
4 Literally, 'above your own soul.' Cf. Barnabas 1.4.

---

1 Ps. 36.11; Matt. 5.5.

patient, merciful, guileless, and mild and gentle, and in every regard 'fearful of the words,'[2] which you have heard. 9 Do not exalt yourself or allow impudence in your soul. Your soul shall not cling to the proud, but associate with good and humble men. 10 Accept the troubles that come to you as good, knowing that nothing happens without God.

Chapter 4

1 My child, day and night keep in memory him who speaks the word of God to you,[1] and you shall honor him as the Lord, for the Lord is there wherever the doctrine of the Lord is preached. 2 And every day look for the company of holy men, that you may find comfort in their conversation. 3 Do not desire any schism, but make peace among those who fight. Judge justly, and do not show any favor to any one in correcting offences.[2] 4 Do not waver whether a thing shall be or not be.

5 Do not hold your hands open for receiving and closed for giving.[3] 6 If you possess something by the labor of your hands, give it for the redemption of your sins. 7 Do not be reluctant in giving, or murmur when you give, for you well know who He is who gives a good reward. 8 Do not turn away from the needy,[4] but share all with your brother and do not claim that it is your own.[5] For, if you are sharers in immortal things, how much more in mortal.[6]

9 Do not take your hand from your son or your daughter,

2 Isa. 66.2.

1 Heb. 13.7.
2 Deut. 1.16 f.; Prov. 31.9.
3 Eccli. 4.36.
4 Eccli. 4.5.
5 Acts 4.32.
6 Rom. 15.27.

but teach them the fear of God from their youth. 10 Do
not with bitterness command your servant or maid, who trust
in the same God, lest they should cease to fear God who is
above both of you, for, without respect of persons, He comes
to call those whom the Spirit has prepared. 11 And you who
are servants, be subject to your masters, as being the repre-
sentatives of God, with modesty and reverence.[7]

12 You shall hate all hypocrisy and everything that dis-
pleases the Lord. 13 Do not abandon the commandments of
the Lord, but keep what you have received, without adding
or subtracting.[8] 14 You shall confess your offences in church,[9]
and shall not come forward to your prayer with a bad conscience.[10] This is the way of life.

Chapter 5

1 On the other hand, this is the way of death. First of all,
it is evil and full of cursings, murders, adulteries, evil desires, fornications, thefts, idolatries, magical practices, sor-
ceries, robberies, false witnessings, hypocrisies, double-mindedness, guile, pride, malice, arrogance, covetousness, filthy
talk, envy, insolence, haughtiness, boastfulness [and lack
of fear of God].[1] 2 [Those who walk the way of death]
persecute good people, hate the truth, love lies, do not
acknowledge any reward of justice, do not follow goodness or just judgment, and are vigilant not for good but for
evil, from whom meekness and patience are far removed,

---

7 Eph. 6.5.
8 Compare Deut. 4.2; 13.1 (12.32).
9 Eccli. 4.31.
10 Eccli. 18.23.

---

1 This list of vices may be compared with similar enumerations in:
  Matt. 15.19; Gal. 5.20; Rom. 1.29 f.; Col. 3.8; Hermas, Mand. 8.3-5.
  The *Didache* here has five more vices than the parallel passage in
  Barnabas 20-1.

who love vanities, pursuing gain, without pity for the poor and without care for those who are oppressed. They do not acknowledge their Creator,[2] they are murderers of children, corrupters of the image of God; they turn away from the needy, oppress the afflicted; they are flatterers of the rich, unjust judges of the poor, and are full of all sins.[3] May you be saved, children, from all these.

Chapter 6

1 Beware lest anyone lead you astray from the way of the Teaching, since his teaching would be without God.[1] 2 If you are able to carry the full yoke of the Lord, you will be perfect; but if you are not able, do whatever you can. 3 With regard to food, abstain as much as you can, and from whatever has been offered to idols abstain completely, for this is to worship dead gods.[2]

---

2 Deut. 32.18.
3 This is the end of the parallel with Barnabas (Barnabas 30.2).

---

1 Matt. 24.4. This is the end of the parallel with the ancient Latin version of the 'Two Ways.' The Latin omits the prohibition of eating meats offered to idols, and has a conclusion of its own: 'See that no one leads you astray from this teaching; otherwise you will be taught "outside the rule of discipline." If you perform these things daily, you will be close to God; if you do not, you will be far from the truth. Keep all these things in mind and be not deceived in your trust; by these holy struggles you will gain a crown. Through the Lord Jesus Christ who lives and reigns with God the Father and the Holy Spirit forever and ever. Amen.'
2 Acts 15.29 contains a similar prohibition. St. Paul in 1 Cor. 8 shows that the prohibition was neither absolute nor permanent. The importance of the question in everyday life arose from the fact that large quantities of meat offered in the daily sacrifices of pagan temples could not be consumed by the priests and found their way into the local meat market. Perhaps the bulk of fresh meat in large cities came from pagan sacrifices. Some Christians would be inclined to buy it without question. Others would be scandalized at the thought of touching it.

Chapter 7

1 Regarding baptism, baptize thus. After giving the foregoing instructions,[1] 'Baptize in the name of the Father, and of the Son, and of the Holy Spirit'[2] in running water.[3] 2 But if you have no running water, baptize in any other;[4] and, if you cannot in cold water, then in warm.[5] 3 But, if the one is lacking, pour the other three times on the head[6] 'in the name of the Father, and Son, and Holy Spirit.' 4 But, before the baptism, let the one who baptizes and the one to be baptized fast, and any others who are able to do so. And you shall require the person being baptized to fast for one or two days.

Chapter 8

1 But do not let your fasts be with the hypocrites;[1] for they fast on Monday and Thursday; but you shall fast on

---

1 The literal text, 'these things,' is rather indefinite.
2 Matt. 28.19.
3 Literally, 'in living water,' as in John 4.10 f. From the beginning Christians seem to have preferred to baptize in the waters of springs and flowing rivers. The ancient baptisteries were constructed so that the water could flow through them. Such water was probably considered to be more pure than still water.
4 'Any other water' means a lake, pool or reservoir where the water would not be flowing.
5 Cold water is preferred to warm probably because of its greater apparent purity and of its being in a more natural state.
6 Baptism was usually by immersion of the whole body. But, in case there was not sufficient water for immersion, it was sufficient to baptize by pouring water on the head of the person to be baptized. This is the earliest explicit reference to Baptism by infusion, although the circumstances in Acts 16.33 and elsewhere would seem to suppose it.

---

1 The word 'hypocrites,' found in Matt. 6.16, refers to Pharisees. The present reference may be either to the Pharisees or to some Jewish Christians who continued the practices of the Pharisees.

178   THE DIDACHE

Wednesday and Friday. 2 And do not pray as the hypocrites,[2] but as the Lord directed in His Gospel, 'Thus shall you pray: "Our Father[3] in heaven, hallowed be Thy name, Thy kingdom come, Thy will be done on earth just as in heaven; give us this day our bread from above,[4] and forgive us our debt as we also forgive our debtors, and lead us not into temptation, but deliver us from evil," ' for Thine is the power and glory forever.[5] 3 Three times in the day pray thus.

Chapter 9

1 In regard to the Eucharist,[1] you shall offer the Eucharist thus: 2 First, in connection with the cup, 'We give Thee thanks, Our Father, for the holy vine[2] of David Thy son, which Thou hast made known to us through Jesus Thy Son; to Thee be glory forever.' 3 And in connection with the breaking of bread, 'We give Thee thanks, Our Father, for the life and knowledge which Thou hast revealed to us through Jesus

2 Matt. 6.5.
3 This is the oldest transcription of the Lord's Prayer outside the New Testament. It is closer to Matt. 6.9-13 than to Luke 11.2-4.
4 'From above,' Greek *epiousion*, is a word of uncertain meaning. It is usually translated 'daily.' The word does not occur in any Greek author prior to the New Testament, and Origen remarked in the third century that it was a very rare word (*De Oratione* 27.7). The early Greek Fathers are about equally divided between the two meanings, 'daily' and 'supernatural.'
5 This ending, which is very ancient, does not occur in the best manuscripts of the New Testament. It is. first found in Syrian liturgical usage, whence it was borrowed by the Byzantine Church, which prefixed 'kingdom' to 'power and glory.' It is used as an ending for two other prayers in the *Didache*.

1 Although some editors think that these prayers were intended for the ancient Christian banquet known as the *agápe*, or love-feast, it is more likely that they are prayers to be said by the congregation immediately before Communion.
2 John 15.1.

Thy Son; to Thee be glory forever. 4 As this broken bread was scattered upon the mountain tops and after being harvested was made one, so let Thy Church be gathered together from the ends of the earth into Thy kingdom, for Thine is the glory and the power through Jesus Christ forever.' 5 But let no one eat or drink of the Eucharist with you except for those baptized in the name of the Lord, for it was in reference to this that the Lord said: 'Do not give that which is holy to dogs.'[3]

Chapter 10

1 But, after it has been completed, give thanks in the following way: 2 'We thank Thee, holy Father, for Thy holy name which Thou hast caused to dwell in our hearts, and for the knowledge and faith and immortality, which Thou hast made known to us through Jesus thy Son; to Thee be glory forever. 3 Thou, Lord Almighty, has created all things for Thy name's sake[1] and hast given food and drink to men for their refreshment, so that they might render thanks[2] to Thee; but upon us Thou hast bestowed spiritual food and drink, and life everlasting through Thy Son.[3] 4 For all things we render Thee thanks, because Thou art mighty; to Thee be glory forever. 5 Remember, O Lord, Thy Church, deliver it from all evil[4] and make it perfect in Thy love and gather it from the four winds,[5] sanctified for Thy kingdom, which Thou hast prepared for it; for Thine is the power and the

---

3 Matt. 7.6. This injunction seems to favor the Eucharistic interpretation of this whole passage.

---

1 Wisd. 1.14; Eccli. 18.1; 24.8; Apoc. 4.11; Isa. 43.7.
2 *Render thanks* in Greek is the same as 'celebrate the Eucharist.'
3 John 6.27.
4 Matt. 6.13; John 17.15.
5 Matt. 24.31.

glory forever. 6 Let grace come, and let this world pass away, "Hosanna to the God of David."[6] If anyone is Holy, let him come; if anyone is not, let him repent. Marantha.[7] Amen.' 7 But allow 'prophets' to render thanks as they desire.[8]

Chapter 11

1 If anyone, therefore, comes to you and teaches all the aforesaid things, receive him. 2 But, if a wicked person comes and teaches another doctrine to contradict this, do not listen to him.[1] But, if one teaches so as to increase justice and the knowledge of the Lord, receive him as the Lord.[2]

3 In regard to 'apostles' and 'prophets,' act according to the doctrine of the Gospel.[3] 4 Let every apostle who comes to you be received as the Lord. 5 But he shall not remain more than one day. But, if necessary, let him remain a second day. But, if he stays for three, he is a false prophet. 6 And when the apostle departs, let him take only enough bread to last until he reaches shelter; but, if he asks for money, he is a false prophet.

7 And you shall not tempt any prophet who speaks in the spirit, or judge him; for every sin shall be forgiven, but this

---

6 Matt. 21.9, 15.
7 1 Cor. 16.22, an Aramaic phrase meaning 'Lord, come.' See Apoc. 22.20.
8 'Prophets' might compose their own prayers in different words and at greater length.

---

1 2 John 10.
2 Meaning 'in the name of the Lord.'
3 An 'apostle' here is not one of the Twelve. but an intinerant mission-ary who traveled from church to church preaching and exhorting. See. St. Paul, 1 Cor. 12.28. The 'prophet' seems at times to have enjoyed special inspiration to speak in the public assemblies of Chris-tians. See St. Paul 1 Cor. 14.22,29; Acts 13.1. The phrase, 'speak in the spirit,' which will occur several times in connection with 'pro-phets.' may mean to speak 'in ecstasy' or to speak 'by inspiration of the Holy Spirit.'

sin shall not be forgiven.[4] 8 But not everyone who speaks in the spirit is a prophet, but only if he follows the conduct of the Lord. Accordingly, from their conduct the false prophet and the true prophet will be known.[5] 9 No prophet who in the spirit orders a meal to be prepared eats of it; but, if he does, he is a false prophet. 10 And every prophet who teaches the truth and fails to do what he teaches is a false prophet. 11 Anyone who has been proved to be a true prophet and who does something purporting to be an outward mystery of the Church (so long as he teaches you not to do what he does) is not to be judged by you, for his judgment is with God. For the ancient prophets also acted in this manner.[6] 12 And, whoever says in spirit: 'Give me money,' or anything like it, do not listen to him. But, if he asks that it be given to others in need, let no one judge him.

Chapter 12

1 Let everyone who 'comes to you in the name of the Lord'[1] be received; but, after testing him, you will know him, for you know right and wrong. 2 If the one who comes to you is a traveler, help him as much as you can; but he shall not remain with you more than two or three days, unless there is need. 3 But, if he wishes to settle among you and is a craftsman, let him work and eat. 4 But, if he has no trade, provide according to your conscience, so that no Christian

---

4 Matt. 12.31. It is not certain that the *Didache* is making a correct interpretation of Christ's famous saying that 'the blasphemy of the Spirit shall not be forgiven.'
5 False prophets and lying teachers had already given anxiety to the Apostles: 2 Pet. 2.1; 1 John 4.1.
6 The meaning of this verse and the reference to the Old Testament are equally obscure.

---

1 Matt. 21.9; Ps. 117.26.

shall live among you idle. 5 But, if he does not agree to do this, he is trading on the name of Christ; beware of such men.

Chapter 13

1 Every true prophet who desires to settle among you is worthy of his food. 2 Likewise, a true teacher is worthy, as a workman, of his food.[1] 3 Accordingly, take all the first-fruits of the winepress and of the harvest, of the cattle and of the sheep, and give them to the prophets, for they are your high priests. 4 But, if you have not a prophet, give it to the poor. 5 If you make bread, take the first share and give according to the commandment. 6 Likewise, when you open a jar of wine or oil, take and give the first share to the prophets. 7 Also of silver and of clothes and every other possession, take the first share as it seems best to you and give according to the commandment.[2]

Chapter 14

1 And on the Lord's Day,[1] after you have come together, break bread and offer the Eucharist, having first confessed your offences, so that your sacrifice may be pure. 2 But let no one who has a quarrel with his neighbor join you until he is reconciled, lest your sacrifice be defiled.[2] 3 For it was

1 Matt. 10.10; 1 Tim. 5.18.
2 These injunctions concerning the first-fruits seem to imply that the audience was very familiar with Jewish practices. Cf. Exod. 22.29 f. Num. 1519 f.; 18.11 f.; Deut. 18.3 f.

1 Literally, 'On the Lord's Day of the Lord,' which indicates that 'Lord's Day' had already become a word of common usage for Sunday. Outside of the Apocalypse (1.8) this is the oldest use of the term 'Lord's Day' for the first day of the week.
2 Matt. 5.23 ff.

said by the Lord: 'In every place and time let there be offered to me a clean sacrifice, because I am the great king'; and also: 'and my name is wonderful among the Gentiles.'[3]

Chapter 15

1 Elect, therefore, for yourselves bishops and deacons worthy of the Lord, humble men and not covetous, and faithful and well tested; for they also serve you in the ministry of the prophets and teachers. 2 Do not, therefore, despise them, for they are the honored men among you, along with the prophets and teachers. 3 And correct one another, not in anger but in peace, as you have it in the Gospel. And let no one speak with anyone who has harmed his neighbor, nor let him be heard until he repents.[1] 4 Offer your prayers and alms and do all things according to the Gospel of our Lord.

Chapter 16

1 'Be vigilant' over your life; 'let your lamps' not be extinguished, or your loins be ungirded, but be prepared, for you know not the hour in which our Lord will come.[1] 2 Come together frequently, and seek what pertains to your souls: for the whole time of your faith will not profit you, unless in the last hour you shall be found perfect.[2] 3 For, in the last days, false prophets and seducers will increase,[3] and sheep will be turned into wolves, and charity will be changed into hate. 4 For, as lawlessness grows, men will hate one another

---

3 Mal. 1.11,14.

---

1 Compare Matt. 5.22-26; 18.15-35.

---

1 Matt. 24.42,44; 25.13; Luke 12.35.
2 Barnabas 4.9.
3 2 Pet. 3.3.; Matt. 24.10 ff; 7.15.

and persecute one another and betray one another, and then will appear the Deceiver of the world, as though he were the Son of God, and will work signs and wonders; and the world will be delivered into his hands, and he will do horrible things, which have not been done since the beginning of the world.[4] 5 Then shall all created men come to the fire of judgment, and 'many will be scandalized'[5] and perish; but those who persevere in their faith will be saved[6] from the curse itself.[7] 6 And then will appear the signs of the Truth:[8] first, the sign of confusion in the heaven; second, the sign of the sound of the trumpet;[9] and third, the resurrection of the dead—7 not the resurrection of all men, but, as it was said: 'The Lord will come and all His saints with Him.'[10] 8 Then shall the world see the Lord coming on the clouds of heaven.[11]

---

4 Apoc. 12.9; 2 John 7; Matt. 24.24; 2 Thess. 2.4,9; Apoc. 13.2, 13 f.; 19.20.

5 Matt. 24.10.

6 Matt. 10.22; 24.13.

7 'From the curse' is a conjecture of Klauser, based on the Georgian version of *Didache,* instead of the more usual 'by the accursed thing,' which is the reading of the Jerusalem manuscript.

8 Matt. 24.30.

9 Matt. 24.31; 1 Cor. 15.52; 1 Thess. 4.16.

10 Zachary 14.5. The author of the *Didache* seems to believe that only the just will arise in the future resurrection. But he may possibly be thinking of the Millenium, according to which Christ and the saints would reign on earth for a thousand years before they all go to heaven. Other Fathers, including Papias, shared this erroneous opinion.

11 Matt. 24.30; 26.64. The ideas of this last chapter, although not altogether clear to us, show the interest which many early Christians manifested in analyzing the signs that should foretell the end of the world.

THE LETTER

OF

BARNABAS

Translated

by

FRANCIS X. GLIMM, S.T.L.

Seminary of the Immaculate Conception

Huntington, N. Y.

INTRODUCTION

THE TRACT which goes by the name of the *Letter of Barnabas* is really anonymous. There is no indication that its author intended to pose as the Barnabas who was St. Paul's companion.[1] How it came by this name is unknown, unless the author's name might also have been Barnabas.

The Greek text is extant in two manuscripts, the Codex Hierosolymitanus, and the famous Codex Sinaiticus, once in St. Petersburg, now in the British Museum.[2] An early Latin translation (Imperial Library at Leningrad) and a Syriac version (Library of Cambridge University) are incomplete.

Two dates of composition are possible. The years A. D. 70-79 are suggested by a veiled reference to Vespasian (4.4)). This possibility is not contradicted directly by anything else in the letter. There is no explicit quotation of any writing of the New Testament and there is a hint that the destruction of the Temple was still a living memory. A second date is suggested by the reference to the rebuilding of the Temple (16.3-4). This could refer to the insurrection of Bar-Cochba against the Romans, when the Jews, for a brief time in 132, thought that the revolt might be successful and enable them to rebuild the Temple. It is now agreed that the *Letter of Barnabas* could not be any later than 150 and might be as early as 70 or 71. It is older than the present form of the *Didache,* which contains more New Testament quotations or allusions.

---

1 Eusebius *(Historia ecclesiastica* 3.25.4) and St. Jerome *(De viris illustribus* 6) recognize the letter to be apocryphal.
2 See note 1, p. 61.

187

The *Letter of Barnabas* was much read in the second and third centuries, and is quoted by the name of Barnabas by Clement of Alexandria and by Origen. This connection with writers of Alexandria suggests that this city is the probable place of its origin. Its peculiar method of interpreting the Old Testament has been called the allegorical method, proper to the Alexandrian School. It should rather be called a rabbinical method or a cabbalistic method. It finds a hidden meaning, not simply in certain sentences and words, but even under the single letters of certain words. The author's familiarity with the Old Testament suggests that he might have been a rabbi or rabbinical student. He was almost surely a convert from Judaism.

The announced purpose of the 'epistle' is to warn Christian readers against accepting the Old Testament in its literal sense, particularly where that meaning seems to indicate the permanent validity of Jewish religious practices. The writer's tone is strong, but not bitter. There is no reference to any contemporary difficulty with the Jews, but the writer sets up as a thesis that the revelations in the Old Testament were misunderstood by the Jews from the beginning. The thesis, of course, is false, and the method of proof is extremely tortuous. This accounts for the difficulty of reading this epistle and for its many obscurities of meaning. Copyists have increased this difficulty by numerous attempts to correct it.

To understand the writer's difficulty, we must remember that the divinely inspired Scriptures known to Christians at the moment were only the Old Testament, the writings of the New Testament not being yet collected into a canon. As the Jews were in possession of this Bible, and as its promises were quite plainly made to them, many uninstructed Christians were at a loss to understand their own relation to it. Some of them, as the heretic Marcion, threw the Old Testament over altogether. Others, like Barnabas, relying on their own imagination, simply read an unhistorical meaning into it. But the Church, not forgetting that the Jews were the Chosen People and that the Savior would come from them, knew that the Old Testament was not a complete revelation, but only a preparation for the salvation, not only of a Chosen People, but of the whole world.

The text followed in the present translation is that of Bihlmeyer, *Die apostolischen Väter* (Tübingen 1924). Mention should be made of the English rendering of Kirsopp Lake, which in many instances has been of service.

SELECT BIBLIOGRAPHY

Texts and Translations:

    K. Bihlmeyer, *Die apostolischen Väter*, Neubearbeitung der Funkschen Ausgabe (Tübingen 1924).

    G. Bosio, *I Padri Apostolici,* (Torino 1940) *Parte 1.*

    T. Klauser, *Doctrina duodecim Apostolorum; Barnabae epistula* (Florilegium Patristicum, Fasc. 1, Bonn. 1940).

    K. Lake, *The Apostolic Fathers* (Loeb Classical Library, New York 1912) 1.

    J. B. Lightfoot, *The Apostolic Fathers* . . . revised texts with short introductions and English translations . . . edited and completed by J. R. Harmer (London 1891).

Secondary Works:

    O. Braunsberger, *Der Apostel Barnabas, sein Leben u. der ihm beigelegte Brief* (Mainz 1876).

    H. Connolly, O.S.B., *Journal of Theological Studies*, 33 (1931-32), 237-253.

    F. X. Funk, 'Die Zeit des Barnabasbriefes,' *Kirchengeschichtl. Abhandl. u. Untersuch.* II,(1899) 77/108.

    J. Muilenburg, *The Literary Relations of the Epistle of Barnabas and the Teaching of the Twelve Apostles* (Marburg 1929—Dissertation).

THE LETTER OF BARNABAS

Chapter 1

GREETINGS, sons and daughters, in the name of the Lord who loves us, in peace.

2 Since the ordinances of God in your regard are great and rich, I rejoice very greatly and exceedingly at your blessed and glorious spirits; so deeply engrafted is the grace of the spiritual gift you have received. 3 For this, also, I congratulate myself in the hope of salvation, because I truly see in you the Spirit poured out upon you from the fount of the bounteous Lord. So greatly on your account has the long-desired sight of you astonished me. 4 With this conviction, then, and the consciousness that, while speaking much among you, I understand the Lord was my fellow traveler on the road of righteousness, I am completely bound to this: to love you more than my life, because great faith and charity dwell in you due to the hope of His life. 5 Considering this, then, that, if I take care to share something with you of what I have received, it will be [turned to] a reward for having ministered to such spirits, I hasten to send you a brief message, in order that with your faith you may have perfect knowledge.

6 The doctrines of the Lord are three: hope of life, the beginning and end of our faith; righteous life, the beginning and end of judgment; love [that comes] from joy and gladness, the witness of the words of a righteous life. 7 For the Lord by His prophets made known to us things past and things present, and gives us the foretaste of things to come;

and, as we see these things coming to pass one by one, as He foretold, we are bound to make a more generous and higher offering to reverence Him. 8 Now, not as a teacher, but as one of yourselves, I will point out a few things by which you shall be made happy in the present circumstances.

Chapter 2

1 Since the times are evil and the Worker of evil himself holds sway, we must give heed to ourselves and search out the commandments of the Lord. 2 The helpers of our faith are fear and patience; our allies are long-suffering and self-control. 3 While these [virtues], then, persist in their purity in matters relating to the Lord, Wisdom, Prudence, Understanding and Knowledge rejoice with them. 4 For He has made known to us through all the Prophets that He does not need holocausts or oblations, saying at one time:[1] 5 'What is the multitude of your sacrifices to Me?' Says the Lord, 'I am sated with holocausts and desire neither fat of lambs nor blood of bulls and goats, not even when you come to appear before Me. For who has demanded these things from your hands? You shall no longer tread My court. If you bring flour, it is in vain. Incense is an abomination to Me. I cannot suffer your new moons and Sabbaths.' 6 This He accordingly did away with, so that the new law of our Lord Jesus Christ might be without restraining yoke and without man-made offering. 7 Again he says to them:[2] 'Did I command your fathers when they came out of the land of Egypt to offer Me holocausts and sacrifices? 8 Rather I did command them

---

1 Isa. 1.11-13 .
2 A loose quotation, keeping the substance, however, of Jer. 7.22-23. Barnabas apparently quotes from memory.

this:[3] Let none of you cherish evil in his heart against his neighbor, and love not a false oath.' 9 We ought therefore to understand, if we are not senseless, the kindly intention of our Father, for he speaks to us, desiring us not to err like them, but to seek how to make our offering to Him.

10 To us He accordingly speaks thus:[4] 'A contrite heart is a sacrifice to the Lord; an odor of sweetness to the Lord is a heart which glorifies its Maker.' We ought, therefore, to watch carefully after our salvation, brethren, lest the evil one, sneaking in among us deceitfully, push us away from our life.

Chapter 3

1 So, again He says to them concerning these matters:[1] 'Why do you fast for Me, says the Lord, so that your voice is heard today crying? This is not the fast which I have chosen, says the Lord, not a man humbling his soul; 2 Not if you bend your neck like a hoop, and put on sackcloth, and make your bed of ashes, not even so shall you call it an acceptable fast.' 3 But, to us He says: 'Behold, this is the fast which I have chosen, says the Lord, give up every attachment to wickedness, release the chains of forced agreements, send away the bruised with forgiveness, and tear up every unjust contract. Break thy bread for the hungry, and if thou seest a naked man clothe him, bring the homeless into thy house, and if thou seest a humble man despise him not, nor shall any of thy house or of thy family. 4 Then will thy light break forth at dawn, and thy healing shall rise quickly, and thy justice

---

3 Zach. 8.17. Cf. n. 2.
4 Ps. 50.19.

---

1 Isa. 58.4-10.

shall go before thee, and the glory of God will surround thee. 5
Then thou shalt cry and God shall hear thee; while thou
art still speaking He shall say, "Behold, I am here,"[2] if thou
puttest away from thee bondage [enslavement] and stretch-
ing out the hands and words of discontent, and dost give the
hungry thy bread heartily and dost pity the soul that is humbled.' 6 For this reason, therefore, brethren, the long-suffering
One foresaw that the people whom He prepared in His Beloved would believe with simplicity. So He made a revelation
beforehand concerning all things, that we should not be ship-
wrecked, like the uninitiated, by their law.

Chapter 4

1 We, then, must earnestly look into the present, and seek
out what can save us. Let us completely flee from all works
of lawlessness, lest the work of lawlessness overcome us; let
us hate the error of the present time, that we may be loved in
the time to come. 2 Let us give no leeway to our souls and
so enable them to associate with sinners and evil men, lest we
become like them. 3 The final stumbling block is at hand,
concerning which it is written, as Enoch[1] says: 'For to this
purpose the Lord has shortened the seasons and the days, that
His beloved should hasten and come to His inheritance.' 4 And
the Prophet also speaks thus:[2] 'Ten kingdoms shall reign on
the earth, and after them shall rise up a little king, who shall
humble three of the kings under one.' 5 Likewise, Daniel

---

2 'Behold I am here,' also quoted in 2 Clem. 15.3.

---

1 On the Book of Henoch and its use cf. 'Apocryphes de l'ancien Testament,' in Vigouroux, *Dict. de la Bible*, Suppl. Vol. 1, cols. 354 ff.

2 Dan. 7.24. The quotation is according to the substance, not the exact
wording, either of Septuagint or Vulgate.

speaks of the same thing:[3] 'And I beheld the fourth beast,
evil and powerful and fiercer than all the beasts of the sea,
and how ten horns sprang from it, and from them a small
horn, a mere excrescence and that it subdued three of the
great horns under one.' 6 You ought then to understand.
Furthermore, I also beg this of you, as one of yourselves,
one who loves you all individually more than my own life:
Be careful for yourselves now, and do not become like some;
do not add to your sins and say that the covenant is both
theirs and ours. 7 Yes! it is ours; but they thus lost it forever
when Moses had only just received it, for the Scripture says:[4]
'And Moses was on the mountain fasting forty days and forty
nights, and he received the covenant from the Lord, tablets of
stone written by the finger of the hand of the Lord.' 8 But
they, by turning away to idols, lost it. For the Lord speaks
thus:[5] 'Moses, Moses, come down quickly, for thy people,
whom thou has brought out of the land of Egypt, have broken
the law.' And Moses understood and threw the two tablets out
of his hands and their covenant was broken in order that
the covenant of Jesus, the Beloved, should be sealed in our
hearts by the hope which faith in Him gives. 9 Though
wishing to write much to you, not as a teacher, but as one who
loves you should write, I, dirt under your feet,[6] have made
haste to write without omitting anything from our common
possessions. So, let us be on the watch in the last days, for
the whole time in which we believe will profit us nothing,
unless in this present lawless period, in the temptations to
come, we resist as becomes children of God. Thus, the Black
One may have no opportunity of stealing in [upon us]. 10 Let

3 Dan. 7.8. Cf. n. 2.
4 Exod. 31.18; 34.28.
5 Exod. 32.7; Deut. 9.12.
6 Perípsema, literally, 'off-scouring'; cf. Ignatius of Antioch, p. 90, note 8.

us flee all vanity, let us hate completely the deeds of the evil way. Do not retire and live apart by yourselves, as if you had already achieved justification, but come together and seek the common good. 11 For, the Scripture says:[7] 'Woe to them that are wise in their own eyes and prudent in their own conceits.' Let us become spiritual, let us become a temple perfect for God. So far as is in our power, let us 'exercise ourselves in the fear' of God, and let us strive to keep His commandments in order that we may rejoice in His ordinances. 12 The Lord will judge the world 'without respect of persons.' Each man will receive according to his deeds. If he be good, his goodness will lead him, if he be evil, the reward of injustice is before him. 13 And so, since we are called, let us never slacken and slumber in our sins, lest the Prince of evil gain power over us and cast us out from the Kingdom of the Lord. 14 And remember this also, my brethren, when you see how, after such great signs and wonders were done in Israel, even they were finally cast off;—let us be careful lest, as it is written, it should be found with us that 'many are called but few chosen.'[8]

Chapter 5

1 For this reason the Lord endured the sacrifice of His flesh to corruption, that we might be sanctified by the forgiveness of sin, that is, by the sprinkling of His blood. 2 For the Scripture concerning Him refers partly to Israel, partly to us, and it speaks thus:[1] 'He was wounded for our sins and bruised for our iniquities, by his wounds we were healed. He was led as a sheep to the slaughter, and as a dumb lamb

---

7 Isa. 5.21.
8 Matt. 22.14.

---

1 Isa. 53.5,7.

before its shearer.' 3 We ought therefore to be extremely
thankful to the Lord that He has revealed to us the past and
has made us wise in the present, and for the future we are
not without understanding. 4 The Scripture says:[2] 'Not unjustly are the nets spread out for the birds.' This means that
a man perishes deservedly who, although he has knowledge of
the way of justice, thrusts himself into the way of darkness.
5 Furthermore, my brethren, if the Lord endured suffering
for our souls although He is the Lord of the whole world,
to Whom God said at the foundation of the world:[3] 'Let us
make man in our image and likeness,' how then did He
allow Himself to suffer at the hands of men? 6 Here is the
reason. The Prophets, with His grace, prophesied concerning
Him, and He, to destroy death and manifest the Resurrection
from the dead, allowed Himself to suffer because He must
necessarily be manifested in the flesh. 7 It was also to fulfill
the promise made to the fathers, and prepare for Himself
the new people; also to show, while still on earth, that, having effected the Resurrection, He Himself will be the judge.
8 Over and above this He taught Israel and preached by
performing such great signs and wonders. Yes! He loved them
exceedingly. 9 But when He chose as His special Apostles to
preach His Gospel men lawless beyond all others, and showed
that 'he came not to call the just, but sinners,'[4]—then He
showed Himself to be God's Son. 10 For, if He had not come
in the flesh, there is no conceivable way in which men could
be saved by beholding Him, since, even when they look at
the sun, which will perish and is a work of His hands, they
cannot gaze straight at its rays. 11 For this purpose, therefore,
the Son of God came in the flesh, that He might round out

2 Prov. 1.17.
3 Gen. 1.26.
4 Matt. 9.13.

the total of the sins of those who persecuted His Prophets to death. 12 For this purpose He allowed Himself to suffer, For God says that they are the authors of the wound of His flesh:[5] 'When they smite their shepherd, then the sheep of the flock shall be destroyed.' 13 It was His will to suffer thus, for it was necessary that He should suffer on a tree, for the Prophet says of Him: 'Spare my soul from the sword,'[6] and 'Nail my flesh, for the congregations of evil-doers have risen against me.'[7] 14 And again He says:[8] 'Behold, I have given my back to scourges, and my cheeks to strokes, and I have set my face as a hard rock.'

Chapter 6

1 When, therefore, He gave the commandment, what does He say? 'Who is the man to dispute with me? Let him oppose Me. Or, who comes to law against Me? Let him approach the servant of the Lord. 2 Woe to you, for you shall all become old as a garment and the moth shall consume you.'[1] And again, on being assigned as a strong stone for crushing, the Prophet says: 'Behold, I will put down for the foundations of Sion a precious stone, specially chosen, a corner-stone.'[2] 3 Then what does He say? 'And he that shall put his hope in it shall live forever.'[3] Is our hope therefore set on a stone? Not at all. But he means that the Lord set his flesh in strength. For he says:[4] 'And He set me as a hard

---

5 Zach. 43.7; Matt. 26.31.
6 Ps. 22.21; 119.120; 22.17.
7 Isa. 50.6,7.
8 Isa. 50.6,7 (Septuagint).

---

1 Isa. 50.8,9 (Septuagint).
2 Isa. 28.16 (Septuagint).
3 Isa. 28.16 (The sense of the Septuagint.)
4 Cf. n. 1.

rock.' 4 And again the Prophet says: [5] 'The stone which the builders rejected, this has become the head of the corner,' and again he says: [6] 'This is the great and wonderful day which the Lord has made.' 5 I write to you more simply that you may understand. I, mean token of your love.[7] 6 What, then, does the Prophet say again? 'The congregation of them that do evil has surrounded me, they encircled me as bees the honeycomb'[8] and 'For my clothing they cast lots.'[9] 7 Since, then, He was to be revealed in the flesh and to suffer in the flesh, His suffering was revealed in advance. For the Prophet speaks concerning Israel, 'Woe to their soul, for they have plotted an evil plan against themselves, saying,[10] "Let us bind the just one, for he is unprofitable to us." ' 8 What does the other Prophet, Moses, say to them? 'Behold, thus says the Lord God, enter the good land which the Lord swore to give to Abraham, Isaac, and Jacob, and inherit it, a land flowing with milk and honey.'[11] 9 But what does knowledge[12] say? Let me tell you! Hope [it says,] in the one who will be revealed to you in the flesh, in Jesus. For man is earth suffering, for the creation of Adam[13] was effected from the face of the earth. 10 What, then, does 'into the good land, a land flowing with milk and honey' mean? Blessed be our Lord, brethren, who has put in us wisdom and understand-

---

5 Ps. 118.22 (= 117 in Vulgate) .

6 Ps. 118.25 (= 117 in Vulgate); Vulgate: 'This is the day which the Lord has made; let us be glad and rejoice at it.'

7 The sense seems to be: 'I on whom you have expended your love and who deserve it so little.'

8 Ps. 22.17 (= 21 in Vulgate); Ps. 118.12 (= 117 in Vulgate) .

9 Ps. 22.19 (=21 in Vulgate) .

10 Isa. 3.9,10.

11 Exod. 23.13.

12 I.e., real penetration and understanding of the Scriptures.

13 'Adam' is the Hebrew for 'earth.'

ing of his secret. Yes! the Prophet speaks a parable of the Lord: 'Who will understand except the wise and learned, the lover of his Lord?' 11 Since, then, he has renewed us by the forgiveness of sins, He made us another product, and we have the soul of children, as though he were creating us again. 12 For the Scripture says of us, as He says to the Son:[14] 'Let us make man after our image and likeness, and let them rule over the beasts of the earth, and the birds of heaven, and the fishes of the sea.' And, on seeing the beauty of our creation, the Lord said:[15] 'Increase and multiply and fill the earth.' This He addressed to the Son. 13 Again I will show you how He refers to us. He made a second creation in the last days. And [in this connection][16] the Lord says:[17] 'Behold, I make the last things as the first.' The Prophet referred to this, then, when he preached:[18] 'Enter into a land flowing with milk and honey, and be lords over it.' 14 See, then, we have been recreated as, once more, He says in another Prophet:[19] 'Behold says the Lord, I will take out from them (that is, from those whom the Spirit of the Lord foresaw) their hearts of stone and will put in hearts of flesh.' Because He Himself was going to be manifested in the flesh and dwell among us. 15 For, my brethren, the dwelling of our hearts is a temple sacred to the Lord. 16 For the Lord says again: 'And in what shall I appear before the Lord my God and be glorified?'[20] I will confess to thee in the assembly of my brethren, and I

---

14 Gen. 1.26.
15 Gen. 1.28.
16 Words in brackets are not in original text.
17 Matt. 20.16.
18 Exod. 33.1,3.
19 Ez. 11.19; 36.26. The substance, as usual, is quoted.
20 Ps. 42.3 (= Vulgate 41.3).

will sing to thee in the midst of the congregation of saints.'[21]
We, then, are the ones whom He brought into the good land.
17 What, then, is the milk and honey? Because the child is
made to live first with honey, and afterwards with milk. So
then, we, also, being nourished on the faith in the glad tidings
and by the word, shall live and rule over the earth. 18 As
we have said above:[22] 'Let them increase and multiply and
rule over the fishes.' Who, then, is it who is able now to rule
over beasts or fishes or birds of heaven? For we ought to
perceive that to rule is a sign of authority, and that one who
gives orders really rules. 19 If, then, this is not happening
at present, He has told us when it will happen—when we
ourselves also shall become perfect and become heirs of the
covenant of the Lord.

Chapter 7

1 Realize, therefore, children of gladness, that the good
Lord made all things known to us in advance, that we might
know Him to whom we must give thanks and praise for
all things. 2 If, then, the Son of God, Lord as He is, and future judge of the living and dead, suffered that His wound
might make us live, let us believe that the Son of God could
not suffer except for our sakes. 3 But, being crucified, He was
also 'given vinegar and gall to drink.' Let me tell you how
the priests of the Temple threw light on this. A commandment was written:[1] 'Whoever does not keep the fast shall
certainly perish,' and the Lord commanded this because He
Himself was going to offer the vessel of His spirit as a sacri-

---

21 Ps. 22.23 (= Vulgate 21.23).
22 Gen. 1.28.

---

1 Lev. 23.29. A Hebraism; literally, 'Shall die (or perish) in death.'

fice for our sins that the *type*[2] signified by Isaac, offered on the altar, might be fulfilled. 4 What, then, does He say in the Prophet? 'And let them eat of the goat which is offered in the fast for all their sins.'[3] Note carefully—'and let all the priests alone eat the entrails unwashed by vinegar.'[4] 5 Why?— Because you are going to give Me gall and vinegar to drink when I offer My flesh for My new people. But you shall eat alone, while the people fast and mourn in sackcloth and ashes—to show that He must suffer at their hands. 6 Note the things which He commanded: 'Take two sound, similar goats, and offer them, and let the priest take the first one as a holocaust for sins.'[5] 7 But what are they to do with the other? 'The other,' he says, 'is accursed.'[6] Notice how the type of Jesus is manifested. 8 'And spit on it, all of you, and kick it, and put the scarlet wool around its head, and then let it be cast out into the desert.'[7] And when this has been done in this manner, he who takes the goat into the desert leads it away and takes the wool, and puts it on a shrub which is called 'Rachia,' whose shoots we usually eat when we find them in the country. That is why the fruit of the thorn-bush alone is sweet. 9 What then does this mean? Note well: 'The one is for the altar, and the other is accursed';[8] besides, the accursed one is crowned, because then 'they will see Him' on that day with the long scarlet robe on His body, and they will say, 'Is not this He whom we once despised and pierced and spit upon and crucified? Truly, He is the One who then

---

2 Cf. A. J. Maas, S. J., *Christ in Type and Prophecy.*
3 An unidentified quotation.
4 Throughout this chapter Barnabas has completely jumbled the text and meaning of Lev. 16.
5 Lev. 16.7,9.
6 Lev. 16.8.
7 An unidentified quotation.
8 Lev. 16.8.

said He was the Son of God.' 10 But how is He like to this [goat]? In this way—'the goats are to be alike and beautiful,' that, when they see Him coming at that time, they may be astounded at the likeness of the goat. See, then, the *type* of Jesus Who was to suffer. 11 But why did they put the wool in the middle of the thorns? It is a type of Jesus, displayed for the Church: Whoever wishes to take away the scarlet wool must suffer much, because the thorns are terrible and one gets hold of it through pain. Thus, He says: 'those who wish to see Me and come to My kingdom must lay hold of Me through affliction and suffering.'

Chapter 8

1 But what kind of *type* do you think this is? A commandment was given to Israel, that men whose sins are complete should offer a heifer, kill and burn it; then boys take the ashes and put them into containers and bind the scarlet wool around a tree (see again the type of the cross and the scarlet wool!), and hyssop; after this the boys sprinkle the people one by one that they may be purified from their sins. 2 Observe how he speaks to you in simplicity: The calf is Jesus; the men who offer it, since they are sinners, are those who offered Him for the slaughter. Then there are no longer men [who offer]; there is no longer glory for sinners.[1] 3 The boys who sprinkle are those who preached to us forgiveness of sins and purification of the heart. They are those to whom He gave authority, based on the Gospel, to preach. There are twelve, as a witness to the tribes (for there are twelve tribes of Israel). 4 But why are there three boys who sprinkle? As a witness to Abraham, Isaac, and Jacob, because they are great in the sight of God. 5 But why the wool on the tree?

---

1 Text is corrupt.

Because the Kingdom of Jesus is on the tree[2] and those who hope in Him shall live forever. 6 But why are the wool and the hyssop together? Because in His Kingdom there shall be evil and dark days, in which we shall be saved, because a person who has a bodily ailment is cured by the foulness of hyssop. 7 For this reason the things that were so done are plain to us, but obscure to them because they did not hear the voice of the Lord.

Chapter 9

1 And again He speaks concerning the ears, [meaning] how he circumcised our hearts, for the Lord says in the Prophet:[1] 'In the hearing of the ear they obeyed.' And again He says: 'They who are far away shall surely hear, they shall know what I have done,'[2] and 'Be circumcised in your hearts, says the Lord.'[3] 2 And again He says:[4] 'Listen, O Israel, thus says the Lord thy God. . . . '[5] 'Who is the man who desires to live forever?[6] Let him hear carefully the voice of my servant.'[7] 3 And again He says:[8] 'Hear, O heaven, and give ear, O earth, for the Lord has spoken these things for a testimony.' And again He says: 'Hear the word of the Lord, you rulers of the people.' And again: 'Hear, O children, the voice of one crying in the desert.'[9] So, then, he circumcised

2 I.e., the tree of the Cross.

1 Ps. 18.45 (= 17.45).
2 Is. 33.13.
3 Jer. 4.4.
4 Jer. 7.2,3.
5 The Latin translation and many Greek manuscripts have: and again the Spirit of the Lord prophesies' after 'the Lord thy God.'
6 Ps. 34.13 (= 32.13).
7 Ex. 15.26.
8 Is. 1.2.
9 Is. 40.3.

our ears that we might hear the word and believe. 4 But the circumcision in which they trust has also been abolished. For He said that circumcision was not of the flesh. But they were mistaken because an evil angel was teaching them [vain] cleverness.[10] 5 He says to them: 'Thus says the Lord your God' [here I find a commandment], 'sow not among thorns, be circumcised to your Lord.'[11] And what does He say? 'Circumcise the hardness of your heart, and do not stiffen your neck.'[12] Take this again: 'Behold, says the Lord, all the Gentiles are uncircumcised in the foreskin, but this people is uncircumcised in their heart.' 6 But you will say: The people surely has been circumcised to seal[13] the covenant. Yes, indeed, but every Syrian and Arab and all priests of the idols have been circumcised; are they also [part] of their covenant? Why, even the Egyptians belong to the circumcision. 7 Learn fully, then, children of love, on all points that [because] Abraham, who first instituted circumcision, did it looking forward in spirit to Jesus, for he received the doctrines [implicit in][14] three letters. 8 For it says:[15] 'And Abraham, circumcised from his household eighteen men and three hundred.' What, then, was the special knowledge taught him? Notice that he first mentions eighteen, and, after a pause, three hundred. Eighteen is I, and H—you have Jesus (IH)—and, because the cross in the T was to have grace, he says 'and three hundred' (T).[16] So he indicates Jesus in the two letters and the cross in the other. 9 He who placed the innate gift of

10 The Greek is equivalent to: 'plays the sophist.'
11 Jer. 4.3,4.
12 Deut. 10.16.
13 The Greek has 'For a seal.'
14 Greek: 'Doctrines of three letters.'
15 Gen. 14.14; 17.23. The actual words of the Septuagint are: Three-hundred ten and eight.
16 Letters have numerical value in Greek: TIH=318.

His teaching in our hearts knows this. No one has heard from me a more excellent teaching, but I know that you are worthy.[17]

Chapter 10

1 When Moses said:[1] 'You shall not eat swine, nor eagle, nor hawk, nor crow, nor any fish which has no scales on it,' he included three doctrines in his meaning. 2 Moreover, he says to them in Deuteronomy:[2] 'And I will lay My commandments as a covenant on this people.' So then it is not a commandment of God to abstain from eating these creatures, but Moses spoke spiritually. 3 Accordingly, he mentioned the swine for the following reason: You shall not cling, he means, to men who are like swine; that is, when they prosper they forget the Lord, but when they are in need acknowledge the Lord, just as the pig when it eats ignores its master, but when it is hungry cries out, and after receiving food is again silent. 4 'Nor shalt thou eat the eagle, nor the hawk, nor the kite [?], nor the crow.'[3] He means that thou shalt not live with or become like such men as know not how to provide their food by labor and sweat, but take other people's property in their lawlessness, and lie in wait for it, though they give the impression of walking in innocence, and look around to see whom they may strip bare in their greed, just as these birds by their own efforts provide no food for themselves, but sit idle and seek how to devour the flesh of others, a pest in their wickedness. 5 'Thou shalt not eat,' he

---

17 Possibly an indication that Barnabas felt that his interpretation was strained.

1 Lev. 11.7,10,13-15; Deut. 14.8,10,12-14.
2 Deut. 14.10,13.
3 Lev. 11.13-15; Deut. 14.12-14.

says, 'lamprey nor polypus nor cuttlefish.'[4] He means that you should not become like men who are utterly ungodly and already condemned to death, just as these fish alone are accursed and swim in deep water, and do not rise like the others, but live on the mud below in the depths. 6 Furthermore, Thou shalt not 'eat the hare either.'[5] Why? You shall not become, he means, a corrupter of boys, nor shall ye become like such persons. For the hare gains a passage in the body each year, and every year it lives, it has that many passages. 7 Nor shalt thou eat the hyena.'[6] You shall not, he means, become an adulterer or fornicator, nor become like such persons. Why? Because this animal changes its nature every year, and becomes now male, now female. 8 Moreover, he hates the weasel, and rightly so. You shall not, he means, become like those men who, we are told, work iniquity with their mouth in their uncleanness nor shall you associate with impure women who work iniquity with their mouth. For this animal conceives by the mouth. 9 So Moses received three decrees concerning foods, and spoke them in a spiritual sense, but the Jews received them as referring to food in their carnal desires. 10 David also received special knowledge concerning the same decrees and says:[7] Blessed is the man who has not walked in the council of the ungodly,' as the fishes go in darkness into the deep waters, 'and who has not stood in the way of sinners' like those who, appearing to fear the Lord, sin like swine, 'and sits not in the company of the insolent,'[8]

---

4 Not identified.
5 Lev. 11.5.
6 Not identified.
7 Ps. 1.1.
8 Ps. 1.1. Vulgate: *et in cathedra pestilentiae non sedet*. Lightfoot translates: 'and has not sat in the seat of the destroyers.'

like the birds who sit for their prey. Now grasp fully also the teaching about food. 11 Moses says again:[9] 'Eat of every animal that divides the hoof and chews the cud.' What does he mean? [He means] that whoever receives food recognizes him who feeds him and, relying upon him, seems to rejoice. He spoke well in regard to the commandment. What then does he mean? He means: Associate with those who fear the Lord, with those who meditate in their heart on the meaning of the word which they have received, with those who speak of and keep the commandments of the Lord, with those who know that meditation is a work of joy, and who ponder over[10] the word of the Lord. But what does 'that divideth the hoof' mean? It means that the righteous both walks in the world and looks forward to the holy age. See how well Moses wrote the law. 12 But how could the Jews understand or comprehend these things? At any rate we, rightly recognizing them, announce the commandments as the Lord intended. For this reason He circumcised our hearing and hearts that we should understand these things.

Chapter 11

1 But let us inquire if the Lord took care to give a revelation beforehand about the water [of baptism] and the Cross. Concerning the water, Scripture says with regard to Israel that they will not receive the baptism that brings forgiveness of sins, but will build for themselves. 2 For the Prophet says:[1] 'Be astounded, O heaven, and let the earth shudder the more at this, that this people has done two evil things: they have

---

9 Lev. 17.3; Deut. 14.6.
10 The Greek original reads 'ruminate' here.

---

1 Isa. 1.2.

deserted me, the fountain of life, and they have dug for themselves a pit of death. 3 Is my holy mountain Sinai a desert rock? For you shall be as young birds, fluttering about when they are ejected from the nest.' 4 And again the Prophet says:[2] 'I will go before thee and I will level mountains, and I will break the gates of brass, and will shatter bars of iron, and I will give thee treasures, dark, secret, invisible, that they may know that I am the Lord God.' 5 And 'Thou shalt live in a lofty cave of a strong rock.' And, 'His water is sure; you shall see the King with glory, and your soul shall meditate on the fear of the Lord.'[3] 6 And again, He says in another Prophet :[4] 'And he who does these things shall be like a tree which is planted near the running waters, which shall bring forth its fruit in due season. And his leaf shall not fall off, and all whatsoever he shall do shall prosper. 7 Not so the wicked, not so; but like the dust which the wind driveth from the face of the earth. Therefore the wicked shall not rise again in judgment; nor sinners in the council of the just. For the Lord knoweth the way of the just, and the way of the wicked shall perish.' 8 Notice how he described the water and the Cross together. He means this: Blessed are they who put their hope in the Cross and descended into the water. For He speaks of their reward 'in due season'; at that time, He says, I will repay. But now, when He says: 'Their leaves shall not fall off,' He means that every word which shall come from your mouth in faith and charity shall profit many for conversion and hope. 5 And again, another Prophet says :[5] 'And the land of Jacob was praised above every land.' He

---

2 Isa. 45.2.3.
3 Ps. 33.16-18.
4 Ps. 1.3-6.
5 Vague reference to Sophonias 3.19.

means this: He glorifies the vessel of His spirit. 10 What does He say next? 'And there was a river flowing on the right hand, and beautiful trees grew out of it, and whoever shall eat of them shall live forever.'[6] 11 This means that we go down into the water full of sins and foulness, and we come up bearing fruit in our hearts, fear and hope in Jesus in the Spirit. 'And whoever shall eat of them shall live forever.'[7] This means: Whoever hears these things spoken and believes shall live forever.

Chapter 12

1 In a similar way again, He describes the Cross with precision[1] in another Prophet, who says:[2] 'And when shall these things be done? says the Lord. When a tree shall fall and rise again, and when blood shall drip from a tree.' Again you have a reference to the Cross and to Him who would be crucified. 2 And again He speaks in [the books of] Moses,[3] when Israel was attacked by strangers, in order to remind those that were attacked that they were delivered to death because of their sins. The Spirit speaks to the heart of Moses, [telling him] to make a *type* of the Cross, and of Him who would suffer, because, He says, unless they put their hope in Him, they shall be warred upon forever. Moses, therefore, piled arms on arms in the midst of the struggle, but stood

---

6 Ezech. 47.1-12.
7 Ezech. 47.9.

---

1 'He defines.'
2 4 Esdras, regarded by early Christian writers as canonical, was later universally rejected as apocryphal. Therefore it is usually printed as an appendix at the end of the Vulgate.
3 I.e., in the Pentateuch, spoken of as Moses.

high above them all and kept his hands outstretched; thus
Israel began again to win, then. But, whenever he let them
fall, they began to be killed. 3 Why? That they might know
that they cannot be saved unless they hope in Him. 4 And
again, He says in another Prophet: [4] 'I have spread forth
my hands all the day to an unbelieving people, who walk in
a way that is not good after their own thought.' 5 Once more
Moses makes a *type* of Jesus: He must suffer, and He Himself
will give life, though they shall think that He has died by
the sign given when Israel was falling. For the Lord made
every serpent bite them, and they were dying—for the Fall[5]
took place in Eve through the serpent, in order to convince
them that they would be delivered to the tribulation of death
because of their transgression. 6 Moreover, after Moses had
commanded them, 'You shall have neither a carved nor a
molten [cast] statue for your God,'[6] yet he makes one himself
to show a *type* of Jesus. Moses, therefore, made a carved serpent, and set it up conspicuously, and called together the
people by a proclamation. 7 So they came together and begged
Moses to offer a prayer for their recovery. But Moses said to
them, 'Whenever one of you,' he said, is bitten, let him come
to the serpent that is placed on the tree, and let him hope
and believe that, though dead, the serpent is able to vivify, and
he shall immediately be saved.' And they did so. In this,
again, you have the glory of Jesus, for all things are in Him
and for Him. 8 Again, what does Moses say to Josue,[7] the
son of Nun, when, as a prophet, he gave him this name that
the whole people should listen to him alone? It was because

---

4 Isa. 65.2.
5 Literally, 'transgression.'
6 Deut. 27.15.
7 Josue = Jesus = Savior.

the Father revealed everything concerning His Son Jesus.
9 Moses says to Josue, the son of Nun, after giving him this
name, when he sent him to explore the land:[8] 'Take a book
in your hands, and write what the Lord says, that the Son of
God shall in the last days tear up by the roots the whole
house of Amalek.' 10 See again Jesus, not as son of man, but
as Son of God, manifested by a *type* in the flesh. So, since
they will say that Christ is David's son, David himself prophesies, fearing and realizing the error of sinners. 'The Lord
said to my Lord, Sit at my right hand until I make thy enemies thy footstool.'[9] 11 And again Isaias speaks as follows:[10] 'The Lord said to Christ my Lord, whose right hand
I hold, that the nations should obey in his presence, and I
will break the strength of kings.' See how 'David calls Him
Lord' and does not say 'Son.'[11]

Chapter 13

1 Let us see whether this new people or the former people
is the heir, and whether the covenant refers to us or to them.
2 Hear, then, what the Scripture says concerning the people:[1]
'And Isaac prayed for Rebecca his wife, because she was
barren; and she conceived. Then Rebecca went to consult the
Lord, and the Lord said to her, "Two nations are in thy
womb, and two peoples in thy belly, and one people shall

---

8 Exod. 17.14.
9 Ps. 110.1 (= Vulgate 109.1); Matt. 22.44.
10 Isa. 45.1. By adding one letter in the word for 'Lord'—Kyrios instead
of Kyros—the reference, otherwise accurately quoted, becomes closely
Messianic.
11 Cf. Matt. 22.45.

---

1 Gen. 25.21-23. The Biblical text is not quoted in full by Barnabas.

overcome the other people, and the older shall serve the younger." ' 3 You must understand who is Isaac and who is Rebecca, and in regard to whom He has shown that this new people is greater than the former. 4 And, in another prophecy, Jacob speaks more plainly to Joseph his son, saying:[2] 'Behold, the Lord did not deprive me of your presence; bring me your sons, that I may bless them.' 5 And he brought Ephraim and Manasses, desiring that Manasses be blessed because he was the elder; for Joseph brought him to the right hand of Jacob his father. But Jacob saw in spirit a *type* of [the] people to come. And what does he say? 'And Jacob crossed his hands, and placed his right hand on the head of Ephraim, the second and younger son, and blessed him. And Joseph said to Jacob, change your right hand to the head of Manasses, for he is my first born son. And Jacob said to Joseph, I know, son, I know; but the elder shall serve the younger, and this one shall be blessed.'[3] 6 Note in what cases He decided that this [new] people is the first and the heir of the covenant. 7 If, then, this people is commemorated also in the case of Abraham, we reach the perfection of our knowledge. What, then, does He say to Abraham, when he alone believed and it was set down to his justification? 'Behold, I have made you, Abraham, the father of the Gentiles who believe in God in uncircumcision.'[4]

Chapter 14

1 So it is. But, let us see whether He has really given the covenant which He swore to the fathers He would give to the people. He did give it. But, they were not worthy to receive

2 Gen. 48.11,9.
3 Gen. 48.14,18,19.
4 Rom. 4.11.

it because of their sins. 2 For the Prophet says:[1] 'And Moses was fasting on Mount Sinai, to receive the covenant of the Lord for the people, forty days and forty nights. And Moses received from the Lord the two tablets, written allegorically by the finger of the hand of the Lord; and Moses took them and was carrying them down to give to the people. 3 And the Lord said to Moses: "Moses, Moses, go down quickly, for your people whom you brought out of the land of Egypt have broken the law." And Moses realized that they had once more made molten statues for themselves, and he threw them out of his hands, and the tablets of the covenant of the Lord were broken in pieces.'[2] 4 Moses received the covenant, but they were not worthy. Well! how did we receive it? Let me tell you. Moses, a mere servant, received it, but the Lord Himself gave it to us, as the people of the inheritance, by suffering on our account. 5 Now He was made manifest both that they should be 'perfected' in their sins and that we should receive the covenant through Jesus the Lord who inherited it. For He was prepared for this purpose, that, having appeared in person, He might redeem from darkness our hearts already surrendered to death and delivered to the iniquity of error, and might by His Word make a covenant with us. 6 For the Scripture tells how the Father commands Him to redeem us from darkness and prepare a holy people for Himself. 7 The Prophet accordingly says:[3] 'I the Lord, thy God, have called thee in justice, and taken thee by the hand, and preserved thee. And I have given thee for a covenant of the people, for a light of the Gentiles: That thou mightest open the eyes of

---

1 Exod. 24.18.

2 Exod. 32.7,8,19.

3 Isa. 42.6,7.

the blind, and bring forth the prisoner out of prison, and them that sit in darkness out of the prison-house.' We realize then from what we have been redeemed. 8 Again the Prophet says:[4] 'Behold, I have given thee to be a light of the Gentiles, that thou mayest be my salvation to the farthest part of the earth. Thus says the Lord the God who redeemed thee.' 9 And again, the Prophet says:[5] 'The Spirit of the Lord is upon me, because he anointed me to preach the gospel to the humble, he sent me to heal the contrite of heart, to proclaim release to the captives, and recovery of sight to the blind, to announce the acceptable year of the Lord, and a day of recompense, to comfort all who mourn.'

Chapter 15

1 Furthermore, it is also written concerning the Sabbath in the ten commandments which He spoke on Mount Sinai face to face to Moses:[1] 'Sanctify also the Sabbath of the Lord with pure hands and a pure heart.' 2 And, in another place, He says:[2] 'If my sons keep the Sabbath, then I will bestow my mercy on them.' 3 Concerning the Sabbath He speaks at the beginning of Creation:[3] 'And God made in six days the work of His hands, and on the seventh day He ended, and rested on it and sanctified it.' 4 Note, children, what 'He ended in six days' means. It means this: that the Lord will make an end of everything in six thousand years, for a day with Him means a thousand years. And He Himself is my witness, saying:[4] 'Behold, the day of the Lord shall be as a thousand

4 Isa. 49.6.7.
5 Isa. 61.1.2.

1 Exod. 20.8.
2 Jer. 17.24.
3 Gen. 2.2.
4 2 Pet. 3.8.

years.' So, then, children, in six days, that is, in six thousand years, everything will be ended. 5 'And he rested on the seventh day.'[5] This means: When His Son will come and destroy the time of the lawless one and judge the godless, and change the sun and the moon and the stars—then He shall indeed rest on the seventh day. 6 Furthermore, He says:[6] 'Thou shalt keep it holy with pure hands and a pure heart.' If, then, anyone is able *now* to hallow the day which God sanctified, by being pure in heart, we are completely deceived. 7 See that we shall *then* indeed sanctify it when we enjoy true repose, when we shall be able to do so because we have been made just ourselves and shall have received the promise, when there is no more sin, but all things have been made new by the Lord; then we shall be able to sanctify it, having been made holy ourselves. 8 Furthermore, He says to them:[7] 'I will not abide your new moons and your Sabbaths.' You see what He means: The present Sabbaths are not acceptable to Me, but that [Sabbath] which I have made, in which, after giving rest to all things, I will make the beginning of the eighth day, that is, the beginning of another world. 9 Therefore, we also celebrate with joy the eighth day on which Jesus also rose from the dead, was made manifest, and ascended into heaven.[8]

Chapter 16

1 I shall speak to you further about the Temple. These wretched men in their error set their hope on the building, and not on their God who made them, for they are the house of

---

5 Gen. 2.2.
6 Exod. 20.8.
7 Isa. 1.13.
8 This is the earliest attempt to explain why Christians observed the Lord's Day on Sunday rather than Saturday.

God. 2 For, they confined Him by consecration[1] within the Temple almost like the heathen. But, what does the Lord say to make it empty of meaning? Let me tell you: 'Who has measured the heaven with a span, or the earth with his hand? Have not I?'[2] The Lord says:[3] 'Heaven is My throne, and earth is the footstool of My feet; what kind of house will you build for Me, or what is the place of My rest?' You realize now that their hope was vain. 3 Besides, He says again,[4] 'Behold, they that destroyed this Temple shall themselves build it.' 4 It is happening now.[5] For, because they went to war, it was destroyed by their enemies; now, the very servants of the enemy will build it up again. 5 Again, it was revealed that the city and the Temple and the people of Israel would be surrendered. For, the Scripture says:[6] 'And it shall come to pass in the last days that the Lord will deliver the sheep of His pasture, and the sheepfold, and their tower to destruction.' And it happened according to what the Lord said. 6 But, let us inquire whether any temple of God exists. Yes, it does, where He Himself says that He is making and perfecting it. For, the Scripture says:[7] 'And it shall come to pass when the week is ended that a temple of God shall be built gloriously in the name of the Lord.' 7 I find, accordingly, that a temple exists. Let me tell you, then, how it will be built in the name of the Lord. Before we believed in God, the habitation of our heart was corrupt and weak, as is a

---

1 The Greek word (aphiérosan) contains two ideas: (1) deem holy = consecrate; (2) segregate.

2 Isa. 40.12 (quotation of substance).

3 Isa. 66.1.

4 Isa. 49.17.

5 The first destruction of the Temple in Christian times took place under Titus in 70; the second in 132.

6 Apocryphal book of Henoch 89.56,66.

7 Dan. 9.24-27. The substance very loosely quoted.

temple actually built with hands, because it was full of idolatry and was the house of demons from doing things contrary to God. 8 'But it shall be built in the name of the Lord.'[8] Now, make sure that the temple of the Lord be built gloriously. How? I shall tell you. When we received forgiveness of sins, and put our hope in the Name [of Jesus], we were renewed, totally re-created; and so God truly dwells in us as in His habitation. 9 How? His word of faith, the call of His promise, the wisdom of His ordinances, the commandments of the teaching, Himself prophesying in us, Himself dwelling in us, opening the door of the temple—that is, the mouth—to us who were enslaved to death, granting us repentance; [thus] He leads us into the incorruptible temple. 10 For, he who desires to be saved looks not at the man, but at Him who dwells and speaks in him, and is amazed at him, for neither has he ever heard such words from his mouth, nor has he himself ever desired to hear them. This is the spiritual temple being built for the Lord.

Chapter 17

1 So far as in my power lies to give a simple explanation, my soul hopes that none of the things necessary to salvation has been omitted, according to my desire. 2 For if I write to you concerning things present or future, you will not understand because they are put in parables. The foregoing is enough.

Chapter 18

1 Let us turn now to another kind of Knowledge and Teaching. There are two ways of Teaching and of Power: that

---

8 *Ibid.*

of Light and that of Darkness; and there is a great difference between the two ways. Over the one are stationed the light-bringing angels of God; over the other, the angels of Satan. 2 And the first is Lord from eternity to eternity; the latter is the ruler of the present world of lawlessness.

Chapter 19

1 The way of Light, then, is this: If anyone wish to follow the path to the appointed goal, let him be zealous in what he does. This, then, is the Knowledge given to us to walk in this path: 2 Thou shalt love thy Creator, thou shalt fear thy Maker, thou shalt glorify Him who redeemed thee from death. Thou shalt be simple in heart and generous in spirit. Thou shalt not join those who walk in the way of death. Thou shalt hate everything which is not pleasing to God. Thou shalt not abandon the command of the Lord. 3 You shall not exalt yourself, but shall be humble-minded in all things; you shall not take glory to yourself. You shall not take evil counsel against your neighbor; you shall not allow arrogance into your soul. 4 You shall not commit fornication, you shall not commit adultery; you shall not corrupt boys. The word of God shall not be spoken by you among the impure. You shall not respect persons in rebuking any for transgression. You shall be meek, you shall be quiet, 'you shall fear the words' which you have heard.[1] You shall not bear malice against your brother. 5 You shall not doubt whether a thing shall be or not.[2] 'Thou shalt not take the name of the Lord in vain.'[3] You shall love your neighbor more than your own soul. You shall not murder a child by

---

1 I.e., the words of God. Cf. Isa. 66.2.
2 I.e., doubt God's veracity.
3 Exod. 20.7.

abortion, nor again kill it after birth. You shall not remove
your hand from your son or from your daughter, but shall
teach them the fear of God from their youth. 6 You shall
not be found coveting your neighbor's goods, nor showing
avarice. You shall not be associated in soul with the haughty,
but shall associate with humble and righteous men. You shall
receive the trials that befall you as benefits, knowing that
nothing happens without God's permission. 7 You shall not
be double-minded nor gossipping.[4] You shall obey your masters
as a type of God in modesty and fear; you shall not with
bitterness command your servant or maid who hope in the
same God, lest perhaps they cease to fear the God who is
above you both. For He came not to call men with respect
of persons, but those whom the Spirit prepared. 8 You shall
not be quick to speak, for the mouth is a snare of death. So
far as you can, you shall be pure for your soul's sake. 9 Be
not one who holds out his hands to receive, but shuts them
for giving. You shall love as the apple of your eye every man
who speaks to you the word of the Lord. 10 Remember the
day of judgment day and night, and seek each day the company of the saints, either laboring by speech, and going out
to exhort, and striving to save souls by the word, or working
with your hands for the ransom of your sins. 11 Do not hesitate to give and, when you give, do not grumble; but you
shall know who is the good paymaster of your reward. Keep
the teachings which you have received, adding nothing and
subtracting nothing. Hate the Evil One thoroughly. Pass
righteous judgment. 12 Do not cause quarrels, but bring
together and reconcile those who quarrel. Confess your sins.

---

4 K. Lake's text is here followed: *glossodes*. Another reading is 'double-
tongued.'

Do not go to prayer with an evil conscience. This is the way of Light.

Chapter 20

1 But the way of Darkness is devious and accursed. For it is a way of eternal death with punishment, and in it are the things that destroy the soul: idolatry, arrogance, exaltation of power, hypocrisy, double-heartedness, adultery, murder, robbery, pride, transgression, fraud, malice, stubbornness, evil charms, magic, covetousness, lack of the fear of God. 2 Those who walk this way are persecutors of good men, haters of the truth, lovers of lies, who acknowledge no reward of justice, not 'cleaving to the good,'[1] nor to just judgment, who pay no attention to the cause of widow and orphan. They spend wakeful nights not for the fear of God, but in the pursuit of vice. Meekness and patience are far distant from them; they love vanity and seek rewards; are without pity for the poor; do nothing for him who is oppressed by toil. Ready to speak evil, they ignore their Maker, are murderers of children, corrupters of God's creation. They repel the needy and oppress the afflicted, are advocates of the rich, unjust judges of the poor, altogether sinful through and through.

Chapter 21

1 It is good, therefore, that a man who has learned all the commandments of God, which are written here, should walk in them. For, he who does this shall be glorified in the Kingdom of God; he who prefers the others shall perish together with his works. For this reason there is the resurrec-

---

1 Rom. 12.9.

tion; for this reason there is the reward. 2 I beg those of you who are in high positions, if you will accept advice that comes from my good will, keep those among you to whom you may do good. Do not fail to do this. 3 The day is near when all things shall perish with the Evil One. 'The Lord is at hand and His reward.'[1] 4 I beg you again and again: be good lawgivers one to another, remain faithful advisers of one another, take all hypocrisy out of yourselves. 5 And may God who is Lord over all the world give you wisdom, understanding, prudence, knowledge of His commandments, patience. 6 Be taught of God, searching out what the Lord asks of you, and act so that you may be found worthy in the day of judgment. 7 If there is any recollection of good [from my words], meditate on this and remember me, that both my desire and my vigilance may lead to some good. I beg you and ask it as a favor. 8 While the good vessel of the body is still with you, do not fail in any of these matters, but seek these things steadily, and fulfill every commandment; for they deserve it. 9 Therefore, I have been all the more eager to write to you as best I could, to make you glad. May you gain salvation, children of love and peace. The Lord of glory and all grace be with your spirit.

---

1 Isa. 40.10; Apoc. 22.12. Cf. *Didache* 16.7.

THE SHEPHERD

OF

HERMAS

Translated

by

JOSEPH M.-F. MARIQUE, S.J., Ph.D.

Holy Cross College
Worcester, Massachusetts

IMPRIMI POTEST:

F. A. McQUADE, S.J., PRAEP. PROV.

Neo Eboraci
die 24 Oct., 1946

INTRODUCTION

HE SHEPHERD OF HERMAS is longer than the rest of the Apostolic Fathers and quite distinctive in form and content. The external division into five Visions, twelve Mandates and ten Parables does not rest on valid internal reasons. Both Mandates and Parables are also visionary in character, and the ninth Parable is only a more pointed repetition of the Visions,[1] as the author himself clearly points out in one of the Visions.[2] In accordance with these directions of the author himself, the more apt division of the work would be: (1) Vision 1 to Vision 4; (2) Vision 5 to the end of the ninth Parable. The conclusion of the work is supplied by the tenth Parable.

In the first of the two divisions mentioned above, from the first to the fourth Vision, the Church appears to Hermas as a venerable lady, who in the successive Visions gradually sheds the marks of age, until at the end of the fourth Vision she appears as a young woman, dressed in bridal apparel, a symbol of God's elect. There then comes on the scene the angel of penance, sent by the most exalted angel. His shepherd's dress and his remark, 'I am the shepherd to whom you have been committed,' have given the name *Shepherd of Hermas* to the work.

The *Shepherd* is basically an exhortation to penance in apocalyptic form. In the first Vision the Church appears to Hermas and bids him do penance for his own sins and for

---

1 Cf. Parable 9.1.1.
2 Vision 5.5.

225

the transgressions of his household. In the following he receives a booklet to transcribe, which comments on the necessity of doing penance and gives some detailed indications about the coming persecution. After the third Vision, Hermas is to spread the booklet among the faithful. In this Vision the elderly lady points out the fortunes of the Church under the symbolism of the tower from which useless stones are excluded, just as sinners who do no penance are excluded from the Church. The urgency of penance is also stressed because of the little time left for it. Finally, in the fourth Vision, Hermas is shown by the elderly lady a symbol of the coming trials and persecutions of the Church, a huge monster 'who came on with a rush capable of destroying a city.' Then the Church appears as a youthful bride, symbol of the cleanness and purity of God's elect.

The deeper explanation of the foregoing is given Hermas in the Mandates and Parables which he is commanded to write down by the angel of penance.

The Mandates command belief in (1) one God, (2) simplicity of heart, (3) love of truth, (4) chastity and the sanctity of marriage, (5) meekness. The sixth Mandate makes clear the characteristics of the angel of justice and of the angel of wickedness. In the following, (7) fear of God, (8) continence and (9) confident prayer are enjoined. The Mandates close with admonitions (10) against sadness, (11) false prophets and (12) covetousness. Throughout, the Mandates are not severe, stressing the avoidance of sadness and despair of salvation, and encouraging the faithful to drive the Devil from their hearts.

Especially toward the end, the Parables are quite similar to the Mandates in their didactic character. (1) Man has not

in this world a 'lasting city' and should not attach his heart
to transitory goods. (2) The rich should give to the poor and
the poor in return should give the alms of his prayer for the
benefactor. They thus mutually support each other as the elm
does the vine. (3 and 4) Just as the difference between dead
and living trees is not discernible in winter, so the difference
between sinners and just is apparent, not in this world, but in
the world to come. The following three make interesting
observations on fasting and the meritoriousness of good
works (5), on luxury and deceit (6) and on the value of
penance (7). In the eigth Parable the Archangel Michael
is presented as cutting branches from a huge elm and present-
ing a branch to one and all. The elm is a symbol of the
Church; the branches typify the various classes of the good
and the bad. The branches of the good are in bloom; those
of the bad are withered and have to be watered abundantly
on being planted in the ground. An admonition to penance is
directed to them. In the ninth Parable the symbolism of the
tower is developed and the admonition given to sinners to
become useful stones in its building. In conclusion, the exalted
angel appears again and repeats his admonition to Hermas
and the community.

There are different opinions about the date of composition
of the *Shepherd*. Those who identify Hermas with the person
of the same name mentioned in Rom. 16.14, as did Origen[3]
and Eusebius[4] in antiquity, put the date of the writing in
Apostolic times. Other scholars, influenced by the mention of
Clement,[5] date the work toward the end of the first century.
However, the testimony of the Muratorian Canon deserves to
be followed, since it is the deposition of a person almost con-

3 Commentary on Rom. 16.14.
4 *Hist. eccl.* 3.3.6.
5 Vision 2.4.3.

temporary and from the same city of Rome. According to the Canon, it was written 'quite recently, in our own time in the city of Rome, by Hermas, while his brother Pius was sitting on the throne of the church of the city of Rome.' This brings the date to the years 140-154. Furthermore, the moral conditions depicted[6] in the *Shepherd* fit this date better than the years of fervor either in the time of St. Clement or, *a fortiori*, contemporaneous with St. Paul. Besides, there are palpable indications that the Montanist heresy is being combated: the considerations on the permissibility of a second marriage,[7] the symbolic explanation of fasting, the earnestness of the discussion of forgiveness after repeated sin, and the affirmative answer to the question whether this was possible.[8] These facts seem to make the time of the Antonines a much more probable date.

From the remarks in the text itself some scraps of information as to the identity of the author can be gleaned. He tells[9] that he had been sold at a very early age to a certain Rhode. From the style, as Bardenhewer[10] has pointed out, there are indications of Jewish influences, or perhaps even of Jewish birth. The author is an unaffected man of the people, as is learned from his casual remarks about his relatives, his business, the loss of his property and his farming—all told with childlike simplicity.[11] With the same simplicity he recounts the defection of his children from the faith, his wife's talkativeness, and his own sin of thought with respect to Rhode.[12]

---

6 Vision 2.2.3; Parable 6.
7 Mandate 4.4.1-2.
8 Vision 8.7.1; Parable 8.6.5; 9.22.1.
9 Vision 1.1.4; 2.2.2.
10 *Geschichte der altkirchlichen Literatur* I 473.
11 Vision 1.3.2; 4.1.6; Mandate 11.15.18; 12.5.3; Parable 8.1.2-4.
12 Vision 2.2.1-3; 1.1.2.

His style betrays numerous non-Greek elements, Latin loan-words, Latinisms and Hebraisms, thus justifying the conclusion that Hermas' education was not of a high order. The same holds for his reasoning and for his esthetic sense. He is an earnest man with singleness of purpose. That purpose is to frighten the evil and comfort the afflicted. With it all, Hermas has a certain *joie de vivre* which gives lightness to his whole admonition. All these marks of lowly upbringing are so many arguments against the thesis of Bardenhewer that the *Shepherd* is a literary fiction, composed by some distinguished member of the Roman clergy to depict the ravages of the times within the Church. The lowly style pervading the entire work points to a single author, even though it could be admitted that the publication and writing took place in successive stages.

The dogma in the *Shepherd* revolves primarily about the practical question of penance and forgiveness of sins. An apparent contradicition in the section between Mandate 3. 1-2 and 4-6 presents itself. The angel of penance first declares that only baptism brings about a valid remission of sins, but later admits that penance after baptism is possible. The answer probably is that the stricter injunction is directed at catechumens, who are supposed to come to the sacrament of baptism with such a disposition, namely, that they are not going to need a second remission. The second and milder doctrine is directed toward Christians already baptized. The expression used is 'he will live *with difficulty*';[13] but 'he *will* live. . . .'[14] Furthermore, in his doctrine on penance Hermas clearly indicates that justification by penance produces an interior sanctification of man[15] and that good works are cer-

---

13 Mandate 4.3.6.
14 Bardenhewer, *op. cit.* I 481-483.
15 Vision 4.3; Parable 5.7.1-2; 6.5-7.

tainly meritorious.[16] The person who keeps the commandments is pleasing to God, but the one who goes beyond the
commandments gains greater honor in God's sight.[17]

Though Hermas' doctrine of the Trinity is not unambig-
uous and has called forth considerable exegesis—in particular
the phrases, 'The Son is the servant of the Lord,' 'the Holy
Ghost was made to dwell in the flesh of His choice,' 'He took
the Son and the angels as advisors,' 'the Son is the Holy
Ghost,'[18]—it cannot be proved that he puts the Archangel
Michael on the same plane. They have the same offices in
Hermas' symbolism, but their dignities are quite different.
The Son of God is Lord of His people and Owner of the
Tower, whereas the angel is not; Michael constantly appears
as an angel, but the Son never; Michael is the servant of the
Law, but the Son is the Law and the very subject of Hermas'
preaching.

The *Shepherd* enjoyed extraordinary popularity in antiquity, especially in the Greek Church. Irenaeus,[19] Tertullian[20]
before his Montanist period, and Pseudo-Cyprian[21] all put this
writing in the category of Sacred Scripture and it is in the
Codex Sinaiticus. Clement of Alexandria quoted the *Shepherd*
very frequently[22] and Origen equated *Hermas* with the inspired Scriptures.[23] The Latin poet Commodian was also
familiar with him. Against these champions of the *Shepherd*
there is the Montanist Tertullian,[24] the Muratorian Canon,

---

16 Parable 2.
17 Parable 5.3.2-3.
18 Cf. Parable 5.5.2; 5.6.5-6; 9.1.1.
19 *Adv. haer.* 4.30.2.
20 *De orat.* 16.
21 *Adv. Aleat.* c. 2; cf. ch. 4.
22 Cf. the list in Bardenhewer's *Geschichte der altkirchlichen Literatur.*
23 Commentary on Rom. 16.14.
24 *De pud.* 10.

and St. Athanasius.[25] St. Jerome informs us that the work soon lost its popularity in the West,[26] although the numerous manuscripts of the old Latin translation seem to prove that even among the Latins it was not quite neglected.

The *Shepherd* has been transmitted in the following manuscripts: The *Codex Sinaiticus* (together with most of the Sacred Scriptures), containing from Vision 1.1.1 to Mandate 4.3.6. This dates back to the fourth century.[27] The whole work, with the exception of its conclusion (Simil. 9.30.3-10.4.5), is contained in a manuscrit of the late fourteenth or early fifteenth century, of which six leaves are preserved in the monastery of St. Gregory on Mt. Athos, and three in the University Library at Leipzig, the tenth and final leaf being lost.[28]

Eight fragments, which range in date from the third to the sixth century, have been discovered among the papyri or on vellum. They have been edited as follows:

Grenfell, B.P., and Hunt, A.S., *The Amherst Papyri* II (London 1901), No. 190. (Simil. 9.2.1-5).

――――――――, *The Oxyrhynchus Papyri* III (London 1903), No. 404. (Simil. 10.3.3-4.3).

Schmidt, C., und Schubart, W., 'Fragment des Pastor Hermae aus der Hamburger Stadtbibliothek,' *Sitzungsberichte der preussischen Akademie der Wissen-*

---

25 *De Decretis Nic. Syn.* 18; *Epist. Fest.* 39 a. 365.

26 *De vir. ill.,* 10.

27 It has been excellently reproduced in facsimile from photographs by Helen and Kirsopp Lake, *Codex Sinaiticus Petropolitanus, The New Testament, The Epistle of Barnabas,* and the *Shepherd of Hermas* (Oxford 1911) foll. 142-3.

28 Kirsopp Lake, *Facsimiles of the Athos Fragments of the Shepherd of Hermas* (Oxford 1907).

schaften zu Berlin, 1909, i. Hlbbd. 1077-81. Vellum.
(Simil. 4.6-5.5).

——————, *Berliner Klassikertexte* VI: *Altchristliche Texte. ii.* Der Hirt des Hermas' (Berlin 1910), Nos. 5513 (Simil. 2.7-10 and 4.2-5) and 6789 (Simil. 8.1-12).

Hunt, A. S., *The Oxyrhynchus Papyri* IX (London 1912) No. 1172. (Simil. 2.4-10).

Grenfell, B. P., and Hunt, A. S., *The Oxyrhynchus Papyri* XIII (London 1919), No. 1599. (Simil. 8.6.4-8,3).

——————, *The Oxyrhynchus Papyri* XV (London 1922), No. 1828. Vellum. (Simil. 6.5.3 and 5). [29]

Bonner, Campbell, *A Papyrus Codex of the Shepherd of Hermas* (Similitudes 2-9) *with a Fragment of the Mandates* (University of Michigan Studies. Humanistic series, XXII, Ann Arbor 1934).

For centuries, however, the work was known in the West in Latin translation only, two versions being extant: the *Vulgata*, which was made in the second century not long after the *Shepherd* was published and is found in numerous manuscripts,[30] and the *Palatina*, a work of the fifth century, published from a fourteenth century manuscript in 1857.[31] An Ethiopic translation, which may date as early as the sixth century, was published in 1860, about thirteen years after it had been discovered by d'Abbadie in the

---

29 This fragment was identified by Giovanni (now Cardinal) Mercati, *Biblica* VI (1925) 336-8.
30 Critically edited by A. Hilgenfeld in 1873, but a new edition is sorely needed.
31 A. R. M. Dressel. *Patrum Apostolicorum Opera*, Ed. I (Lipsiae 1857); Ed. II (*ibid.* 1863).

Abyssinian monastery, Guindaguinde,[32] and more recently still, fragments of a Coptic (Sahidic) translation of the *Shepherd* have come to light.[33]

The text on which the present translation is based is that of J. B. Lightfoot and J. R. Harmer, *The Apostolic Fathers* (London 1891). Occasionally, as indicated in the notes, the text, as edited by Kirsopp Lake in *The Apostolic Fathers* (New York 1912)2, is preferred. The few references to the history of Christian Greek and Latin literature are to Otto Bardenhewer's *Geschichte der altkirchlichen Literatur*. A. Stahl's *Patristische Untersuchungen* (Leipzig 1901) and other relevant works have been used. On many points the splendid volume, *Die apostolischen Väter* (translated by F. Zeller in the series *Bibliothek der Kirchenväter,* under the general editorship of Bardenhewer, Weyman and Zellinger) has been consulted.

---

32 Antonius d'Abbadie, *Hermae Pastor.* Aethiopice primum edidit et aethiopica latine vertit A. d'A. (*Abhandlungen für die Kunde des Morgenlandes,* hrsg. von der Deutschen Morgenländischen Gesellschaft, II, No. 1, Leipzig 1860).

33 Siml. 2,7-3,3; 4 (end) -5.2.1 (edited by L. Delaporte, *Revue de l'Orient chrétien* X (1905) 424-33); Mand. 12,3,4-4,4; Sim. 6,2,1-7; Sim. 8,10,3-11,5 (*ibid.* deuxième série I (XI) 1906, 301-11). Mand. 12,3,4-4,4; Sim. 2,7-3,3; Sim. 9,5,1-6,1 (J. Leipoldt, 'Der Hirt des Hermas in saidischer Ubersetzung,' *Sitzungsberichte d. preussischen Akademie der Wiss. zu Berlin* 1903, 1 Hlbbd. 261-8); Sim. 9,2,7-4,2 (*Id. Ztsch. für ägypt. Sprache u Altertumskunde* XLVI [1909-19] 137-9).

THE SHEPHERD OF HERMAS

First Vision

I. Appearance of the First Woman

THE PERSON who brought me up sold me to one Rhode in Rome. After many years I met her again and began to love her as a sister. 2 Some time later I saw her bathing in the Tiber and gave her my hand to lead her out of the river. At the sight of her beauty I thought to myself and said: 'How happy I would be if I had a wife of such beauty and character!' My reflections went thus far and no further. 3 A little later, on my way to Cumae, while praising the magnitude, splendor, and power of God's creatures, I fell into a trance as I walked. And a spirit seized me and carried me through a pathless region where no man could make his way, because it was steep and broken into ridges by the waters. So, when I had crossed that river and came to level ground, I knelt down and began praying to the Lord and confessing my sins. 4 During my prayers I saw the heavens open and that woman of whom I was enamored saluting me with the words: 'Greetings, Hermas!' 5 With my eyes fixed on her, I said: 'Lady, what are you doing here?' Her answer was: 'I have been taken up to convict you of your sins before the Lord.' 6 To this I said: 'Are you my accuser at this moment?' 'No' she said, 'but you must listen to what I am about to tell you. God who dwells in Heaven,[1] the Creator of beings out of nothing, He who increases[2] and multiplies them for the sake of His holy Church, is angry with you for your of-

---

1 Ps. 2.4; 122.1; Tob. 5.17.
2 Gen. 1.28; 8.17.

fenses against me.' 7 For answer I said: 'Offenses against you!
How so? Have I ever made a coarse remark to you? Have
I not always regarded you as a goddess? Did I not always
show you the respect due to a sister? Lady, why do you make
these false charges of wickedness and uncleanness against
me?' 8 With a laugh she said: 'In your heart there has arisen
the desire of evil. Surely, you think it evil that an evil desire
arises in the heart of a good man. It is a sin,' she said, 'yes, a
great sin. For the good man aims at justice. And in this aim
at justice his good name in Heaven is secure and he keeps
the Lord propitious in every action of his, while those who
pursue evil draw death and captivity on themselves, in particular those that reach out for this world and glory in their
riches and do not hold fast to the blessings to come. 9 Their
souls will be sorry, for they have no hope. Instead, they have
abandoned their [true] selves and their [real] life. As for
you, pray God and He will heal[3] you of your sins, yours, your
whole household's, and those of all the saints.'

II. Appearance of the Second Woman

1 After these words of hers the heavens closed, and I sat
shuddering and grieving in my whole person. I said to myself: 'If even this sin is down on the record against me, how
can I be saved? How can I win God's forgiveness for out-and-
out sin? With what prayer shall I ask God's indulgence?' 2
As I was weighing and debating this with myself, I saw before
me a great white chair of snow-white wool. Then there came
a lady advanced in years, in an exceedingly brilliant garment,
with a book in her hand. She was sitting alone and saluted
me: 'Greetings, Hermas!' In grief and tears I said to her:
'Greetings, lady!' 3 She then said: 'Why this gloom, Hermas?

---

3 Deut. 30.30; Jer. 3.32.

You are always so patient and slow to anger, always merry; why so downcast in looks and woe-begone?' My answer was: 'Because a very excellent lady declares that I sinned against her.' 4 Then she said: 'This does not refer at all to the servant of God. However, the thought concerning her *did* really enter your heart. For God's servants, such a thought induces to sin. It is a shockingly evil purpose, you know, so far as a devout soul, already tried and tested, is concerned, if there be a desire for evil action, especially [when that soul is] Hermas, the mortified, who has abstained from all desire and is full of holy simplicity and great innocence.

III. Speech and Prophecy of the Second Woman

1 'But this is not the reason why God's anger is stirred against you. Rather, it is in order that you may convert your household that has sinned against the Lord and against you, their parents. Now, because of your love for your children, you do not admonish them, but allow them to fall into dreadful corruption. This is the reason for the Lord's anger. Yet, He will bring a remedy for all past evils committed in your household. Their sins and transgressions are the reason why you have fallen under the corruption of temporal affairs. 2 But the great mercy of the Lord has taken pity on you and on your household and it will give you strength and establish you in His glory. At all events, do not relax, but encourage and strengthen your household. For, just as a smith by hammering his work obtains mastery of it for his purposes, so also does the righteous, daily-repeated sermon overcome all evil. So do not let up—admonish your children, for I know, if they repent with their whole heart, they will be inscribed in the books of life with the saints.' 3 After these remarks she said to me: 'Do you wish to hear me read?' Yes, lady,'

I said. 'Be attentive and hear God's glories.' The great and wondrous things I heard I am unable to remember, for all her words inspired fear which no mortal can endure. But her last remarks I do remember, for they were helpful for us and gentle: 4 'Behold the God of Hosts,[4] who has created the world with His invisible power,[5] strength, and surpassing wisdom, and who in His glorious good-pleasure has clothed His creation with beauty and by His mighty Word has firmly fixed the heavens and set earth's foundations on the waters,[6] who in the wisdom and providence that is His alone has founded His holy Church and blessed it; behold! He is moving away the heavens, the mountains,[7] the hills, and seas, and all is becoming level for His elect, to fulfill the promise He made in fullness of glory and joy—provided they observe the commands of God which they have received in great faith.'

IV. ENCOURAGEMENT

1 Now, when she had finished reading and had risen from her throne, there came four young men who took the throne and went away to the east. Then she beckoned me and, touching my breast, said: 'Were you pleased by what I read?' To which I answered: 'Yes, lady, the last part pleased me, but the first part was difficult and stern.' She answered as follows: 'The last part was for the just; the first for pagans and apostates.' As she was still speaking with me, two unknown men appeared, lifted her in their arms, and went away in the same direction as her throne, to the east. However, she went away with a smile and turned to say to me: 'Courage, Hermas!'

---

4 Ps. 58.6 and *passim.*
5 Acts. 17.24.
6 Ps. 135.5.6 and *passim.*
7 Ps. 45.3; 1 Cor. 13.2.

Second Vision

I. HERMES RECEIVES A BOOKLET TO COPY

1 While making my way to Cumae at the same time as last year, I recalled, as I was walking, last year's vision, and once more the spirit seized me and bore me off to the same spot as in the past. 2 So, when I came to the place, I got down on my knees and began praying to the Lord and praising His Name,[1] since He had deemed me worthy of receiving the knowledge of my former sins. 3 On rising from prayer, I beheld before me the elderly lady I had seen last year. She was walking and reading a little book. Then she said to me: 'Can you report this to God's elect?' 'Lady,' I said, 'I cannot remember so many things. Give me the book and I shall copy it.' 'Take it,' she said, 'and return it to me.' So I took it, and went to some part or other of the field, and copied everything letter by letter, for I could not make out the syllables.[2] As I finished the last letters of the book, it was suddenly snatched from my hands—by whom I could not see.

II. EXHORTATION TO PENANCE

1 After fifteen days of fasting and many prayers to the Lord, the knowledge of the writing was revealed to me. This is what was written: 2 'Your offspring, Hermas, have rebelled against God and blasphemed against the Lord. They have betrayed their parents in notorious evil-doing. They pass for traitors to their parents, yet their betrayal has done them no good. Instead, they have added still more to their iniquities:

---

1 Ps. 85.9; 2 Thess. 1.12.
2 Hermas evidently refers to the continuous script of ancient manuscripts.

dissoluteness, a mass of wickedness. In this way they made full the measure of their lawlessness. 3 Now, make this message known to your children, every one of them, and to your wife who in future is to be as your sister. Yes, she also fails to put a check on her tongue and thus she commits sin. However, after hearing this message she will control herself and obtain mercy. 4 As soon as you have made known to them this message the Master has commanded me to reveal to you, all the sins that they previously committed will be forgiven. Yes! and the saints who have sinned up to this time will be forgiven, provided they repent whole-heartedly and rid themselves of divided purposes. 5 For, the Master has taken this oath by His glory concerning His elect: If, after this day has been determined, there is any sinfulness, they shall not obtain salvation; for repentance for the just is at an end; the days of repentance for all the saints have reached their fullness. But, for pagans there is repentance until the last day. 6 So, tell the leaders of the Church to rectify their ways in justice, that they may fully receive the promises with great glory. 7 Stand firm, then, you who work righteousness[3] and have singleness of purpose, that your entrance [into Heaven] may be in the company of the holy angels. Blessed are those of you who will endure the great persecution that is to come and those of you who will not deny their life. 8 For, the Lord has sworn by His Son that those who have denied their Christ have been rejected from their Life; I mean those who are on the point of denying in the days to come. However, to those who have denied Him formerly, mercy has been granted because of His great mercy.

---

3 Ps. 14.2; Acts 10.35.

III. Hermas Is Encouraged and Comforted

1 'Now, Hermas, do not hold a grudge against your children any longer and do not allow your sister to have her way, that they may be cleansed of their former sins. For, by just punishment they will be corrected, provided you do not hold a grudge against them. For, a grudge is the worker of death. As for you, Hermas, you have had many trials of your own, from the transgressions of your house and your lack of concern about them. Yes, you were absorbed by other matters, you were involved in your own evil doings. 2 However, your refusal to fall away from the Living God,[4] your simplicity, and your great continence are saving you. This saved you, if you endure, and it is saving all who do the same and who walk in innocence and simplicity. These shall gain the mastery over all evil and are going to stand fast until life everlasting. 3 Blessed are all those who do righteousness.[5] They will not perish forever. 4 Tell Maximus: "See! Persecution is coming, if you decide to deny the faith again." "The Lord is close to those who turn to Him," as it is written in Eldat and Modat,[6] who prophesied to the people in the desert!'

IV. The Copying of the Book

1 Brethren, a revelation was made to me in my sleep by an exceedingly beautiful young man, who said: 'Who, do you

---

4 Heb. 3.12.
5 Ps. 105.2; 14.2.
6 These 'prophets' are mentioned in Num. 11.26-27. The 'Prophecy of Eldat and Modat' is frequently cited by the Fathers. St. Cyril cites it in *Cat.* XVI. 25.26 and St. Basil the Great in *De Spir. Sancto* ch. 26. It is mentioned among the Apocrypha in the Athanasian Synopsis and in the Stichometry of Nicephorus. It is probably quoted in 2 Clem. 11.2.

think, is the elderly lady from whom you took the book?' 'The
Sibyl,'[7] I said. 'No,' he said, 'you are mistaken.' 'Who is she,
then?' I said. 'The Church,' he said. 'Why is she elderly?' I
asked. 'Because she was created before all things,' he said.
'For this reason she is elderly and for Her sake the world
was erected.' 2 After this I had a vision in my house. The
elderly lady came and asked me whether I had already given
the book to the Presbyters. I said that I had not. 'That is well,'
she said, 'for I have remarks to add. So, when I shall complete all the words, with your help they will be made known
to all the elect. 3 Write, then, two small booklets, one for
Clement and one for Grapte. Clement will then send it
to the cities abroad since this is his duty, and Grapte will
instruct the widows and orphans. But you shall read it
to this city together with the Presbyters, who are in charge of
the church.'

Third Vision

I. THE APPEARANCE IN THE FIELD

1 Brethren, this is the vision I had. 2 After much fasting
and prayer to the Lord that He grant me the revelation He
promised to manifest through the elderly lady, on that very
night she appeared to me and said: 'Since you are so helpless,
yet eager to know all, go to the field where, while you are
farming,[1] I shall appear to you about the fifth hour and
show you what you have to see.' 3 Then I asked her a question: 'Lady, in what part of the field?' 'Wherever you please,'
she said. I chose a beautiful and retired spot. But, before I

---

7 The *Shepherd of Hermas* is the first Christian writing in which the
'Sibyl' is mentioned.

1 The reading, *chondrizeis*, is preferred to *chronzeis*.

could speak and tell her the spot, she said: 'I shall come wherever you please.' 4 I was in the field, then, brethren, counted the hours, and came to the place where I had told her to come, when I saw an ivory couch placed there. On the couch was placed a linen cushion and on top a coverlet of finely woven linen was spread out. 5 When I saw these objects thus arranged and that not a person was in the place, I was amazed and a shudder, so to speak, took hold of me; my hair stood on end and unreasoning fear came upon me, because I was alone. When I recovered, then, recalling God's glory, I took courage and knelt down; once more, as on the former occasion, I confessed my sins to the Lord. 6 At this point she came with six young men whom I had also seen before, and they stood by me. As I prayed and confessed my sins to the Lord, she listened. Then she touched me and said: 'Hermas, cease saying all these prayers for your sins. Ask also for righteousness in order that you may take some of it to your household.' 7 Then she raised me up by the hand and led me to the couch, saying to the young men: 'Go away and build.' 8 After the young men's departure, when we were alone, she said to me: 'Sit here.' 'Let the elders sit down first, lady,' I said. 'Do as I tell you,' she said; 'sit down.' 9 Then, when I wished to sit down on the right side, she did not allow me, but motioned with her hand to sit on the left. As I was reflecting and brooding about this that she would not allow me to sit on the right, she said to me: 'You are sad, Hermas? The place at the right belongs to others who have already been pleasing to God and have suffered for His Name. To sit with them, there remains much for you to do. But, persist in your singleness of purpose, as you now do, and you will sit with them. So also will all who do what they have done and who endure what they have endured.'

II. The Building of the Tower

1 'What have they endured?' I said. 'Let me give you the list,' she said: 'Scourgings, detention in prison, heavy afflictions, crucifixions, exposure to wild beasts for the sake of the Name. For this reason, theirs is the right side of the Holiness, as for anyone who suffers for the Name. The left side is for the rest. But the same bounty and the same promises are reserved for both those sitting on the right and those sitting on the left. Only this difference |exists|, that those who have suffered sit at the right and enjoy a certain distinction. 2 Now you are eager to sit with those on the right, but your short-comings are numerous. However, you will be purified of shortcomings, as will all who are single in purpose. You will be purified of all sins up to this day.' 3 With these remarks, she wished to go away. But, I fell at her feet and besought her by the Lord to show me the vision she had promised. 4 So, she took me again by the hand, raised me, and made me sit on the couch at the left, while she sat down to the right. Then she raised a shining wand and said to me: 'Do you see something big?' 'Lady,' I said, 'I see nothing.' Then she said to me: 'Look! Do you not see before you a large tower built on the waters out of shining square stones?' 5 Now, the tower was being built in the shape of a square by the six young men who had accompanied her, but innumerable other men were bringing along stones, some of them out of the depths of the sea, others from the land, and they were distributing them to the six young men, who were taking them and building. 6 All the stones dragged out of the sea they were putting into the building just as they were, for they had been shaped and fitted in the joining with the other stones—in fact they fitted so snugly with one another that the line of contact did not

show up. The structure of the tower seemed really to be of one single stone. 7 Of the other stones, those taken from the dry land, some they put into the building, while others were broken up and thrown far away from the tower. 8 But, many other stones were lying about the tower and were not being used in the building. For, some of them had spots, others cracks, some were chipped and some white and round, unable to fit into the building. 9 Moreover, I saw other stones thrown at a great distance from the tower and coming to the road without staying on it, but rolling into waste lands. Other stones fell into fire and were burned. While others still fell near water and yet were unable to roll into the water, in spite of their desire to roll and come to the water.

III. First Revelations about the Tower

1 After showing me this, she wished to rush away. I said to her: 'Lady, what good is it to see and not to know what this means?' 'Insistent fellow!' she said. 'You do wish to know about the tower.' 'Yes,' I said, 'in order that I may tell my brothers, lady, and they may have greater joy and upon this message may know the Lord in great glory.'[2] 2 She said: 'Many will listen and some will rejoice for having listened, but some, too, will weep. But, even the latter, if they listen and repent, will also rejoice. Let me tell you now the parables of the tower. I shall reveal everything to you. And do not importune me any more about the revelation, since these revelations are at an end. They have been fulfilled. Yet you will not cease asking for revelations, shameless as you are. 3 The tower which you see being built, that is I, the Church,[3] who has appeared to you now and formerly. So, ask me what-

---

2 Lake's text has been followed here.
3 The Church symbolized by the tower comprises only the just, either those still living or those who have entered into internal beatitude; cf. Vis. 3.5.1.

ever you wish about the tower and I shall reveal it to you, that you may rejoice along with the saints.' 4 I said to her: 'Lady, since, on one occasion, you considered me worthy of the whole revelation, make it.' She said: 'Whatever can possibly be revealed to you will be revealed. Only let your heart be directed to God and do not doubt whatever you see.' 5 Then I asked her: 'Why, lady, is the tower built on waters?' 'Yes,' she said, 'as I told you before, you do enquire persistently. With your enquiries you are finding the truth. The reason why the tower is built on water is this: Your life has been saved by water and will be so saved.⁴ The tower has been put on a foundation by the omnipotent and glorious Word of the Name and it is held together by the Lord's invisible power.'

IV. The Builders Are Exalted Angels of God

1 In answer I said to her: 'Lady, this is a great and marvellous thing. But, lady, the young men, the six who are building, who are they?' 'These are the holy angels of God, the first to be created, to whom He has committed His whole creation, to give increase, and to build, and to have complete control of creation. By their agency the building of the tower will be perfected.' 2 'Who are the others who are dragging along stones?' 'These also are God's holy angels, but the former six are superior to them. With their help, then, the tower will be perfected and all together will rejoice around the tower and give glory to God because the building of the tower has been perfected.' 3 I spoke and asked her: 'Lady, I would like to know what is the destination and meaning of the stones.' In answer she said to me: 'Not that you are worthier

---

4 Baptism, of course, is meant.

to receive the revelation than all the rest of men, for others are ahead of you, and worthier, and it would be right for them to have the revelation. But, that God's Name may be glorified,[4] the revelation has been made and will be made to you, for the sake of those who are doubting and those who are debating in their hearts whether this is so or not. Tell them that all this is true and nothing is beside the truth, but thoroughly secure, firm, and well-established.

V. The Stones Symbolize Various Classes of Believers

1 'Now let me tell you about the stones that go into the building. The square, white stones that fit accurately in their joinings, these are the apostles, bishops, teachers, and deacons who walk in accordance with God's reverence by administering with purity and sanctity the office of bishops, of teachers, and deacons for God's elect. Some of them rest in the Lord and some are still living. Now, they have always been in mutual agreement; they are at peace with one another and listen to one another. For this reason in the tower-building their joinings fit accurately.' 2 'Who are the stones dragged from the sea to be put into the building, whose joinings fit into the other stones already used in the building?' 'They are those who have suffered for the Name of the Lord.' 3 'Lady, please let me know who are the other stones taken from the dry land.' She said: 'Those going into the building without being cut are the ones the Lord has approved, because they walk in the straight way of the Lord and observe strictly His commandments.' 4 'Who are those that are brought and placed in the building?' 'They are young in the faith and faithful. But they are reminded by the angels to do good, because

---

4 Ps. 85.9,12.

wickedness was discovered in them.' 5 'Who are the ones whom they rejected and threw away?' 'They are sinners who wish to repent. Because they will have their uses in the building, in case they repent, they are not thrown at a great distance from the tower. Now, those who are to repent will be strong in the faith when they actually do, provided they repent now, while the tower is in process of building. But, if the building has been completed, they no longer have a place and will be castaways. Their only advantage is to be lying close to the tower.

VI. THE SYMBOLISM OF THE DISCARDED STONES

1 'Do you wish to know who those are that have been broken up into fragments and thrown far from the tower? They are the sons of lawlessness. Their belief was a sham and wickedness in its fullnesss has not been wanting in them. Because of their wickedness, therefore, they have no salvation because they are of no use for the building. Hence, they have been broken into fragments and thrown far from the tower, because of the Lord's anger and because they roused Him to anger. 2 The many other stones which you see lying around without going into the building are the stones with spots, who knew the truth, but failed to persist in it and did not cling to the saints. Consequently, they are useless.' 3 'Who are the stones with cracks in them?' 'They are those opposed in their hearts[5] and not at peace with one another. They have only a semblance of peace, but when they leave one another, discord is still in their hearts. These are the cracks in the stones. 4 The stones that are chipped are believers, just for the most part, but a certain portion of lawlessness lingers

---

5 1 Thess. 5.13; Mark 9.50; 2 Cor. 13.11.

in them. Hence, they are chipped and not perfect in every respect.' 5 'Lady, who are the white, round stones that do not fit into the building?' She answered and said: 'How long are you going to be foolish and senseless? All these questions! Do you not understand anything? They are those who have the faith, but also the riches of this world. When persecution comes, they deny their Lord, because of their riches and their business.' 6 I answered and said to her: 'Lady, when will they be useful for the building?' 'Whenever riches that lead their hearts astray have been torn from them,' she said, 'then will they be useful to God. Just as the round stone cannot be made square, unless it be cut and lose something, so also the rich in this world cannot be made useful for the Lord, unless their riches have been cut out of them. 7 Learn from your own experience: When you were rich you were useless, but now you are useful and a help to life. Be useful to God, for you yourself have drawn profit from these same stones.

VII. THE SYMBOLISM OF THE REMAINING STONES

1 'The other stones which you see thrown far from the tower, falling on the road and rolling off it into waste lands, are the believers. But, in their doubt, they have deviated from their true road, because they thought they could find a better. So, they wander in distress, walking about in waste lands. 2 Those who fall into fire and are burned are the ones who have finally rebelled[6] from the living God, into whose hearts repentance no longer enters, because of their unbridled lust and the impious acts they put into execution. 3 Do you wish to know who are the other

---

6 Heb. 3.12.

stones that have fallen near the waters and cannot roll there?
They are the ones who hear[7] the word and wish to be baptized in the Name of the Lord,[8] but then change their mind
when they recall the purity of the truth and return to their evil
desires.'[9] 4 With this, she finished her explanation of the
tower. 5 Unabashed, I asked her another question: 'All these
stones that have been thrown away and do not fit into the
tower—is there no repentance and no place in this tower for
them? 'They can repent,' she said, 'but they cannot fit into
this tower. 6 They will fit into another place much less honorable, but only after they have been chastised and fulfilled
the days [of penance for] their sins. But, since they have
been partakers of the just word, their place will be changed.
Then, also, it will be their good fortune to be relieved of
their chastisements, if they recall the evil deeds that they
performed. But, if they do not recall them, they will not be
saved because of their hardness of heart.'

VIII. THE VISION OF THE SEVEN WOMEN

1 When I ceased asking questions about all these matters,
she said to me: 'Do you want to see something else?' Eager
as I was to behold, I was overjoyed at the prospect of seeing
visions. 2 She looked at me with a smile and said: 'Do you
see seven women around the tower?' 'Yes, lady,' I said. 'This
tower is being supported by them in accordance with the
Lord's command. 3 Now let me tell you their functions. The
first of them, with the strong hands, is called Faith. God's
elect are saved by her. 4 The second, with the girdle, who
looks like a man, is called Continence. She is the daughter of

---

7 Mark 4.18; Matt. 13.20-22.
8 Acts 19.5.
9 Eccles. 18.30; cf. also Prov. 17.3 (earliest example); Wisd. 3.6.

Faith. Whoever follows her will be happy in his life, because
he will abstain from all evil deeds in the assurance that, by
abstaining from all evil desire, he will inherit eternal life.
5 'Who are the others, lady?' 'They are the daughters one
of the other. Their names are: Simplicity, Knowledge, Innocence, Reverence, and Love. When you perform all the acts
of their mother then you are able to live.' 6 'Lady,' I said,
'I would like to know what power each of them has.' 7 'You
shall be told. Each has the other's and they follow one another in the order in which they are born. Continence is the
daughter of Faith, Simplicity of Continence, Innocence of Simplicity, Reverence of Innocence, Knowledge of Reverence,
Love of Knowledge. Their acts then, are pure, reverent and
divine. 8 Whoever serves them and succeeds in mastering
their acts will have a dwelling in the tower along with God's
saints.' 9 Then I asked her whether the consummation of time
had arrived yet. And she cried out with a loud voice, saying:
'Stupid man, do you not see that the tower is still being built?
Whenever the building of the tower is completed, that will be
the end. But, it will be quickly built up. Do not ask me anything any more. This reminder and the renewal of your souls
is sufficient for you and for the saints. 10 Now, this revelation
is not made for you alone, but to have you make it known to
everybody—11 after three days [for you must understand
this first]. My command, Hermas, is for you to speak all
the words I am about to tell you to the ears of the faithful.
Thus, when they hear and do them, they will be cleansed from
their wickedness—you along with them.'

IX. Warning to the Rich and to the Leaders of the Church

1 'My children, listen to me. I brought you up in great simplicity and innocence and reverence, because of the Lord's mercy. He instilled justice into you, that you might be justified and sanctified from all wickedness and all perversity. But, you did not wish to desist from your wickedness. 2 Now, then, hear me: Be at peace among yourselves,[10] look after one another,[11] help one another. Furthermore, do not partake of God's creatures superabundantly by yourselves, but give a share also to those who have less. 3 For some people, from the abundance of things to eat, bring on sickness to their flesh and weaken it; while others, who have not things to eat, are weakened in the flesh from lack of sufficient food and their body is ruined. 4 So this failure to share is harmful to you who have and fail to distribute to the indigent. 5 Keep your eyes on the judgment to come. Seek out those who are hungry so long as the tower is not yet finished, you who have a superabundance! For, after the completion of the tower, you will be wishing to do good and will not have an opportunity. 6 Now, then, you who pride yourselves on your wealth, take care lest the indigent groan at any time, and their groan mount up to the Lord, and you and your goods be shut out from the door of the tower. 7 At this point it is to you—the leaders of the Church and to those in the first seats—that I speak: Do not be like poisoners. They carry their poison in boxes, whereas you carry venom and poison in your hearts. 8 You are hardened and do not wish to cleanse your hearts. You do not wish to mix together your wisdom in a clean

10 1 Thess. 5.13.
11 Rom. 15.17.

heart, that you may obtain mercy from the Great King.[12]
9 Watch then, my children, lest these dissensions deprive you
of your life. 10 How do you expect to correct the elect of the
Lord, if you have no instruction yourselves? Correct yourselves, then, and live in peace[13] with one another, that I for
my part may take my stand before the Father and joyfully
give an account of you to your Lord.'

X. The Different Appearance of the Woman in the Three Visions

1 Now, when she finished speaking with me, the six young
men who were builders came and took her to the tower, while
four others took up the couch, also, and brought it to the
tower. I did not see their faces, because they were turned
away. 2 As she was going away, I asked her to give me a
revelation about the three forms in which she had appeared
to me. 'About this matter you have to ask another for a
revelation.' 3 In the former vision last year, brethren, she
had appeared to me as very old and sitting on a chair. 4 In
the second vision she had a younger appearance, but her flesh
and hair were old, though she had spoken to me standing up.
5 But, in the third vision she was youthful in every respect
and of surpassing beauty; only her hair was that of an old
lady and, towards the end, she was quite joyful and sitting
on a couch. 6 I was very deeply depressed, because I wished
to know the revelation on these matters. Now in a night-
vision I beheld the elderly lady saying to me: 'Every question
requires humility of spirit. Fast, then, and you will receive
from the Lord what you ask.' 7 So I fasted for a day, and
that same night there appeared to me a young man, who

12 Ps. 46.3; 47.3.
13 1 Thess. 5.13.

said to me: 'Why do you ask for instant revelations in your prayer: Be careful lest you injure your flesh by heavy requests. 8 The present revelations are all you need. Can you see greater revelations than those you have seen?' 9 In answer, I said to him: 'Sir, I am only asking for a revelation complete in every detail about the three forms of the elderly lady.' For answer, he said to me: 'How long are you going to be without perception? It is your doubts that make you so and the failure to have your heart directed to the Lord.' 10 Again, I said in answer: 'Well, we shall know this more accurately with your help, sir.'

XI. Explanation of the First Appearance

1 'I shall tell you,' he said, 'about the three forms about which you are enquiring. 2 Why did she appear to you as an elderly lady sitting on a chair in the first vision? Because your spirits were old, and already wasting away, and infirm from your softness and divided purposes. 3 For, just as old men, without hope of renewing their youth, have no other thing to look forward to except their final rest, so you also, weakened by temporal affairs, surrendered to indifference, instead of throwing your cares on the Lord.[14] Yes! your spirit has been broken and you have grown old with your griefs.' 4 'Sir, I would like to know why she was sitting in a chair.' 'Because every weak person sits in a chair on account of his weakness, that his weak body might find support. Here you have the meaning of the first vision.

XII. Interpretation of the Second Appearance

1 'In the second vision you saw her standing, younger in

_____
14 Ps. 54.23; 1 Pet. 5.7.

appearance and more cheerful in comparison with the first
time, although her flesh and hair were those of an old lady.
Now, listen to this parable, also. 2 When an old man, who
has already given up hope, because of his weakness and
poverty, and waits for nothing more except the last day of
his life, suddenly has an inheritance left him, he rises at the
news, is exceedingly happy, and gathers strength; he does not
lie down any more, but stands up and his spirit is rejuvenated,
though it was broken by his former practices. He no longer
sits, but takes courage. In the same way you also were rejuvenated, when you heard the revelation which the Lord made
to you. 3 Because the Lord has had mercy on you and has
made your spirits young again, you put aside your weak-
nesses, strength returned to you, and you were made mighty
in the faith, while the Lord at the sight of your strengthening
rejoiced. For this reason He made clear to you the building
of the tower and will clarify other matters, provided you live
whole-heartedly[15] at peace with one another.

XIII. Explanation of the Third Appearance

1 'In the third vision you saw her as a younger lady, beautiful and joyous, and her appearance, too, was beautiful.
2 For a man immediately forgets former sorrows when good
news comes in the midst of grief; he excludes everything
except the good news he has heard; he gets strength to do
good in the future; in his joy his spirit is rejuvenated. So,
also, did you receive a rejuvenation of soul at the sight of these
benefits. 3 Now, the fact that you saw her sitting on a couch
means the position is secure, for the couch had four feet and
was securely fixed, just as the world is supported by four

---

15 1 Thess. 5.13.

elements. 4 Therefore, those who repent thoroughly will become young and firmly established; I mean those who repent with their whole heart. Here you have the complete revelation. Do not ask for anything more about a revelation, but if anything is necessary it will be revealed to you.'

Fourth Vision

I. VISION OF A MONSTER

1 Brethren, the vision which I saw twenty days after the former had been made is a type of the persecution to come. 2 I was leaving for the country by the Via Campana. The place is about a mile off the public road and easily reached. 3 So, as I was walking alone, I thanked the Lord for the revelations and visions He had shown me through His holy Church and begged Him to round them out; I begged Him to strengthen me and to grant repentance to His servants who had stumbled, for the glory of His great and glorious Name.[1] For He deemed me worthy to have these marvellous secrets pointed out to me. 4 As I was praising and giving thanks to Him, an echo, as it were, of my voice answered me: 'Do not be divided in purpose, Hermas.' I had begun to weigh this and to say to myself: 'How can I be divided in purpose, after having been so firmly established by the Lord and after having seen glorious things? 5 So, I approached a little closer, brethren, and behold, I saw a cloud of dust reaching up, as it were, to the heavens. I then began to say to myself: 'Cattle are now approaching and raising a cloud—six hundred feet away from me.' 6 As it was getting ever bigger, I suspected it was some supernatural apparition. The sun

---

1 Ps. 85.9.

shone a little and, behold, I saw a huge beast something like a whale, with fiery locusts coming out of its mouth. The size of the beast was about a hundred feet and its head seemed to be of earthenware. 7 As I began to cry and to ask the Lord to deliver me from the beast, I recalled the remark I had heard: 'Hermas, do not fear in your heart.' 8 I put on, then, the faith of the Lord and, recalling the wonderful things He had taught me, I faced the beast with courage. Now the beast came on with a rush capable of destroying a city. 9 I came close to it and, for all its size, the monster only stretched itself on the ground, without doing anything except project its tongue. In fact, there was not stir in it at all, until I had passed by. 10 There were four colors on the head of the beast: black, then the color of fire and blood, next gold, finally white.

II. THE INTERPRETATION OF THE MONSTER BY THE VIRGIN

1 After I had gone approximately thirty feet past the beast, behold, there met me a virgin, decked out like a lady coming from a bridal chamber,[2] all in white and with white sandals. She was veiled to the forehead and her headdress was a turban. But her hair was white. 2 I knew from former visions that it was the Church, and so I became more cheerful. She saluted me with the words: 'Greetings, my good man.' My salutation in turn was: 'Greetings, lady.' 3 For answer, she said to me: 'Have you met anything?' 'Lady,' I said to her, 'a huge beast met me, capable of destroying peoples, but by the power of the Lord and His abundant mercy I escaped from it.' 4 Yes, indeed,' she said, 'you escaped, because you

---

2 Ps. 18.6; Apoc. 21.2.

cast your care on God[3] and you opened up your heart to the Lord,[4] in the assurance that you can be saved by nothing except His great and glorious Name.[5] Hence, the Lord has sent His angel who is set over the beasts, whose name is Segri. He has shut its mouth, that it may not hurt you.[6] By your faith you have escaped great persecution, because at the sight of such a great monster you were not swayed by doubt. 5 Go off, then, and explain to the Lord's elect His wonders and tell them that this beast is a symbol of the great persecution that is to come. If you prepare in advance and repent to the Lord with all your hearts, you will be able to escape the persecution, provided your hearts become pure and sinless and you serve your Lord blamelessly the rest of the days of your life. Cast your cares on the Lord and He will set them straight.[7] 6 Put your faith in the Lord, you men of divided purpose, because He can do all things and turns aside His wrath from you, while he sends scourges on you who doubt in your heart. Alas for those who hear these remarks and disobey them! It were better for them that they had not been born.'[8]

III. The Interpretation of the Four Colors

1 I asked her a question about the four colors on the head of the beast. She answered and said: 'Still curious about such matters!' 'Yes, lady,' I said. 'Tell me what this means.' 2 'I will tell you,' she said. 'The black is this world in which you

---

3 Ps. 54.23.
4 Ps. 61.9.
5 Acts 4.12.
6 Dan. 6.22. 'Segri' or 'Thegri' occurs nowhere else in Christian or Jewish literature; cf. K. Lake, *op. cit.,* II 65.
7 Ps. 54.23.
8 Mark 14.21.

live. 3 The color of fire and blood stands for this, that this world must be destroyed in fire and blood. 4 You who flee this world are the golden section. For, just as gold is tried by fire[9] and becomes useful, so also you who live in the world are tried in it. So, then, you who remain in it and pass through the flames will be purified. For, just as gold casts off its dross, so you also will cast off all sorrow and tribulation, becoming pure and useful for the building of the tower. 5 Finally, the white section is the world to come in which the elect of God dwell; for those chosen by God for eternal life will be without spot and pure. 6 Do not let up, then, but speak to the ears of God's saints. You have also the symbol of the persecution that is to come. But, if you have good will, it will not mean a thing. Remember what was written before.' 7 With this, she went away, but I did not see where she went, for there was a cloud and I turned back in fear, thinking that the beast was coming.

Fifth Vision

THE ANGEL OF REPENTANCE

1 As I was praying in my house and sat on my bed, a man of glorious appearance entered. He was dressed like a shepherd, a white skin wrapped around him, a bag over his shoulders and a staff in his hand. He greeted me and I returned his greeting. 2 Sitting beside me, he said immediately: 'I have been sent by the most venerable angel to dwell with you for the rest of your life.' 3 Thinking he was here to tempt me, I said to him: 'Who are you? I know to whom I was entrusted.' He said: 'Do you not recognize me?' 'No,'

---

9 2 Pet. 2.20; 1 Pet. 1.7.

I said, I am the shepherd to whom you have been entrusted.' 4 As he was still talking, his form changed and I recognized that he was the person to whom I had been entrusted. I was confounded at once and fear took hold of me. I was completely overcome with grief for having answered him so wickedly and senselessly. 5 But he answered and said to me: 'Do not be confounded, but draw strength in the command I am going to give you. For I have been sent,' he said, 'to show you once more all that you saw before, the most important matters, those useful to you. First of all, write my commands and parables. Write the rest in the order I shall indicate to you. The reason,' he said, 'why I command you to write first the commands and parables is that you may have them to read at once and then keep them.' 6 So I wrote the commands and parables as he bade me. 7 If you hear and keep them, and walk in them, and fulfill them in a pure heart, you will receive from the Lord what He promised you. But if you hear them and do not repent, or even add to your sins, you will receive the contrary from the Lord. All this the shepherd, the angel of repentance, commanded me to write as follows.

First Mandate

BELIEF IN ONE GOD—FEAR OF GOD

1 First of all, believe that there is one God, that He created all things and set them in order, that He caused all things[1] to pass from non-existence to existence,[2] and that, though He contains all things, He is Himself uncontained. 2 Trust Him, then, and fear Him, and in this fear be continent. Observe this mandate and throw far from you all wickedness. Clothe yourself with every excellence that goes with justice and you will live to God provided you observe this command.

Second Mandate

AVOID SLANDER—DO GOOD

1 He said to me: 'Hold fast to simplicity of heart and innocence. Yes! Be as infants who do not know the wickedness that destroys the life of men. 2 In the first place, do not speak against anybody and do not listen readily to a slanderer. Otherwise you, the listener, will be guilty of the sin of the slanderer, in case you believe the slander you hear. For, by believing it you yourself will hold a grudge against your brother and thus you will be guilty of the sin of the slanderer. 3 Slander is wicked, a restless devil, never at peace, but always dwelling amid dissensions. Keep away from it and you will always be on good terms with all men. 4 Clothe yourself with reverence in which there is no evil, which gives no

---

1 Eph. 3.9; Ps. 67.29.
2 2 Mac. 7.28.

offense, which is all smoothness and cheerfulness. Do good, and from the fruit of your labors, God's gift, give to all those in need, without distinction, not debating to whom you will and to whom you will not give. Since it is God's will that we give to all from His bounties, give to all. 5 Those who have received will give an account to God why they received and for what purpose. For, those that receive in distress will not be judged, but those that receive under false pretenses will pay the penalty. 6 Under these circumstances, the giver is innocent. For, on receiving from the Lord a service to perform, he performed it with simplicity, without distinguishing to whom to give and to whom not to give. The service, then, performed with simplicity, becomes honorable in God's eyes. Therefore, the man who thus serves with simplicity will live to God. 7 Keep this commandment as I have told you, that you and your house may be found sincere in your repentance and your heart clean and unsullied.'[1]

Third Mandate

Do Not Lie

1 Again he spoke to me: 'Love truth and let nothing but truth issue from your mouth, in order that the spirit which God has settled in this flesh of yours may be found to be truthful in the sight of all men. Thus, the Lord who dwells in you will be glorified, since the Lord is truthful in every word and there is no lie in Him. 2 This is why liars ignore the Lord and defraud Him, since they do not return the deposit received from Him, namely, a spirit in which there is no lie. If they return this falsified, they have besmirched the command of the Lord and become robbers.' 3 On hearing

1 James 1.27.

this I wept copiously. At sight of my tears he said: 'Why do you weep?' 'Because, sir,' I said, 'I do not know whether it is possible for me to be saved.' 'Why?' he said. 'Because, sir,' I said, 'I have not yet spoken a true word in my life; at all times I have lived like a villain among all men and have dressed up my lie as the truth in the eyes of all. At no time have I been contradicted by anybody, but they have put faith in my word. How,' I said, 'can I live, sir, after having done this?' 4 'Your intentions are noble and true,' he said. 'It was really your duty, as the servant of God, to walk in truth and not allow an evil conscience to dwell in the company of the Spirit of truth. Neither ought you to cause grief to the Spirit of truth and holiness.' 'Sir,' I said, 'I have never correctly understood these commands.' 5 'Well, now you do,' he said. 'Keep them, that even the lies formely uttered in your business transactions may become credible, now that your present remarks have been found true. It is really possible for these business "lies" to become credible. For, if you keep watch over what you say and speak nothing but the [strict] truth from now on, you can obtain life for yourself. And anybody who hears this command and abstains from that most pernicious habit, lying, will live to God.

Fourth Mandate

I. PRESERVE CHASTITY

1 'I command you,' he said, 'to guard purity. Let it not enter your heart to think of another man's wife, nor about fornication, nor any such thing. If you do, you will commit a serious sin. Keep your wife in mind always and you will never fall into sin. 2 For, if this desire comes into your heart, you will make a slip and you will commit sin, if any other

such wicked thought enters you heart. For, a desire of this kind is a serious sin for the servant of God and, if anyone puts into execution such a wicked thought, he draws death upon himself. 3 Be in your guard then: Keep this desire from you. Where holiness dwells, there, in the heart of a just man, lawlessness should not enter.' 4 I said to him: 'Sir, allow me to ask you a few questions.' 'Ask them,' he said. 'Sir,' I said, 'if a man has a wife who believes in the Lord and surprises her in adultery, does he commit sin if he lives with her?' 5 'Before he finds out,' he said, 'he does not. But, if her husband knows the sin, and she does not repent, but persists in her fornication, he becomes guilty of her sin, as long as he lives with her, and an accomplice in her adultery.' 6 'Sir,' I said, 'what then is he to do, if the wife continues in this passion?' 'Let him divorce her,' he said, 'and remain single. But, if he divorces her and marries another woman, he himself commits adultery.'[1] 7 'But, if, sir, I said, 'after the divorce the wife repents and wishes to return to her husband will he refuse to receive her?' 8 'No, indeed,' he said. 'If the husband does not receive her, he sins. He incurs a great sin. The sinner who has repented must be received. However, not often, for there is only one repentance for the servants of God. To bring about her repentance, then, the husband should not marry. This is the course of action required for husband and wife. 9 Not only is it adultery,' he said, 'for a man to pollute his flesh, but it is likewise adultery for anyone to act in imitation of the pagans.[2] So, if anyone persists in acts of this kind and does not repent, keep away from him, do not live with him; otherwise you also have a part in his sin. 10 This is the reason why you were com-

---

1 Matt. 5.32; Mark 10.11; 1 Cor. 7.11.
2 In other words, if one member of the Christian married couple lapses into paganism, this is to be considered tantamount to adultery.

manded to live by yourselves, whether husband or wife be guilty. For, under these circumstances, repentance is possible. 11 I am not giving an excuse,' he said, 'that this may be the conclusion of the matter, but merely that the sinner may sin no more. There is One who can give a remedy for his former sin and He has power over all things.'

II. PENANCE IS UNDERSTANDING

1 Once more I asked him and said: 'Since the Lord has thought me worthy of having you live with me always, bear with me for a few more words, since I do not understand anything at all and my heart has been hardened by my past. Give me understanding, for I am exceedingly stupid and understand absolutely nothing.' 2 He answered in these words: 'I am in charge of penance,' he said, 'and give understanding to all who repent. Do you not think,' he asked, 'that this very act of repentance is understanding? Repentance,' he continued, 'is deep understanding. For, the man who has sinned, then, understands that he has done evil before the Lord,[3] the deed he committed enters his heart, and he repents, never to commit evil again. Instead, he does good perfectly by humbling his soul and putting it to the torture, because it has sinned. Do you see now how repentance is deep understanding?' 3 'Sir,' I said, 'the following are the reasons why I am making accurate enquiries into everything: In the first place I am a sinner and then I do not know what works I am to perform to live, for my sins are numerous and varied.' 4 'You will live,' he said, 'if you keep my commandments and walk in them. Whoever hears my commandments and keeps them will live to God.'

---

3 Judges 2.11; 3.12 and *passim;* 1 Cor. 15.19; 3 Kings 14.22.

III. Penance Is for Those Who Have Been Baptized

1 'May I press on with my questions, sir?' I asked, 'Yes,' he said. 'Sir,' I said, 'I have been told by some teachers that there is no other repentance except the one [that was vouchsafed us], when we went into the water and received remission of our former sins.' 2 He said to me: 'You have been correctly told; such is the case. For, the person who has received remission of sins must no longer sin, but live in purity. 3 However, since you are enquiring accurately into everything, I shall also clarify this matter for you, without giving an excuse either to those who now believe or are destined to believe in the Lord. For, those who now believe or are destined to believe do not have repentance for sins, but they do have remission of their former sins.[4] 4 The Lord, then, has prescribed repentance for those who were called before these days. For, the Lord has knowledge of hearts and knows all things in advance, the weakness of human beings and cunning craft of the Devil, the evil he will do to the servants of God and his wickedness against them. 5 Therefore, the Lord in His exceeding mercy took pity on His creatures and prescribed this occasion for repentance. Authority over this repentance has been given to me. 6 But this I say to you,' he said. 'After that solemn and holy call, if a man sins after severe temptation by the Devil, he has one chance of repentance. But, if he sins and repents offhandedly, it is unprofitable for such a man.[5] Only with difficulty will he live.' 7 I said to him: 'I have been restored to life by hearing these accurate statements of yours. For, now I know that, if I do not commit additional sins, I shall be saved.' 'You will be saved,' he said, 'as well as all those who do this.'

---

4 Cf. Introduction, pp. 229-30.
5 'It is unprofitable . . . ' with a view to his reacceptance in the Church.

IV. Second Marriage Is Not Recommended

1 Once more I spoke and asked him: 'Sir, since you have borne with me once, make this also clear to me.' 'What is it?' he said. 'Sir,' I said, 'if a wife or husband is deceased and either one of the survivors marries again, does he or she sin by marrying?' 2 'There is no sin,' he said. 'But, anyone who remains single achieves greater honor for himself and great glory before the Lord. But, even in remarriage, there is no sin. 3 Keep a watchful eye, then, on purity and modesty and live for God. All that I am telling you and am going to tell you observe from now on, from the day on which you have been entrusted to me, and I shall dwell in your house. 4 There will be remission for your former lapses, if you observe my commandments. There will also be remission for all who observe these commandments and walk in like purity.'

Fifth Mandate

I. Praise of Long-suffering

1 'Be long-suffering,' he said, 'and prudent, and you will obtain the mastery over wickedness and accomplish all justice. 2 For, if you are long-suffering, the Holy Spirit dwelling in you will be clear, unobscured by any other spirit of evil. Dwelling in a spacious place, He will rejoice and be glad with the lodging in which He finds Himself. Thus, He will serve God with abundant cheerfulness, because He has His well-being within Himself. 3 However, if violent anger enters, the good spirit in His sensitiveness is immediately confined, since He has not a clean habitation. So, He tries to withdraw from the place. The evil spirit chokes Him; He is unable to serve God in accordance with His wishes; He is befouled by

the violent anger. For, the Lord dwells amid long-suffering, but the Devil has his abode in anger. 4 Therefore, if both spirits dwell in the same place, it is unprofitable and evil for the man in whom they dwell. 5 Take a little wormwood and pour it into a jar of honey. Is not the honey spoiled altogether? Even a great quantity of honey is ruined by the smallest amount of wormwood and its sweetness is lost. It is no longer pleasant to the owner, because it has been mixed and it is no longer enjoyable. Now, if no wormwood is put into the honey, it turns out to be sweet and becomes useful for the owner. 6 You see, then, that long-suffering is very sweet, far more than honey, and useful to the Lord. His dwelling is in long-suffering. Anger, on the contrary, is bitter and useless to Him. So, if anger is mixed with long-suffering, the latter is spoiled and the man's prayer to God is not useful.' 7 'Sir, I would like to know the operation of anger to be on my guard against it,' I said. 'Yes,' indeed,' he replied. 'If you do not guard against it, you and your house, all hope is lost for you. Do guard against it. I shall be on your side. And all who repent with their whole heart will be preserved from it. I shall be on their side and shall watch carefully in their behalf. For all have been justified by the most holy angel.

II. Evil Effects of Anger

1 'I shall tell you now,' he said, 'of the operation of anger; its wickedness; how it destroys the servants of God; how it makes them swerve from justice. Now, it does not cause the majority of those who are in the faith to swerve; neither is it able to operate against them, because the power of the Lord is on their side; but it causes the empty-minded and those of divided purpose to swerve. 2 For, when it sees people of this kind in prosperity, it insinuates itself into the heart of

such a person and, for no reason at all, the man or woman is embittered over worldly concerns, either about food or some trifle, some friend, a benefaction or a gift, or other such foolish matters. All this is foolish, vain, senseless and unprofitable to the servants of God. 3 But, long-suffering is great and steadfast, sturdy and powerful; it prospers expansively, it is cheerful, joyous, carefree; it praises the Lord at all times;[1] it has no bitterness in itself; but in all circumstances it remains meek and calm. So, this long-suffering dwells with those who hold on to the faith in its perfection. 4 Now, in the first place, violent anger is foolish, frivolous, and silly. In the next place, bitterness arises from silliness, from silliness wrath, from wrath anger, and from anger rage. Finally, the rage that has in it such evil elements becomes a serious and incurable sin. 5 For, when all such spirits dwell in one vessel along with the Holy Spirit, it cannot hold them, but overflows. 6 Then the delicate spirit that is not accustomed to dwell with an evil one, nor with uncouthness, departs from a man of this kind and tries to dwell in a gentle, calm abode. 7 Then, when He has left, the man in whom He dwelled becomes emptied of the righteous spirit; he is filled with evil spirits afterwards and disorderly in all his actions, dragged here and there by evil spirits. In a word, he is blind to all good intentions. This is what happens to those subject to violent anger. 8 Keep away from violent anger, the most wicked spirit. Put on long-suffering and oppose violent anger as well as bitterness, and you will be found on the side of holiness, beloved by the Lord. Make sure, then, that you do not forget this command. For, if you master this commandment, you will also be able to keep the other commandments which I am about to lay upon you. Gain strength and power in their ob-

---

1 Tob. 4.19; Ps. 33.2.

servance and let all those who wish to walk in [accordance with] them also gain such power.'

Sixth Mandate

I. THE GOOD AND THE EVIL PATH

[1] 'In the first mandate,' he said, 'I bade you keep the faith, fear [of the Lord], and continence.' 'Yes, sir,' I said. 'But now I wish to explain their nature, that you may know their individual power and effect. Well! Their effects are twofold. For they relate both to the just and to the unjust. 2 Trust righteousness, but distrust unrighteousness. For, the path of righteousness is straight, but wickedness is a crooked path. So, walk in the straight path and leave the crooked path alone. 3 For, there are no beaten tracks on the crooked path. Instead, there is nothing but waste lands and numerous obstacles; it is rough and full of thorns. So, it is injurious to those who walk in it. 4 Those who take the straight path walk smoothly without stumbling, because it is neither rough nor thorny. Hence, you see that it is more advantageous for you to walk in this road.' 5 'Sir,' I said, 'it is on this road that I like to walk.' 'Walk in it, then,' he said, 'and anyone who turns[1] to the Lord wholeheartedly will also walk there.

II. THE ANGELS OF RIGHTEOUSNESS AND OF EVIL

1 'Now I am going to tell you about faith,' he said. 'There are two angels who accompany man, the angel of justice and the angel of wickedness.' 2 'But, how am I to know their operations,' I said, 'if both are dwelling within me?'

---

1 Jer. 24.7; Joel 2.12 and *passim*.

3 'Listen,' he said, 'and you will understand them. The angel
of justice is sensitive, modest, gentle, and calm. So, when
this angel comes into your heart, he will immediately converse with you about justice, purity, holiness, self-control,
every just work and glorious virtue. When all these thoughts
enter your heart, you can be sure that the angel of justice is
within you. These are the deeds of the angel of justice.[2]
Believe him, then, and his deeds, also. 4 Now, observe the deeds
of the angel of wickedness. First of all, he is of a violent
temper, bitter, and silly. His deeds are evil, the undoing of
the servants of God. So, when he enters your heart, know him
from his deeds.' 5 'Sir, I do not know how I shall recognize
him,' I said. 'I shall tell you,' he said. 'When violent anger
comes over you, or bitterness, you can tell that he is within
you. Then there arises the craving for excessive action, extra-
vagance in many things to eat and drink, numerous feasts,
varied unnecessary dishes, the desire for women, covetousness,
arrogance, boasting, and a host of similar, related excesses—
when they arise in your heart you can tell that the angel of
wickedness is with you. 6 So, then, since you know his deeds,
keep away from him and put no trust in him, because his
deeds are wicked and against the interests of God's servants.
Here you have the workings of the two spirits. Understand
them and trust the angel of justice. 7 Keep away from the
angel of wickedness, because his teaching is evil in every
respect. For, even though a person have faith, if the desire
of this angel arises in the heart, that man or woman is bound
to commit some sin. 8 Now, on the other hand, though a
man or woman is very wicked, when the deeds of the angel
of justice suggest themselves, they must necessarily perform a
good action. 9 So you see,' he said, 'that it is good to follow

---

2 Lake's text has been followed here.

the angel of justice and to put yourself out of range of the angel of wickedness. 10 This much this commandment makes clear about faith, that you may believe the deeds of the angel of justice and live to God by performing them. Believe that the deeds of the angel of wickedness are difficult and, if you do not perform them, you will live to God.

Seventh Mandate

ON THE FEAR OF GOD

1 Fear the Lord and keep His commandments,'[1] he said. 'So, by keeping God's commandments you will be powerful in every action, and your action will be beyond criticism. Fear the Lord, then, and you will do everything well; this is the fear you must have to be saved. 2 Do not fear the Devil. By fearing the Lord you will gain the mastery of the Devil, for there is no power in him. For, there can be no fear of him in whom there is no power, but of Him whose might is glorious there must be fear. For, everyone who has power inspires fear, but he who has no power is despised by everybody. 3 However, fear the deeds of the Devil, because they are evil. If you fear the Lord you will fear the Devil's deeds; do not perform them, but keep aloof from them. 4 There are two kinds of fear, then. If you wish to do evil, fear the Lord and you will not do it. So, too, if you wish to do good, fear the Lord and you will do it. Consequently, the fear of the Lord is security, mighty and glorious. Fear the Lord, then, and live for Him. All those who fear Him and keep His commandments will live to God.' 5 'Sir,' I said, 'why do you say about those who observe His commandments, "They will

---

1 Eccle. 12.13.

live to God"?' 'Because,' he said, 'all creatures fear the Lord, but not all creation keeps His commandments. But, life with God is for those who both fear Him and keep His commandments; nor is there life in Him for those who fail to keep His commandments.

Eighth Mandate

ON CONTINENCE

1 'I told you,' he said, 'that God's creatures are twofold; now, temperance also is twofold. For in some things we have to restrain ourselves and in others we do not.' 2 'Let me know, sir,' I said, 'in what we must restrain ourselves and in what we must not.' 'I shall tell you,' he said. 'Restrain yourself from evil, and do not do it; from good, however, do not retrain yourself, but do it. For, if you restrain yourself and keep from doing good, you commit a serious sin; but, if you restrain yourself and abstain from doing evil, you achieve signal righteousness. Restrain yourself from all evil by doing good.' 3 'What are the kinds of evil, sir,' I said, 'from which we must hold off?' 'I shall tell you,' he said. 'From adultery and fornication, from uncontrolled drunkenness, from evil luxury, from excessive food and extravagant wealth, from boastfulness, and pride, from lying, backbiting, and hypocrisy, vengefulness and all blasphemy. 4 These deeds are worst of all in the life of all human beings. From such deeds, then, a servant of God must restrain himself. The person who does not cannot live to God. Now, let me tell you the consequences of such deeds.' 5 'Sir,' I said, 'are there still other evil deeds?' 'Yes indeed, many; and the servant of God must restrain himself from them: theft, lying, robbery, false witness, covetousness, lust, deceit, vainglory, pretense, and similar excesses.

6 Surely you think such sins are wicked, very wicked indeed,'
he said, 'for servants of God? A servant of God should restrain himself from all these excesses. Restrain yourself, then,
that you may live to God and that you may be enrolled with
those who restrain themselves in these matters. So, the foregoing are the matters in which you should exercise self-
retraint. 7 I shall now tell you from what you should not
hold off,' he said, 'and what you ought to perform: Do not
refrain from good, but do it.' 8 'Sir, make clear to me also
the nature of good,' I said, 'that I may walk in it, and be
subject to it, and by doing it may be saved.' 'I shall also tell
you,' he answered, 'the deeds of goodness that you are to perform and from which you are not to hold back,' he said. 9 'In
the forefront are faith, fear of the Lord, love, concord, up-
right speech, truthfulness, patience. There is nothing superior
to these in the life of human beings. If a person keeps these
virtues and does not hold back from them, he will be blessed
in his life. 10 Let me enumerate, also, the consequent good
actions: the assistance of widows, visiting orphans and the
poor, ransoming God's servants in their difficulties, showing
hospitality (for benevolence occasionally finds play in hospitality), non-resistance to anyone, being of a quiet disposition,
being poorer than all men, honoring the aged, practising
justice, exercising fraternal charity, enduring insult, being
long-suffering, abstaining from spite, comforting those who
are troubled in spirit, not rejecting those who have stumbled
in the faith, but winning them back and encouraging them,
calling sinners to order, not oppressing debtors in their needs—
all this and more besides. 11 Do you not think these acts are
good?' 'Sir, there is nothing better than such acts,' I said.
'Walk in them, then, and do not hold back from them,' he
said, 'and you will live to God. 12 Observe this command-

ment: If you do good without restraint, you will live to God, just as all those will live to God who do likewise. So, too, will you live to God, if you avoid doing evil and hold back from it. Whoever observes these commandments and walks in them will also live to God.'

Ninth Mandate

ON CONFIDENT PRAYER

1 He said to me: 'Cast off indecision and doubt not in the least, when asking anything from God. Do not say "How can I ask and receive anything from the Lord after having committed so many sins?" 2 Do not entertain such thoughts, but with your whole heart turn to the Lord[1] and ask Him without wavering. You will learn His superabundant mercy. He will not leave you in the lurch. No! He will fulfill the request of your soul. 3 God is not like human beings who bear a grudge. He is without malice and has mercy on what He has made. 4 Cleanse your heart, then, of all the vanities of this world and of the vices mentioned above. Then ask of the Lord and you will receive all. You cannot fail to obtain all your requests, provided you ask the Lord without wavering. 5 However, if you waver in your heart, you will not receive a single one of your requests. Those who are divided in purpose are they who waver before the Lord and altogether fail to obtain any of their requests. 6 But those who are wholly perfect in the faith ask everything with reliance on the Lord[2] and they receive, because they ask without wavering, without divided purpose. Every man of divided purpose will be saved

1 Jer. 24.7; Joel 2.12.
2 Ps. 2.13; 10.1.

with difficulty, unless he repents. 7 Cleanse your heart, then, of divided purpose, clothe yourself with faith, because it is strong, and put your trust in God, confident that you will receive every request you make of Him. Now, if some time or other, after having made it, you receive your request from the Lord rather slowly, do not doubt because you did not receive your soul's request quickly. In general, you receive your request slowly because of some temptation or some shortcoming of which you are not aware. 8 Do not let up, then, in the request of your soul. But, if in your request you grow faint and doubt, blame yourself and not the Giver. 9 Be on your guard against this divided purpose, for it is evil and senseless. It uproots many from the faith, however strong in faith they are. For, divided purpose is the daughter of the Devil and exceedingly wicked to the servants of God. 10 Despise divided purpose and gain the mastery of it in everything by clothing yourself with strong and powerful faith. For, faith promises all things and accomplishes them, but divided purpose, without confidence in itself, fails in all its works. 11 You see, then,' he said, 'that faith is from above from the Lord, and its power is great, whereas divided purpose is an earthly spirit, from the Devil, lacking in power. 12 Be subject, then, to the faith that has power and hold aloof from divided purpose that lacks power, and you will live to God as well as all who are of the same mind.

Tenth Mandate

I. Sadness Is Worse than Lack of Confidence or Anger

1 'Take sorrow out of your heart,' he said, 'for it is a sister of divided purpose and violent anger.' 2 'How is it a sister of these two?' I said. 'It seems to me that anger is one thing

and divided purpose another and sorrow still another,' 'You are a senseless man,' he said, 'not to know that sorrow is more wicked than all spirits and most dangerous to servants of God. More than all spirits it destroys a human being and wears out the Holy Spirit – but again saves it.' 3 'I am a man without understanding,' I said, 'and do not follow these parables. I do not see how it can wear out and then again save.' 4 'I shall tell you,' he said. 'There are those who have never made deeper enquiry into the truth nor about God. They merely believe, while they are involved in business, wealth, pagan friendship, and many other commitments of this world. People intent on such matters fail to grasp the parables of the Godhead, for these occupations keep their minds in darkness; they are corrupted and become barren. 5 Just as good vineyards, when not cared for, grow barren with thorns and various weeds, so believers, who become involved in the aforementioned numerous occupations, lose their understanding and are altogether without perception for justice. When they hear about the Godhead and truth, their mind is taken up with their business and they understand absolutely nothing. 6 It is different with those who have the fear of God, and make enquiry into the divine nature and truth, with hearts directed to the Lord. They understand more quickly what is told them and penetrate its meaning, because they have the fear of the Lord. Wherever the Lord dwells, there also is much understanding. Cling to the Lord and you will grasp and understand everything.

II. SADNESS HAS EVIL EFFECTS

1 'Let me tell you now, slow-witted man, how melancholy wears out the Holy Spirit and again lightens it. 2 When the man of divided purpose applies himself to any practice

and fails in it because of his divided purpose, this melancholy enters into him and the Holy Spirit is in gloom and is worn out. 3 So, also, when violent anger clings to the man about some matter and he is very much embittered, melancholy enters the heart of the angry man. He is then distressed at the action he performed and repents because he did evil. 4 Now, this melancholy seems to bring salvation, because he repents of having done evil. So, both deeds distress the Spirit: the divided purpose, because he has not succeeded in the action itself; the anger, because he committed evil. The two, then, divided purpose and anger, are saddening to the Holy Spirit. 5 Remove melancholy, then, and do not oppress the Holy Spirit dwelling within you, lest He pray to God to depart from you, 6 For, the Spirit of God that was given to this flesh does not endure melancholy and confinement.

III. Joy Brings Blessings; Sadness Is Harmful

1 'Clothe yourself with cheerfulness, which always finds favor with God and is acceptable to Him. Rejoice in it. For, every cheerful man does good, has good thoughts, and despises melancholy. 2 On the other hand, the melancholy man is always committing sin. In the first place, he commits sin because he brings melancholy to the Holy Spirit that was given to man as a spirit of gladness. In the second place, by bringing melancholy to the Holy Spirit he commits grave sin, because he does not intercede with God nor confess to God.' 3 'Why does not the intercourse of the melancholy man reach up to altar of God?' I said. 'Because melancholy resides in his heart. Consequently, the melancholy mingled with his converse does not let his prayer ascend clean to the altar. Just as vinegar mixed with wine in the same vessel does not have the same agreeable taste, so also melancholy, as-

sociated with the Holy Spirit, has not the same power of impenetration. 4 Cleanse yourself, then, of this wicked melancholy and you will live to God. So, also, will they live to God who cast away melancholy and clothe themselves in complete cheerfulness.'

Eleventh Mandate

ON TRUE AND FALSE PROPHETS

1 He pointed out to me men sitting on a bench[1] and another man sitting on a chair. 'Do you see the men sitting on the bench?' he said to me. 'Yes, sir,' I replied. 'These men are believers,' he said, 'and the man sitting on the chair is a false prophet who corrupts the understanding of God's servants. However, he corrupts the understanding of those who are doubters, not of the believers. 2 These doubtful men, then, come to him as to a wizard and ask him about their future. That false prophet, without having in himself any power from a Divine Spirit, then speaks with them along the lines of their questions, in accordance with their evil desires, and fills their souls just as they wish. 3 Empty as he is, it is empty answers that he gives to empty [minds]. For, whatever enquiry is made, his answer is directed to the emptiness of a man. However, some of the words he utters are true. For the Devil fills him with his own spirit, to see whether he can break down one of the just. 4 So, those who are strong in the faith of the Lord clothe themselves with truth and do not cling to this kind of spirit. No! They keep at a distance from such spirits. But, those who are doubting souls re-

---

1 *Sympsellion*, as Lake points out (*op. cit.*, p. 117), must here be translated 'bench' and not 'couch,' as in Vis. 3.1.4.

pent frequently,[2] consult fortune-tellers like the pagans, and
bring a greater sin upon themselves with their idolatry. For,
the person who consults a false prophet about some action is
an idolater, empty of truth and stupid. 5 For, no spirit
granted by God has to be consulted. It speaks everything
with the Godhead's power, because it is from above, from
the power of the Divine Spirit. 6 But, the spirit that is consulted and speaks according to the desires of men is earthly[3]
and weak, without any power. Besides, it does not speak at
all, unless it be consulted.' 7 'How, sir,' I said, 'is a man to
know which of them is a prophet and which is a false prophet?'
'I shall tell you about both prophets,' he said. 'In accordance
with what I am going to tell you, you can test the true and
the false prophet. Test a man who has the Divine Spirit according to his life. 8 In the first place, the man who has the
Spirit from above is meek, calm, humble. He abstains from
all wickedness and vain desires of this world, and considers
that he is inferior to all men. He does not give answers to
questions, either, nor does he speak by himself (neither does
the Holy Spirit speak when a man wishes Him to speak),
but he speaks then when God wishes him to speak. 9 When
a man who has the Divine Spirit enters a gathering of just men
who have faith in God's spirit, and an entreaty is addressed
to God by such a gathering, at that moment the angel of the
prophetic spirit, who is attached to this man, fills him and in
the fullness of the Holy Spirit he speaks to the gathering in
accordance with the Lord's wishes. 10 In this manner, then,
the spirit of the Deity will be made clear. This, then, is the
power of the Lord's divine spirit. 11 Now I shall tell you,'
he said, 'about the earthly spirit, that is inane, powerless,

2 I.e., their repentance is only momentary in any specific case.
3 James 3.15.

and truly foolish. 12 In the first place, the man who thinks
he has a spirit exalts himself and wishes to have the seat of
honor. Immediately he is reckless, impudent, indulges in considerable luxury and in many other deceits. He also takes pay
for his prophecy and makes no prophecy unless he receives it.
Can the Divine Spirit receive money for prophesying? It is
impossible for a spirit of God to do this, whereas the spirit of
this kind of prophet is earthly. 13 Furthermore, it does not
approach gatherings of just men at all, but avoids them. It
clings to the men who are doubters and to the vain, making prophecies to them in a corner, deceiving them by talk
in accordance with their lusts—all in empty fashion, for
their answers are to be empty. For the empty vessel placed
with other empty vessels does not break, but they match
one another. 14 Now, when he comes to a gathering filled
with just men who have the Divine Spirit, such a man is
emptied after their prayer of petition, the earthly spirit
in fear takes flight from him and he is struck dumb, completely falling to pieces, without the power of saying a thing.
15 For, if you stack wine and oil into a cellar and place an
empty jar among the rest, when you wish to unstack the
cellar, you will find the one you placed there just as empty.
In the same way, also, vacuous prophets: After entering the
souls of just men, they are found to be exactly the same as
when they came in. 16 The life of the two kinds of prophets
has just been given you. Test, then, by life and actions the
man who says he is inspired. 17 Put your faith in the Spirit
that comes from God and has power. But, put no faith in
the earthly, empty spirit, because there is no power in him:
He comes from the Devil. 18 Listen to the parable I am going
to tell you. Pick up a stone and throw it up and see whether
you can touch the heavens. Or again, take a syringe full of

water and squirt up to the heavens and see whether you can bore through.' 19 'Sir,' I said, 'how can this be done? According to you, both these actions are impossible.' 'Just as these actions are impossible,' he said, 'so, too, are the earthly spirits powerless and feeble. 20 Now, compare the power that comes from above. A hailstone is quite a small missile, but, when it falls on a man's head, it causes considerable pain. Another example: A drop of fluid falling from a jug onto the ground bores through a stone. 21 Hence, you see that the lightest possible objects falling from above have great power. So, too, is the Divine Spirit, that comes from above, powerful. Put your trust, then, in this Spirit, and keep away from the other.'

I. Evil Desire Works Havoc with the Imprudent

1 He said to me: 'Remove every evil desire and clothe yourself with good and holy desire. For, if you are clothed in this good desire, you will hate the evil desire and bridle[1] it as you please. 2 For, evil desire is fierce and is tamed with difficulty; it is fearsome in its ferocity and wastes men. In particular, if a servant of God becomes entangled in it and has no prudence, it works dreadful havoc with him. But, it costs a heavy price to those who have not the cloak of good desire and are engrossed with this world. Such men it hands over to death.' 3 'Sir,' I said, 'what are the works of evil desire which hand a man over to death? Tell me, so I may keep away from them.' 'You will hear,' he said, 'by what works evil desire brings death to the servants of God.'

---

1 James 3.2,4.

II. The Bad Effects of Evil Desire

1 'In the forefront are the desire of another man's wife or another wife's husband, the desire of profuse wealth, of many useless foods and drinks, and of numerous other foolish luxuries. For, every luxury is foolish and empty for the servant of God. 2 Such desires, then, are evil and death-dealing to the servants of God. An evil desire of this kind is the daughter of the Devil. Therefore, one has to abstain from evil desires and by abstention live to God. 3 Those who are overpowered by them, and do not resist, finally die, since these desires are deadly. 4 As for you, put on the desire of justice and, armed with the fear of the Lord, resist them. For, fear of the Lord has its dwelling in good desire. If evil desire sees you armed with the fear of God and resisting, it will flee far away and you will not set eyes on it, because it fears your arms. 5 So, after receiving the crown for your victory[2] against evil desire, advance to the desire of justice and attribute the victory to this. Serve the wishes of justice. If you serve and are subject to good desire, you will be able to master evil desire and hold it in subjection as you please.'

III. How Good Desire Is to Be Maintained

1 'Sir,' I said, 'I should like to know how I have to serve good desire.' 'I shall tell you,' he said. 'Practise justice[3] and virtue, truthfulness and fear of the Lord, faith, meekness and all similar good acts. By doing this you will be a pleasing servant of God and will live to Him. So will live to God those who are servants of good desires.' 2 With this he completed the twelve mandates. He then said to me: 'These are

2 Lake's text (op. cit., p. 128) has been followed here.
3 Ps. 14.2; Acts. 10.35; Heb. 11.3.

the mandates. Walk in them and exhort those who hear you, that their repentance may be clean for the rest of their days. 3 Fulfill with utmost care the ministry I have given you and work hard. You will find favor with those who are going to repent and they will obey your words. For, I shall be on your side and will bring them to obey you.' 4 I said to him: 'Sir, these mandates are great, good and glorious, and capable of gladdening[4] the heart of the man who is able to observe them. But, I do not know whether these mandates can be kept by men, because they are exceedingly hard.' 5 For answer he said to me: 'If you persuade yourself that they can be observed, you will do so easily and they will not be hard; but, if you let the thought get into you that they cannot be observed by a human being, you will not observe them. 6 But now I tell you [solemnly]: If you do not observe them, but neglect them, neither you nor your children nor your household will have salvation, since you have passed judgment on yourself by "the impossibility for a human being of observing these mandates." '

IV. MAN SHOULD BE MASTER OF HIS DESIRES

1 He said this with such excessive anger that I was confounded and very much afraid of him. His appearance had so changed that no human being could stand up against his anger. 2 On seeing my utter distress and confusion, he began to address me more gently and cheerfully in these words: 'Foolish man, without understanding and of doubtful heart! You do not realize how great, strong and marvellous is God's glory.[5] It was for man that He created[6] the world and it is

---

4 Ps. 18.9; 103.15.
5 Ps. 137.5.
6 Acts 17.24; 2 Mac. 7.23.

to man that He has subjected all His creation, giving him the mastery over everything that is under the heavens. 3 Now, if man is the master of all creation and has the mastery of everything, certainly he can acquire mastery of these mandates. The man who has the Lord in his heart,' he said, 'can master all things and all these mandates. 4 But, the persons who have the Lord on their lips, while their heart is hardened, who are in fact far from the Lord—for them these mandates are difficult and hard to fulfill. 5 Put the Lord in your hearts, then, you who are empty and fickle in the faith. You will then know that nothing is easier, sweeter, or more gentle than these mandates. 6 Be converted, you who walk in the commandments of the Devil, commandments that are hard, bitter, cruel, and foul. And do not fear the Devil either, because he has no power against you. 7 I, the Angel of Repentance, who have overcome the Devil, am on your side. The Devil only causes fear, but his fear is of no consequence. Do not fear him, then, and he will flee from you.'

V. THE DEVIL CANNOT HARM THOSE OF STRONG FAITH

1 I said to him: 'Sir, let me say a few words.' 'Say what you please,' he answered. 'Sir,' I said, 'man is eager to keep God's commandments and there is not one who does not entreat the Lord to be strengthened in His commandments and to submit to them. But, the Devil is harsh and lords it over them.' 2 'The Devil cannot lord it over those who are servants of God with their whole heart and who place their hope in Him. The Devil can wrestle with, but not overcome them.[7] So, if you resist him, he will flee from you in defeat and confusion. But empty men,' he said, 'fear him, as if he

---

7 James 4.7.

had power. 3 When a man fills an ample number of jars with good wine and among these jars there are a few half-empty, he does not pay attention to the full ones when he comes to his wine-jugs, because he knows that they are full. But, he is concerned lest the empty ones have turned sour, because empty jars quickly turn sour and the wine's good taste is lost. 4 In the same way the Devil comes and tempts all the servants of God. Those who are strong in the faith resist him and he goes away from them, because he cannot find entrance. So, he goes then to the empty and, finding an entrance, he goes into them. Thus he accomplishes in them whatever he pleases and makes them his slaves.

VI. Even Former Sinners Can Overcome the Devil

1 'I, the Angel of Repentance, am telling you: Do not fear the Devil. For I have been sent,' he said, 'to be on the side of you who repent with your whole heart, and to steady you in the faith. 2 Put your faith in God, you who despair of your life because of your sins, you who add to your sins and make your life burdensome. Trust that, if you turn to the Lord with your whole heart and do righteousness[8] for the rest of your life, serving Him uprightly in accordance with His will, He will provide a remedy for your previous failings and you will obtain the power of mastering the Devil's snares. Do not be in the least afraid of the Devil's threats, for they are as powerless as a dead man's sinews. 3 Listen to me: Fear Him who has power to save and to destroy.[9] Keep all the mandates and you will live to God.' 4 I said to him: 'Sir, I have now gained strength in all the justifications of the Lord,

8 Jer. 24.7; Joel 2.12; Ps. 14.2; Acts 10.35; Heb. 11.3.
9 James 4.12. Cf. Matt. 10.28; Luke 6.9; 9.24 and *passim*.

because you are on my side. I know that you will break down
all the Devil's power and we shall have the mastery over him
and overcome all his snares. Sir, I now hope, with the Lord's
help, to be able to keep these mandates you have given.'
5 'You will keep them,' he said, 'if your heart is made pure
to the Lord. All those, also, who cleanse their hearts of the
vain desires of this world will keep them and will live to God."

First Parable

MAN HAS HERE NO ABIDING CITY. WITH HIS POSSESSIONS
HE SHOULD ACQUIRE RICHES BEFORE GOD BY THE
PRACTICE OF FRATERNAL CHARITY

1 He said to me: 'You know that you servants of God
are living in a foreign country, for your city is far from this
city. Now, if you know the city in which you are eventually
to dwell, why do you secure fields, rich establishments, houses,
and superfluous dwellings? 2 The person who secures such
things for this city does not think of turning off to his real
city. 3 Foolish, miserable man of divided purpose, do you
not realize that these superfluities belong to somebody else
and are in the control of another? For, the lord of this city
will say: "I do not wish you to reside in my city. Go out of
it, for you do not live according to my laws." 4 So, if you
have fields, dwellings, and other property, what will you do
with your field, your house and the rest of your accumula-
tions, if you are cast out by Him? The lord of this country
will justly tell you: "Either live according to my laws or
leave my country." 5 What are you going to do, then, since
you are subject to the law of your own city? Are you going,
for the sake of your fields and the rest of your belongings,
to renounce altogether your own proper law and walk according to the law of this city? Take care: It may be against
your advantage to renounce your law. You may not be re-

ceived if you wish to return to your city, because you have denied the law of your city and it will be closed to you. 6 Therefore, you must be careful, while living in a foreign land, not to acquire a bit more than an adequate sufficiency. Be prepared, so that, when the ruler of this city wishes to expel you for resisting his law, you may come out of his city and enter your own and there rejoice without insolence in the observance of your own proper law. 7 Be on your guard, then, you who serve God, and hold Him in your heart. Keep in mind the commandments[1] of God, and the promises He made, and do His works. Be confident that He will fulfill His promises, if His commandments are kept. 8 Instead of fields, then, buy souls that are in trouble, according to your ability. Look after widows and orphans[2] and do not neglect them. Spend your riches and all your establishments you have received from God on this kind of fields and houses.[3] 9 It was for this that the Master bestowed wealth on you, to perform this ministry for Him. It is far better to buy such lands and possessions and houses, for you will find them when you settle in your own city. 10 Such lavishness is good and cheerful, is free from grief and fear, full of joy. Do not perform the "philanthropies" of the pagans. They are of no use for the servants of God. 11 Instead, be lavish in your own special way which can give you joy. Do not counterfeit; do not lay hand on what belongs to another and do not covet his possessions. For, it is wicked to covet another man's possessions. Do your task and you will be saved.'

---

1 Ps. 102.18.
2 James 1.27.
3 To do good to God's poor is to acquire riches in Heaven—a commonplace of Christian virtue.

Second Parable

The Alms of the Rich to the Poor Are Rewarded by God at the Prayer of the Poor

1 As I was walking in the country, I observed an elm and a vine and compared them and their friuts. The shepherd appeared and said to me: 'What are you thinking of by yourself?' 'I am thinking about the elm and the vine,' I said. 'They are very well adapted to one another.' 2 'These two trees,' he said, 'are as a symbol for the servants of God.' 'If only I could know the type which these trees you mention represent,' I said. 'You have the elm and the vine before your eyes?' he said. 'Yes, sir,' I answered. 3 'This vine,' he said, 'bears fruit, but the elm is sterile. However, this vine cannot bear fruit, unless it climbs up the elm. Otherwise, it spreads all over the ground. And, if it does bear, the fruit is rotten, because it has not been hanging from the elm. So, when the vine has been attached to the elm, it bears fruit both from itself and from the elm. 4 So, you see that the elm yields fruit, also, not a bit less than the vine; more, in fact.' 'How does it yield more, sir?' I said. 'Because,' he said, 'the vine that is hanging on the elm yields copious and sound fruit, but, if it is spread on the ground, it bears rotten fruit and little of it. This parable, then, applies to all the servants of God, to both the poor as well as the rich man.' 5 'Sir,' I said, 'how is this the parable of the rich and the poor man? Let me know.' 'I shall tell you,' he answered. 'The rich man has great wealth, but, so far as the Lord is concerned he is poor, because he is distracted by his wealth. His confession, his prayer to the Lord, is very limited; that which he makes is insignificant and weak and has no power above. So, when a rich man

goes up to a poor man and helps him in his needs, he has the assurance that what he does for the poor man can procure a reward from God (for the poor man is rich in his [power of] intercession with God and in his confession). Therefore, the rich man does not hesitate to supply the poor man with everything. 6 On the other hand, the poor man who has been helped by the rich intercedes for him and gives thanks to God for his benefactor. And the latter is constantly solicitous for the poor man, that he may not be in want during his life, because he knows that the poor man's intercession is acceptable and rich in God's sight. 7 Both fulfill their function in this way: The poor man makes intercession—these are his riches—and gives back to the Lord who supplied him; in the same way the rich man unhesitatingly puts the riches he received from the Lord at the disposal of the poor. This is a great and acceptable work in the sight of God. For [the rich man] has understanding in his riches, and out of the bounties of the Lord he works in the poor man's behalf and rightly accomplishes the Lord's ministry. 8 From men's point of view the elm seems not to bear fruit. But, they do not know or understand that in case of a drought the elm holds water and supplies it to the vine. And so the vine with an uninterrupted supply of water yields double the amount of fruit, both for itself and for the elm. In the same way the poor who direct prayer for the rich to the Lord round out their riches, while the rich, by supplying the needs of the poor, make up for the shortcomings of their souls. 9 Both in this way become associates in the just work. By doing this, then, you will not be left in the lurch by God. No! You will be inscribed on the books of the living. 10 Blessed are those who possess such riches and understand that riches are from the Lord. Those who understand this will be able to do some good deed.'

Third Parable

THE JUST AND SINNERS ARE NOT NOTABLY DIFFERENT IN EXTERNALS

1 He showed me many leafless trees that seemed to me to be withered and all alike. And he said to me: 'Do you see these trees?' 'Yes, sir,' I said, 'I do. They are all dry and of the same kind.' In answer he said: 'The trees you see are the people living in this world.' 2 'Why,' I said, 'are they dry and alike?' 'Because,' he said, 'in this world neither the just nor sinners are manifest, but they are alike. For this world is winter for the just, and they are not distinguishable while living with sinners. 3 For, just as in winter trees that have shed their leaves are alike and do not look dry, as they really are, or living, so in this world neither the just nor sinners look as they are, but all are alike.'

Fourth Parable

JUST AS THE SUMMER SEASON BRINGS OUT THE DIFFERENCE BETWEEN TREES, SO IN THE WORLD TO COME WILL THE JUST AND SINNERS BE DISTINGUISHED

1 Once more he showed me trees, some in bloom and some shrivelled, and said to me: 'Do you see these trees?' 'Yes, sir,' I said. 'I see some in bloom and some shrivelled.' 2 'Those that are in bloom,' he said, 'are the just, destined to live in the world to come. For, the world to come is summer for the just, but it is winter for sinners. When the Lord's

mercy shines forth, then will God's servants be made manifest. So will all be made manifest. 3 Just as in summer the fruits of every single tree come to light and we know what they are, so will the fruits of the just be manifest, and it will be known that all are flourishing in that world. 4 Pagans and sinners, the dry trees you see, will be found to be dry and fruitless in that world. They will be burned as firewood and will be manifest, because their activity in life was wicked. Sinners will be burned, because they sinned without repenting; pagans, because they did not know their Creator. 5 Bear fruit, then, so that your fruit may be known in that summer. Keep away from numerous occupations and you will not commit sin. For, those who are engaged in multiple occupations also sin much, because they are distracted by their occupations and fail to serve their Lord. 6 How,' he said, 'can such a person ask and obtain anything from the Lord without serving the Lord? His servants are those who will obtain, but those who do not serve the Lord will not obtain their requests. 7 However, if a person is occupied with only one business, he can also serve the Lord. For his heart will not be corrupted and turned aside from the Lord; he will still serve Him by keeping his heart pure. 8 By doing this you can bear fruit for the world to come. So will every one who does the same.'

Fifth Parable

I. FASTING ON STATION DAYS IS NOT ENOUGH—TRUE AND GENUINE FASTING MEANS KEEPING GOD'S COMMANDMENTS

1 While I was fasting, seated on a mountain and giving thanks to the Lord for all His benefits to me, I saw the shepherd, seated beside me, saying to me: 'Why did you come

here so early in the morning?' 'Because I am keeping a station,[1] sir,' I said. 2 'What is a station?' he said. 'I am fasting, sir,' I said. 'What is this fast you are engaged in?' he said. 'I fast, sir, as I am accustomed,' I said. 3 'You do not know how to fast to the Lord,' he said. 'And this unprofitable fast you keep for Him is not a fast, either.' 'Why do you say this, sir?' I said. 'I declare that this is not a fast, as you think it is,' he said. 'I shall teach you what is a fast complete and acceptable to the Lord. Pay attention,' he said. 4 'God does not wish vain fasting of this kind. When you fast thus for God's sake, you accomplish nothing for justice. Here is the fast you must keep for God:[2] 5 Do not commit any wicked deed in your life and serve the Lord with a pure heart; keep His commandments by walking according to His directions and do not let any evil desire enter your heart; have faith in God. If you do this, and fear Him, and refrain from every evil act, you will live to God. And by doing this you will also perform a fast that is great and acceptable to God.

II. The Industrious Laborer in the Vineyard

1 'Let me tell you the parable I have in mind relative to fasting. 2 A man had a field and numerous servants. One part of the field he planted as a vineyard. Then he chose a dependable, respected, and honest servant, summoned him and said: "Take this vineyard I planted and fence it in till I come. Do not do anything else to the vineyard. Do this and you will receive from me your freedom." Then the master of that slave went off to a foreign country. 3 When he had

---

1 In the *Didache* 8.1 mention has already been made of 'Stations.' There it is stated that Wednesday and Friday are days of fasting.
2 Cf. *Epistle of Barnabas* Ch. 3, where fasting in a spiritual sense is also required, cf. *Shepherd*, Fifth Parable, 3.6.

left, the slave took the vineyard and fenced it in. After finishing it, he noticed that the vineyard was full of weeds. 4 He
thought the matter over to himself and said: "I have done
what my master ordered. I shall next dig this vineyard; it
will be neater after having been dug. Without weeds it will
yield more fruit, since the fruit will not be choked by weeds."
So he went and dug the vineyard and plucked up all the
weeds that were in it. Then the vineyard became very neat
and flourishing, without any weeds to choke it. 5 After a
while the master of the slave and of the field returned to his
vineyard. When he saw that the vineyard had been fenced
in properly and, over and above this, had been dug and
cleared of weeds and that the vines were flourishing, he was
exceedingly glad at the work of his slave. 6 So, he summoned
his beloved son who was his heir and his friends who were his
advisers and told them what he had ordered his slave to do
and what he found. They, also, were happy at the master's
testimony in favor of his slave. 7 The latter said to them:
"I promised freedom to this slave, if he observed the order
I gave him. He has kept my order and, besides, to my great
pleasure, has done a good work in the vineyards. 8 So, as a
reward for this, I wish to make him joint heir with my son,
because, when the good thought came, he did not neglect it,
but put it into execution." With this intention of his the son
of the master agreed: The slave should be joint heir. 9 A few
days later, his master had a banquet and sent him many dainties from the feast. The slave, however, took from the dainties
sent him by his master only what was sufficient for himself and
distributed the remainder to his fellow slaves. 10 Then the fellow slaves, in their joy at receiving the dainties, began praying
in his behalf, that he might find even greater favor with his
master; for he treated them so well. 11 All this his master

heard, and once more was exceedingly pleased with his conduct. So, he called together his friends once more and his
son, and let them know what he had done with the dainties
he had received. Those called together were all the more
agreed that he should be joint heir with the son.'

III. A True and Genuine Fast Has a Necessary Connection with Fraternal Charity

1 I said: 'Sir, I do not know these parables and cannot
understand them, unless you explain them to me.' 2 'I shall
explain everything to you,' he said, 'and any thing I tell you
I shall make clear to you. Keep the commandments of the
Lord[3] and you will be well-pleasing to God; you will be inscribed in the number of those who keep His commandments.
3 But, if you do some good over and above God's commandment, you will acquire all the greater glory and will be held
in that much greater honor in the sight of God, with whom
you are destined to be. Therefore, if you also perform these
additional services, while keeping God's commandments, joy
will be yours, provided you observe them in accordance with
my commands.' 4 I said to him: 'Sir, whatever command
you give I shall observe; for I know that you are on my side.'
'I shall be on your side, because you are zealous in doing
good,' he said. 'I shall also be on the side of all who show
the same zeal. 5 This fasting, which consists in the observance
of the commandments of the Lord,' he said, 'is very beautiful.
This is the way to keep the fast you intend to observe: 6 Before anything else, abstain from every wicked word and every
evil desire, and clear your heart of all the vanities of this
world. If you observe this, your fast will be perfect. 7 Act as

---

3 Matt. 19.17.

follows: After having done what is prescribed, on the day of your fast do not taste anything except bread and water. Compute the total expense for the food you would have eaten on the day on which you intended to keep a fast and give it to a widow, an orphan, or someone in need. In this way you will become humble in soul, so that the beneficiary of your humility may fill his soul and pray to the Lord for you. 8 If you perform your fast, then, in the way I have just commanded, your sacrifice will be acceptable[4] in the sight of God and this fast will be entered in the account [in your favor]; a service so performed is beautiful, joyous, and acceptable in the sight of the Lord. 9 Observe this in the manner explained, together with your children and your whole household. In the observance you will be blessed, and all those who hear and observe this will also be blessed and will receive all they ask from the Lord.'

IV. The Lord Gives His True Servants the Grace to Understand the Parables

1 I urgently asked him to explain the parable of the field, the master, the vineyard, the slave fencing in the vineyard, the fences, the weeds plucked out of the vineyard, the son, and the friendly advisers. For I understood that all this was a parable. 2 He answered and said: 'You are exceedingly persistent in your questions. You do not have to ask anything at all, for, if there is need of explanation, it will be given you.' I said to him: 'Sir, if you do not explain what you show me, there is no use of my seeing it, since I do not understand what it means. Every time you tell me parables, without giving me the key to them, I shall be listening to no purpose.' 3 He

---

4 Phil. 4.18.

answered me again and said: 'Whoever is a servant of God
and has His Lord in his heart asks for understanding and gets
it; he has the key to every parable and the words of the Lord,
told him in parables, become known. But, the weak and
sluggish in prayer ask the Lord hesitatingly. 4 However, the
Lord is abundant in His mercies and gives to those who make
their petition without ceasing. Why do you not ask and receive understanding from the Lord? You have been strengthened by the holy angel, you have received [an answer to]
similar intercessions and you are not sluggish; so, ask of the
Lord and you will receive understanding.' 5 I said to him:
'Sir, since you are with me, I must ask and question you, for
you show me everything and now you are speaking with me.
If I had seen and heard this away from you, I would ask the
Lord to make it clear to me.'

V. Explanation of the Parable of the Vineyard

1 'I have told you only now,' he said, 'that you are shrewd
and persistent in asking meaning of the parables. Since you
are so patient, I shall elucidate for you the parable of the
field and all the other points that follow, so you can make
them known to everybody. Listen,' he said, 'and understand
this. 2 The field is this world.[5] The lord of the field is the One
who has created everything,[6] and fitted things together, and
given them strength. The servant is the Son of God, while
the vines are the people He engendered. 3 The fences are
the holy angels of the Lord who support His people. The
weeds plucked from the vineyard are iniquities of the servants of God. The food He sent are the commandments He

---

5 Matt. 13.38.
6 Eph. 3.9; Apoc. 4.11; Heb. 3.4.

gave to His people through His son. The friends and advisers are the holy angels, His first creation. The departure of the master for a foreign land is the time left over before His coming.' 4 I said to him: 'Sir, all this is marvellous, great, and glorious. Really,' I said, 'I could not have understood this. There is not a single man, no matter how clever he is, capable of understanding this. Once more, sir, explain what I am going to ask,' I said. 'Ask whatever you please,' he said. 'Why is the Son of God represented in the form of a slave in the parable?' I said.

VI. Why the Son of God Has the Part of a Slave in the Parable

1 'Listen,' he said. 'The Son of God is not represented in the form of a slave, but is represented with great power and majesty.' 'How is that?' I said. 'I do not understand.' 2 'Because,' he said, 'God planted the vineyard, that is to say, created His people and gave them over to His Son. The Son appointed the angels to watch over them. He Himeslf cleansed their sins away by undergoing inumerable toils and labors, for, nobody can dig without toil and labor. 3 By cleansing their sins in person, He showed them the ways of life and gave them the law which He received from His Father. 4 So you see,' he said, 'that He Himself is Lord of His people, because He has all power from His Father. Now, let me tell you why the Lord took His Son and the glorious angels as advisers in the question of the slave's inheritance. 5 The Holy Ghost, the Pre-existent, the Creator of all creations, was made by God to dwell in the flesh of His choice. This flesh, then, in which the Holy Spirit dwelt, was beautifully subject to the Spirit, and walked in holiness and purity, and sullied the

Spirit in absolutely nothing. 6 Therefore, the flesh was guided with beauty and purity by the Spirit, and shared His toil and labor in everything. Because the flesh had conducted itself with strength and courage, He associated it with the Holy Spirit, for He was pleased with the career of this flesh which had not been sullied while holding the Spirit on earth. 7 Therefore, He took the Son and the glorious angels as advisers, in order that the flesh might have some place of abode for its blameless subjection to the Spirit and might not seem to have lost the reward of its service. For, all flesh that has been found unsullied and spotless, in which the Holy Spirit has had His abode, will receive a reward. 8 Here you have the solution of this parable.'

VII. Keep Your Body Unsullied

1 'I am delighted, sir,' I said, 'to have heard this solution.' 'Let me tell you further,' he said. 'Preserve this flesh of yours clean and unsullied, in order that the indwelling Holy Spirit may give testimony to it and your flesh may be justified. 2 Make sure that the thought never enters your heart that this flesh of yours is perishable and that you misuse it by some defilement. For, if you defile your flesh, you also defile the Holy Spirit, and if you defile your flesh, you will not live.' 3 'If,' I said, 'before these words were heard, there was some ignorance, how can a man who has sullied his flesh be saved?' 'A remedy for previous ignorance is only possible to God,' he said, 'for He has all power. 4 However, preserve yourself now and the Omnipotent Lord, in His great mercy, will grant a remedy for past ignorance. In the future, sully neither flesh nor spirit, for the two are associates, and one cannot be sullied without the other. Keep both clean, then, and you will live to God.'

Sixth Parable

I. The Parable of the Joyous Shepherd and the Carefree Sheep

1 While seated in my house and praising the Lord for all I had seen, I also reflected on the mandates. I thought that they were noble, possible of fulfillment, joyous, glorious, and capable of saving man's soul. So, I said to myself: 'Happy I shall be if I walk in these mandates; so will anyone be who walks in them!' 2 As I was saying this to myself, I suddenly saw him seated beside me. He said to me: 'Why are you entertaining doubt about the mandates I gave to you? They are beautiful. Put aside all doubt, clothe yourself with faith in the Lord, and walk in them. I shall give you strength to keep them. 3 These mandates are advantageous for those who intend to repent. For, if they do not walk in them, their repentance is worthless. 4 You who repent must cast off the wickedness of this world which wears you down; if you put on every excellence of justice, you can observe these mandates and keep from committing any additional sins. If you do not add to your former sins, you will walk in these mandates and live to God. All this you have been told by me.' 5 After telling me this he said: 'Let us go into the field and I shall show you the shepherds with their sheep.' 'Yes, sir,' I said, 'let us go.' On going into the field, he pointed out to me a young shepherd dressed in a suit of saffron-colored garments. 6 He was feeding an extremely large number of sheep, who were apparently well fed and frisky and gamboling joyously here and there. The shepherd himself was happy with his flock and his whole appearance was joyous as he ran about among his sheep.

II. This Shepherd Is the Angel of Pleasure and Deceit

1 He said to me: 'Do you see this shepherd?' 'Yes, sir,'
I said. 'This,' he said, 'is the angel of luxury and deceit. He
wears down the souls of God's servants and makes them turn
away from the truth by deceiving them with evil desires that
are their death. 2 Consequently, they forget the commandments of the living God and walk in deceits and vain luxury;
thus are they led to destruction by this angel, some to death,
some to corruption.' 3 I said to him: 'Sir, I do not know
what this means: "death" and "corruption." ' 'I shall tell
you,' he said. 'The sheep you see joyously gamboling are
those who have been completely drawn away from God and
have surrendered themselves to the lusts of this world. For
these persons there is no repentance unto life, because God's
Name is being blasphemed by them. Their life is death. 4 The
sheep you see not gamboling, but standing in one place and
grazing, are those who have given themselves up to luxury
and deceit, but have not committed any blasphemy against
the Lord. They are those, then, who have been led away
from the truth. There is hope of repentance for them, and so,
of life. Their perversion, then, holds some hope of renova-
tion, but death means everlasting ruin.' 5 Once more we
went forward a little distance, and he pointed out to me a
shepherd, large and quite savage in appearance. He was
dressed in a white goat's skin, with a bag on his shoulders; in
his hands was a very rough staff with knots in it and a whip.
His look was so fierce that I was afraid of him. 6 This
shepherd was constantly receiving from a young shepherd
sheep that were frisky and well fed, but not gamboling about,
and he threw them into a place that was steep and full of
thorns and thistles. The sheep could not disentangle themselves from the thorns and thistles, therefore, but became

entangled in them. These sheep, entangled in the thorns and thistles, were very miserable, because they were being beaten by him. Though they went here and there, he gave them no rest; they could not lie down at ease anywhere at all.

III. The Avenging Angel Hands Over His Charge to the Angel of Penance

1 When I saw them whipped like this and in misery, I was sorry for them: Such was their torment without any respite whatever. 2 I said to the shepherd who was talking to me: 'Sir, who is this heartless and savage shepherd, so utterly without pity for these sheep?' 'He is the avenging angel,' he said, 'one of the just angels entrusted with punishment. 3 He takes those who have wandered away from God and have walked in the lusts and deceits of this world, and punishes according to their deserts with varied, dreadful punishments.' 4 'I would like to know, sir,' I said, 'what these varied punishments are.' 'I shall tell you,' he said. 'The tortures and punishments are temporal. Some are punished with losses, some by poverty, some by divers sicknesses, some by lack of any permanent abode, some from the insults of unworthy persons and sufferings of all kinds. 5 For, many persons who are unsettled in their plans set their hands at many things, but make no progress at all in them. They say that they are not doing well in their pursuits, but it does not occur to them that they have committed wicked deeds. Instead, they blame the Lord. 6 When they have suffered every affliction, they are handed over to me for sound instruction. Then they are strengthened in the faith of the Lord, and for the rest of their life they serve the Lord with a pure heart. Now,

when they repent, they recall the evil deeds that they committed and at that point they praise God. They declare that God is a just judge and that they suffered each in the measure of his actions. In the future they serve the Lord with pure hearts and prosper in their pursuits, receiving from the Lord everything they ask for.[7] Then, too, they praise the Lord for having been handed over to me and never again suffer any evil.'

IV. The Duration of Pleasure and of Punishment

1 I said to him: 'Sir, explain one more thing to me.' 'What is your question?' he said. 'Sir,' I said, 'are those who live in luxury and deceit tortured for as long a time as they lived in self-indulgence and deceit?' 'Yes, just as long,' he said. 2 'Sir,' I said, 'they are put to the torture a very short time; they ought to be tortured seven times as long for living in self-indulgence and forgetting God as they do.' 3 He said to me: 'You are foolish and do not understand the power of the torture.' 'If I did understand, sir, I would not have asked you to explain it to me,' I said. 'Let me tell you the power of the two. 4 The time of self-indulgence and deceit is one hour, but the hour of torture is the equivalent of thirty days. So, if anyone indulges himself or allows himself to be deceived for a single day, a single day's torture has the effectiveness of a whole year. A man is tortured, then, for as many years as there were days of self-indulgence. So you see,' he said, 'that, though the period of self-indulgence and deceit is very short, the period of punishment and torture is protracted.'

V. There is Harmful and Profitable Pleasure

1 'Sir,' I said, 'I still do not understand fully about the period of deceit and indulgence and the period of torture.

---

7 Matt. 21.22; 1 John 3.22.

Give me a clearer explanation.' 2 For answer he said to me: 'Your foolishness is persistent and you do not wish to cleanse your heart and serve God. Take care,' he said, 'lest the time be fulfilled and it should be found that you are foolish. Let me tell you, then,' he said, 'that you may understand as you wish. 3 The luxurious liver and the man deceived for a single day, who does what he pleases, is clothed in considerable foolishness without realizing his performance. The next day he forgets what he did the day before. For, self-indulgence and deceit have no memory, because of that foolishness in which they are clothed. But, when punishment and torture are imposed on a man for a single day, it is as punishment and torture for a whole year. For punishment and torture have long memories. 4 So, the man who is punished and tortured for a whole year remembers at last his self-indulgence and deceit, and he knows that he suffers evil for that reason. Consequently, every self-indulgent and deceived man is tortured in this way, because, though he had life, he gave himself up to death.' 5 'What kinds of self-indulgence,' I said, 'are harmful, sir?' 'Every act performed with pleasure is self-indulgence for man,' he said. 'For example, the sharp-tempered man, by giving satisfaction to his passion, is self-indulgent. So the adulterer, the drunkard, the slanderer, the liar, the envious, the robber, and anyone who commits similar sins, gives free rein to his individual vice. Consequently, he is self-indulgent in his action. 6 All these [acts of] self-indulgence are harmful to God's servants. It is for these deceits that those who are punished and tortured suffer. 7 However, there are acts of self-indulgence that bring salvation to human beings. For, there are many persons who are self-indulgent in their good actions, who are carried away by the pleasure this gives them. This kind of self-indulgence, then, is advantageous for God's servants and secures life for this type of man. Whereas, the harmful self-indulgence, mentioned above, brings them punishment and torture, and, if they persist without repenting, they bring death on themselves.'

Seventh Parable

HERMAS IS HANDED OVER TO THE AVENGING ANGEL FOR THE SINS OF HIS HOUSEHOLD

1 After a few days, I saw him in the same plain where I had also seen the shepherds, and he said to me: 'What are you looking for?' 'I am here, sir,' I said, 'to have you command the avenging shepherd to leave my house, because he is afflicting me very much.' 'You have to be afflicted,' he said. 'Such is the injunction of the glorious angel in your regard,' he said. 'For, he wants you to be put to the test.' 'What have I done, sir, that is so wicked that I must be handed over to this angel?' I said. 2 'I shall tell you,' he said. 'Your sins are numerous, but not so numerous that you must be handed over to this angel. However, your household has committed many sins and iniquities, and the glorious angel is embittered at their deeds. Hence, he has given orders that you should be afflicted for a while, that they also may repent and cleanse themselves of every lust of this world. When they repent and are cleansed, then the angel will desist from punishment.' 3 I said to him: 'Sir, granted that they have committed acts to embitter the glorious angel, what have I done?' 'They cannot be otherwise afflicted,' he said, 'unless you, the head of the whole household, suffer affliction. For, if you suffer affliction, they also will necessarily be afflicted, but, if you fare well, they suffer no affliction at all.' 4 'But look,

sir, I said. 'They have repented with their whole heart.' 'I
also know,' he said, 'that they have repented with their whole
heart. Do you think, then, that there is immediate remission
from sin with repentance? Not at all. No! The one who
repents must torture his soul and be thoroughly humble in
all his actions and afflicted in a variety of ways. If he endures
the afflictions that come to him, mercy to the full will be
granted by the Creator of all things,[1] who also has given him
strength and who will grant a remedy. 5 This God will do
when He sees the penitent's heart free from all wickedness.
But, it is to the advantage of you and your household that
you be afflicted now. What more need I say to you? You
must be afflicted in accordance with the orders of that angel
of the Lord who handed you over to me. Give thanks to the
Lord also for this, that you were considered worthy beforehand of some indication of the affliction destined for you.
By knowing it in advance you will endure it with fortitude.'
6 I said to him: 'Sir, be on my side and I shall be able to
endure every affliction.' 'I shall be on your side, he said, 'and
I shall also ask the avenging angel to send you milder afflictions. However, you must be afflicted a short time and then
restored once more to your house. Only continue in your
humble service of the Lord with a clean heart—your children,
too, and your household. Walk in the commandments I have
given you, and it will be possible for your repentance to be
strong and clean. 7 If you observe these commandments, together with your whole house, all affliction will pass from you.
So will it pass also from all who walk in these commandments of mine,' he said.

---

1 Eph. 3.9.

Eighth Parable

I. THE PARABLE OF THE WILLOW

1 He showed me an ample willow, covering plains and mountains, and in its shelter came all those called by the Name of the Lord. 2 The glorious, exceedingly tall angel of the Lord stood by the willow with a mighty sickle. He was lopping off branches and distributing them to the people in the shelter of the willow. He also distributed small rods, about two feet long. 3 After every one had received rods,[1] the angel put aside his sickle, yet the tree was as sound as when I had first seen it. 4 I wondered at this to myself and said: 'How can the tree be sound after so many branches have been lopped from it?' The shepherd said to me: 'Do not wonder that the tree remains sound after so many branches have been lopped from it. Let this go until you have seen everything and the meaning will be made clear to you.' 5 The angel who had distributed the rods was asking them back from them. In the order in which they had received the rods they were summoned to him, and each returned his rod to him. The angel of the Lord received them and scrutinized them carefully. 6 From some he took rods dry and apparently worm-eaten. To those who had returned such rods he gave orders to stand apart. 7 Others returned rods that were dry, but not worm-eaten. These persons, also, he ordered to stand aside. 8 Others returned rods that were half-dry and they stood at the side. 9 Another group returned rods with cracks in them and they stood apart. 10 Another class gave up rods green and cracked and stood apart. 11 Others gave him rods half-green and half-cracked and stood apart. 12 Others brought him rods two-thirds green and one-third dry and stood apart.

---

1 On this whole parable cf. Num. 17.6-9.

13 Others returned rods two-thirds dry and one-third green and stood apart. 14 Others returned their rods almost totally green with a very small portion dry, the tip; there were cracks in them also. Then they stood apart. 15 The rods of others were green only in a very small portion and the rest were dry. They also stood apart. 16 Others came and brought rods that were green just as they had received them from the angel. The majority of the crowd returned rods of this kind. With them the angel was exceedingly pleased. They also stood apart. 17 Others returned rods that were green with buds on them. They also stood apart and the angel was likewise highly pleased with them. 18 Others returned rods that were green with buds on them, and the rods apparently had some fruit. The persons whose rods were found to be in this condition were very joyous. The angel also was exultant with them and the shepherd very cheerful.

II. The Bearers of Green Branches Are Rewarded

1 The angel of the Lord ordered crowns to be brought. When the crowns, apparently made of palm, had been brought, he bestowed them on those who had returned rods with buds and some fruit and sent them to the tower. 2 He also sent the rest of them to the tower, those who had returned rods that were green and budding, but without fruit, after giving them a seal. 3 On their way to the tower they all had the same cloak, white as snow. 4 He also sent off those who had returned rods that were green as when they received them, after giving them a white cloak and seals. 5 This finished, the angel said to the shepherd: 'I am going away. Send off these persons to dwell in their place within the walls according to their deserts. Send them off only after having looked carefully at their rods. Yes! Scrutinize them carefully.

Make sure that no one slips by you,' he said. 'But, if someone does go by you, I shall put him to the test at the altar.' With these words to the shepherd he went away. 6 After the departure of the angel, the shepherd said to me: 'Let us take the rods of all and plant them. Perhaps some of them may be able to live.' I said to him: 'Sir, how can these dry rods live?' 7 He answered and said: 'This tree is a willow and naturally tenacious of life. So, if they are planted and get a little moisture, many of the rods will live. Then we shall try to pour water on them, also. If any of them can live, I shall join in its joy. But, if it cannot live, it will be discovered that I was not unsolicitous.' 8 The shepherd ordered me to call them just as they were stationed. They came up rank by rank and returned their rods to the shepherd. On receiving them, the shepherd planted the rods row by row. After planting them, he poured water on them so copiously that the rods could not be seen in the water. 9 After he had watered the rods, he said to me: 'Let us go; after a few days we shall return and look at all the rods. For, He who created this tree wishes all who have taken branches from it to live. I also hope that the majority of these rods, after receiving moisture and having been watered, will live.'

III. EXPLANATION OF THE TREE AND ITS BRANCHES

1 I said to him: 'Sir, tell me what this tree is. I am puzzled about it. After so many branches have been cut, it is sound and does not look as if anything had been cut from it. This really puzzles me.' 2 'I shall tell you,' he said. 'This tree that covers plain and mountain and the whole earth is the law of God, given to the whole world. This law is the Son of God proclaimed to the ends of the earth. The persons under its shelter are the persons who have heard the proclamation and

believed in Him. 3 The great and glorious angel is Michael, who has power over this people and is their captain. For, it is Michael who inspires the law in the hearts of believers. He inspects closely the persons to whom he gave it to see whether they have kept the law. 4 You can see the rods of each individual person, for they are the law. You see that many rods have been made useless, so you can know that all these persons failed to keep the law. You will also see their dwelling.' 5 'Sir,' I said to him, 'why did he send some to the tower, while he left some behind?' 'He has left behind in my power those who violated the law they received from Him, to see whether they will repent. But, those who have already satisfied the law and have kept it he keeps under his own jurisdiction.' 6 'Sir,' I said, 'who are those who have received their crowns and have gone into the tower?' 'They are those who have wrestled with the Devil and have defeated him. They are crowned. They are the ones who suffered for the law. 7 The others, also, who have returned in person green rods, with buds, but without fruit, have endured persecution for the law, but have not suffered; however, they did not deny their law. 8 Those who returned their rods, green as they received them, are holy and just and walk in extreme purity of heart, keeping the commandments of the Lord. The rest you will know when I inspect closely the rods that were planted and watered.'

IV. The Examination of the Branches Planted in the Ground

1 So, after a few days, we came to the spot and the shepherd sat in the place of the angel, while I took a position beside him. He said to me: 'Tie a towel around you and wait on me.' So I tied a clean towel of sack-cloth and was ready to wait on him. 2 'Call the men,' he said, 'whose rods have

been planted according to the rank in which each presented the rods.' And I went to the plain and called everyone; they stood according to their ranks. 3 He said to them: 'Let each one pull up his rod and bring it to me.' 4 The first to return them were those who had had dry and chipped rods, and so they were found—dried and chipped. He commanded them to stand aside. 5 Then those who had dry, but not chipped, rods returned them. Some returned the rods green, but some returned them dried and chipped, apparently by worms. So, he commanded those who had returned them green to stand aside, but those who returned them dried and chipped were to stand with the first class. 6 Then, those who had half-dried and cracked rods returned them; many of them gave back green rods without cracks, but some green rods with buds and fruit on the buds like the persons who had been crowned and had entered the tower. However, some returned them dry and worm-eaten, others dried but not worm-eaten, while some were half-dry and had cracks. And he commanded each one of them to stand aside, some in their own ranks and others by themselves.

V. Further Explanation of the Meaning of the Branches

1 Then those who had green rods with cracks returned them. Since these all had green rods, they stood in their own ranks. The shepherd was pleased with them because their rods had all changed and had lost their cracks. 2 Then those who had half-green and half-dry rods also returned them. The rods of some were found to be completely green, of others half-dried, of others still dried and worm-eaten, but some were green and had buds. All these were sent, each to his rank. 3 Then those whose rods were two-thirds green and

one-third dry returned them. Many of them returned green
rods, many returned half-dried rods, and the rest dried and
worm-eaten rods. All these stood in their ranks. 4 Then those
who had rods two-thirds dry and one-third green returned
them. Many of them returned half-dried rods, but some returned dry and worm-eaten rods; some, rods half-dried with
cracks; a few returned green ones. All these persons stood in
their ranks. 5 Those who had had rods with a very small dry
portion and cracks returned them. Of this number some returned them green and others green with buds. These also
went off to their ranks. 6 Then those who had rods with a
very small portion of green, but otherwise dry, returned them.
In this group the majority were discovered to have rods that
were green with buds and fruit on the buds, while the rest
of the rods were completely green. The shepherd was exceedingly pleased with those whose rods were found in this condition. They all went off, each to his own rank.

VI. The Meaning of the Individuals Bearing Dry Branches

1 After looking closely at all the rods, the shepherd said
to me: 'I told you that this tree clings to life. Do you see,'
he said, 'how many repented and were saved?' 'Yes, I do,'
I said. 'It is,' he said, 'that you may realize that the superabundant mercy of the Lord is mighty and glorious and that
He has granted His Spirit to those who are worthy of repentance.' 2 'Why is it, sir,' I said, 'that all do not repent?'
'He has granted repentance to those whose heart, He sees, is
going to be made pure and who will serve Him with their
whole heart. But, lest His Name be again defiled, He has

not granted repentance to those whose guile and wickedness He saw, for they were making a sham of repentance.' 3 I said to him: Now, sir, explain what sort of persons they are and where is the dwelling of those who returned their rods. In this way believers who have received the seal, but have broken it and failed to keep it whole, may realize what they have done, and repent. Then they will receive a seal from you and will praise the Lord for having had mercy on them and for sending you to renew their souls.' 'I shall tell you,' he said. 4 'The persons whose rods were discovered to be dry and worm-eaten are apostates and traitors to the Church, who blaspheme the Lord by their sins. Furthermore, they were ashamed of the Name of the Lord, the Name invoked upon them.[2] In the end, these persons are lost to God. You see that not one of them has repented, though they heard what you told them at my command. From persons of this kind life has departed. 5 Those, also, are like to them who returned dry rods, not worm-eaten. For they are hypocrites, who introduce strange doctrines and pervert the servants of God. In particular, they pervert sinners by not allowing them to repent, but dissuade them by foolish doctrines. However, there is prospect of repentance for them. 6 Many of them, as you see, have repented since you spoke my commandments to them. More will repent. But, those who will not repent have lost their life. However, those of their number who have repented have become good and their dwelling is within the first walls. Some even went up to the tower. So you see,' he said, 'that repentance for sins means life, but failure to repent means death.

---

2 James 2.7; Gen. 48.18.

VII. THE BEARERS OF HALF-DRIED BRANCHES

1 'Now, let me tell you also about those who returned half-dried rods with cracks in them. Those whose rods were half-dry throughout are the persons of doubtful heart. They are neither dead nor alive. 2 Those who are half-dry and have cracks are persons of divided purpose and slanderers. They are never at peace with one another[3] and always cause dissensions. But, for them also, repentance is possible. You see,' he said, 'some from this class who have repented. There is still,' he said, 'hope of repentance for them. 3 All of this class who have repented,' he said, 'also have a dwelling in the tower. However, those who were slower in their repentance dwell in the walls, while those who do not repent, but persist in their practices, die the death. 4 Those who have returned their rods green though cracked always were faithful and good, but there was some little jealousy among them about first places and points of reputation—foolish to be opposed to one another about first places! 5 But these also, after hearing my commandments, were cleansed and soon repented, since they are good. Their dwelling, therefore, is in the tower. But, if any turn aside again and are divided in purpose, they will be cast out of the tower and will lose their life. 6 Life belongs to all who keep the Lord's commandments. Now, in the commandments there is nothing about first places and any point of honor but about man's long-suffering and humility. The life of the Lord, then, is to be found in men of this kind, but death is among those of doubtful heart and among transgressors.

---

3 Thess. 5.13.

VIII. The Bearers of Partly Green and Partly Dry Branches

1 'Those who gave up rods half dry and half green are the persons engrossed in their business, who fail to cling to holiness. For this reason one half is living and the other half is dead. 2 So many who have heard my commandments have repented. Those that repented, then, have a dwelling in the tower. But, some of them stood off to the end. They, therefore, have no repentance, for they blasphemed the Lord and denied Him on account of their business affairs. Consequently, they lost their life because of their wicked practices. 3 Many of this group were of doubtful heart. These will still have repentance, provided they repent in good time. Then they will have a dwelling in the tower. Even if they repent rather slowly, they dwell within the tower. But, if they fail to repent, they also have lost their life. 4 Those who returned rods two-thirds green and one-third dry are the persons who denied the Lord on divers occasions. Many of this group have repented and returned to the tower to dwell. However, many fell away from God completely. These finally lost life. And some of this group were doubters at heart and caused dissensions. So, they have repentance, if it comes in good time and if they do not persist in their self-indulgence. But, if they do persist in their ways, they also work death for themselves.

IX. The Bearers of the Two-thirds Dry Branches

1 'Those who returned their rods, two-thirds dry and one-third green, are the persons who had been faithful, but became rich and made a name among the pagans. They put on a supercilious demeanor, became haughty, and so abandoned

the truth and did not cling to the just. Instead, they lived in the manner of the pagans and among them, a manner of life more agreeable to them. However, they did not fall away from God, but clung to the faith, without doing its works. 2 Many of them repented and their dwelling was in the tower. 3 But, others who lived and associated constantly with the pagans were corrupted by their vain opinions to fall away from God and act in the manner of the pagans. Such persons are considered pagans. 4 Others in this group were doubting hearts and had no hope of being saved on account of their deeds. Others, again, were doubters at heart and caused divisions among their associates. There is still repentance for those who, because of their actions, doubt. However, if they would have a dwelling within the tower, their repentance must be swift. But, death is at hand to those who do not repent and persist in their pleasures.

X. The Bearers of the Green-tipped Branches

1 'Those who returned their rods green, but dry-tipped and cracked, were always good, faithful, and glorious in the sight of God, but they committed sin in a small degree out of trifling desires or because they had petty quarrels with one another. The majority quickly repented on hearing my words and their dwelling was set in the tower. 2 But, some were doubtful of heart, and in their doubts they created a greater dissension. Still, there is some hope of repentance for them, because at all times they were good. Any of them is hardly likely to die. 3 Those who returned their rods dry, with only the slightest touch of green, are believers, but their actions were those of iniquity. However, they never fell away from God and bore the Name gladly. In their houses they also received God's servants graciously. So, when they

heard of this penance, they repented without hesitation and now they are accomplishing all virtue and justice. 4 Some of them, too, are willing to suffer affliction of their own free will, because they realize the malice of their former actions. The dwelling of all these persons, then, is the tower.'

XI. THE CALL TO CONVERSION IS MADE TO ALL

1 After finishing the explanation of all the rods, he said to me: 'Go off and tell everybody to repent and live to God. The Lord in His mercy has sent me to grant repentance to all, although some are unworthy because of their works. But, in His long-suffering the Lord wishes those that were called through His Son to be saved.' 2 I said to him: 'Sir, I hope that those who have heard this will repent. I am quite sure that each one who realizes his personal acts will repent out of fear of the Lord.' 3 He answered and said: 'Those who repent with their whole heart and cleanse themselves of all the wickedness just described, without ever adding to their former sins, will receive from the Lord a remedy for their former sins. Provided they are not beset by doubt in fulfilling my commandments, they will live to God. But, those who add to their sins and revert to the lusts of this world will bring the judgment of death on themselves. 4 As for you, walk in my commandments and live to God. They, too, will live to God, who walk in these commandments and act uprightly.' 5 After showing and telling me all this he said: 'I shall show you the rest in a few days.'

The Ninth Parable

I. THE APPEARANCE OF THE TWELVE MOUNTAINS

1 When I had written the mandates and the parables of the shepherd, the angel of repentance came and said: 'I want

to point out to you what the Holy Spirit has shown you while speaking to you in the form of the Church. For that Spirit is the Son of God. 2 Since you were rather weak in the flesh, it was not explained to you by an angel. So, when you were given power by the spirit and you grew in strength sufficient even to see an angel, then the building of the tower was revealed to you by the Church. You have looked at everything in a good and reverent manner, as befits what comes from a virgin. Now instruction is being given you by the same spirit through an angel. 3 You are to learn everything from me in greater detail. It was with this intention that I was assigned by the glorious angel to dwell in your house, that you might have powerful insight into everything, without any fear as formerly.'4 Then he led me off to Arcadia to a certain breast-shaped mountain and set me down on top of the mountain. From here he showed me a huge plain with twelve mountains around it, each of a different shape. 5 The first was black as pitch; the second was bare, without any vegetation; the third was full of thorns and thistles; 6 the fourth had half-dried herbage, the top of the grass green, but the part near the roots dry, while some of the vegetation became scorched by the sun; 7 the fifth mountain had green vegetation, in spite of the fact that it was rough; the sixth mountain was full of crevices, some of them small and some large. However, the crevices contained plants, not very flourishing and apparently withered. 8 The seventh mountain contained smiling vegetation and it was flourishing everywhere, with all kinds of cattle and birds feeding on it. And the more the cattle and birds fed, all the more did the vegetation on that mountain blossom. And the eighth was full of springs and every kind of creature of the Lord was provided with water from the springs on that mountain. 9 But the ninth mountain was completely devoid of water and was utterly deserted. However, there were wild beasts and deadly serpents that destroy men. The tenth mountain had huge trees, affording complete shade; under cover of them sheep were resting and chewing their cud. 10 The eleventh mountain was covered with trees, fruit-bearing trees, each adorned with different fruits. A person seeing this fruit would be moved with desire to eat of it. The twelfth mountain was all white and its sight was attractive. It was most imposing in itself.

II. The Rock and the Twelve Virgins

1 In the middle of the plain he pointed out to me a huge rock rising out of it. Now the rock was higher than the mountains, four-square, of a size to hold the whole world. 2 It was old and a door had been cut out of it, but this door seemed to me to have been hewn recently. The glow of the gate was so much beyond that of the sun that I wondered at its brilliance. 3 In a circle around the gate there stood twelve virgins. Now, the four that stood at the corners seemed to me to be more noble than the others, though the others also seemed noble. 4 They stood at the four parts of the gate, two virgins at the center of each side of the gate. They were dressed in linen mantles and had beautiful girdles. Their right shoulders were exposed as if they were about to carry a load. They were ready, cheerful, and eager. 5 On seeing this I said to myself: 'You are looking at something great and glorious.' But, once again I was at a loss to explain how these virgins, delicate though they were, stood their courageously, ready to hold up the whole world. 6 And the shepherd said to me: 'Why are you thinking to yourself and why are you so puzzled? Why are you making yourself sad? What you cannot understand do not try to understand, if you have sense. But, ask the Lord

and you will receive intelligence and understanding. 7 You cannot see what is behind you, but you see what is before you. So, pass over what you cannot see and do not torture yourself. Master what you see and do not concern yourself about the rest. Everything I point out to you I shall explain to you. Now, then, look well at the rest.'

III. The Builders and the Preparations for the Building of the Tower

1 I saw six men coming, tall, noble, and similar in form, and they called a multitude of men. The others, also, who were advancing were tall, handsome, and strong. The latter were commanded by the six to build a tower on top of the gate. The noise of the men who were coming to build the tower was extraordinary, for they were running here and there about the tower. 2 Now, the virgins who were standing around the tower told the men to hurry and build the tower. The virgins stretched out their hands as though they were about to receive something from the men. 3 The six men gave orders for stones to come up from some abyss for the building of the tower. Then ten glistening, uncut, square stones came up. 4 Then the six men called to the virgins and bade them carry all the stones destined to go into the building of the tower, walk through the gate, and pass them on to the men supposed to build the tower. 5 Then the virgins heaped the first ten stones that came out of the abyss on one another and carried them in one load by their united effort.

IV. The Building of the Tower

1 In the same position in which they stood around the tower, those that seemed strong enough got under the corners

of the stone and carried it, while the others got under the sides. This is the way they carried all the stones. They carried them through the gate as they had been bidden and passed them on to the men on the tower. Once the latter had the stones, they built. 2 The tower was built on top of the huge stone over the gate. Then those ten stones were joined together and covered the whole rock, and became the foundation of the tower-building. The rock and gate were the support of the whole tower. 3 After the ten stones others came out of the abyss, twenty-five. These, also, were carried by the maidens like the first, and were joined together in the building of the tower. After these stones there came up thirty-five more, and they were joined together like the rest in the building of the tower. Next, forty more came up and all these also were put into the building of the tower. So there were four stories in the foundations of the tower. 4 Then there was a pause in the ascent of stones from the abyss and the workers also held up for a short while. Then once more the six men gave orders to the masses to bring along stones from the mountains for the building of the tower. 5 Then stones of various colors were brought along from all the mountains. They had been hewn by the men and handed to the virgins, who carried them through the gate and passed them on for the building of the tower. Now, when the varicolored stones were placed into the building, they changed their color and became, all of them, white. 6 However, some stones handed in by the men for the building did not become shining, but turned out to be of the same color as when they were being put into the building. For, they had not been handed along by the virgins, nor had they been carried through the gate. 7 These stones were unsightly in the building of the tower. When the six men saw that the stones were unsightly, they gave orders that they be taken out and carried down to the particular place from where they had come. 8 And they said to the men who were bringing the stones in: 'You must not bring in stones at all into the building. Place them beside the tower for the virgins to carry them through the gate and hand them into the building. For, if these stones have not been carried by the hands of the virgins, they cannot change their colors. So, do not labor to no purpose.'

V. The Interruption in the Building

1 Now, on that day building operations were finished, but the tower was not completed; additions still had to be made. There was a pause in the building. To the builders the six men gave orders to go off for a short while and rest, but to the virgins their orders were not to go away from the tower. It seemed to me that they had been left there to guard the tower. 2 After the departure of everybody to rest, I said to the shepherd: 'Why is it, sir, that the building of the tower is not finished?' 'It cannot yet be finished,' he said, 'unless the lord of the tower comes and inspects the building to find out whether some stones are unsound; then he will change them—for the tower is being built according to his wishes.' 3 'Sir,' I said, 'I would like to know what is the building of this tower. I would like to know about the rock, the gate, the mountains, the virgins and the stones that have come out of the abyss uncut and yet have gone into the building. 4 Furthermore, why are ten stones first put into the foundations, then twenty-five, then thirty-five, and then forty? I would also like to know about the stones that went into the building and were taken out again and placed back in their original place. Quiet my soul on all these points, sir, and let me know.' 5 'If it turns out that you are not idly curious,' he said, 'you will know all.

For, after a few days we shall come and you will see the rest of the materials coming to this tower. Then you will understand the parables accurately.' 6 So, after a few days we came to the place where we had sat, and he said to me: 'Let us go to the tower, for the owner is coming to take a close look at it.' So we went to the tower, but absolutely nobody was with him, except only the virgins. 7 And the shepherd asked the virgins whether the master of the tower had come there. And they answered that he intended to come and look at the building.

VI. Inspection of the Tower by the Master

1 Behold! After a short while I saw an array of many people advancing. And in the midst there was a man taller in stature than the tower. 2 Now, the six men in charge of the building were walking with him on his right and left. All those engaged in the building were with him and many other distinguished persons were about him. The maidens who kept watch on the tower ran forward and kissed him and began to walk beside him around the tower. 3 The very tall man examined the building carefully, even handling the individual stones. Taking a staff in his hand, he struck each individual stone placed in the building. 4 After his blow, some stones became black as soot, some rotten, some showed cracks, some were chipped, some were neither white nor black, some rough and did not fit into the other stones, and some had many spots. Such were the various appearances of the rotten stones found in the building. 5 Therefore, he gave orders that all these stones be transferred from the building and placed beside the tower and other stones be carried in and used as replacements. 6 The builders asked him from what mountain he wished stones to be carried and used in their place. But he did not command stones to be carried from the mountains;

instead, he commanded them from a nearby plain. 7 When the plain was broken, brilliant square stones were found and some spherical ones, also. And any stones that were in the plain were all carried and borne through the gate by the virgins. 8 The square stones were trimmed and put into the place of those that had been removed. The round stones were not fitted into the building, because they were too hard to trim and it took too long. But they were placed beside the tower, because they were destined to be trimmed and placed in the building, for they were extraordinarily brilliant.

VII. THE REJECTED STONES PREPARED FOR USE

1 When he had finished, the distinguished man, the lord of the whole tower, called the shepherd and put him in charge of all the stones lying next to the tower, which had been cast out of the structure. He said to him: 2 'Clean these stones carefully and use them for the building of the tower, those that can fit in with the others. Throw far away from the tower those that do not fit.' 3 After these orders to the shepherd he left the tower in the company of those with whom he had come. But the virgins remained standing around the tower and kept watch over it. 4 I said to the shepherd: 'How can these stones once more be used in the building after having been rejected?' He answered and said: 'Do you see these stones?' 'I do, sir,' I said. 'I shall trim the majority of them,' he said, 'and place them in the building where they will fit in with the rest.' 5 'But, sir, how can they fill the same space, after having been trimmed?' I asked. He answered and said: 'Those found to be too small will find place in the middle of the building, but those that are larger will be put on the outside and will afford support to the former.' 6 After these remarks he said to me: 'Come along. After

two days we shall return and clean these stones and throw them into the building. For, everything around the building must be cleaned, in case the master should suddenly come; for he will be angry, if he finds that the approaches to the tower are dirty and that these stones have not gone into the tower. It would make it appear to the master that I am inattentive.' 7 So, after two days, when we returned to the tower, he said to me: 'Let us examine all the stones and determine those that can go into the building.' 'Yes, sir,' I said.

VIII. The Use of Stones in the Tower

1 At first we examined the black stones and we found that they were the same as when they were put out of the building. The shepherd gave orders that they be moved away from the tower. 2 Then he examined those that were rotten. Many of these he took and trimmed and bade the virgins take and put them into the building. So, they took them and put them in the middle of the tower-building, but the rest he ordered to be placed with the black stones, since they also turned out to be black. 3 Next he examined the stones with cracks. Many of these he trimmed and gave orders that they be carried into the building by the virgins. But they were placed on the outside of the walls, because they turned out to be more sound than the others. But the rest, because of the excessive number of cracks, could not be trimmed. For this reason they were cast aside out of the tower-building. 4 He next looked at the stones that were chipped. Among them many turned out to be black and had developed large cracks. So, he also had these put aside with the rejected stones. But, those left over he cleaned and trimmed and

commanded to be put into the building. And the virgins took up these stones and fitted them into the middle of the tower-building, for they were rather weak. 5 His inspection next turned to the half-white, half-black stones, many of which turned out to be black. And he gave orders that these, also, be taken out with the rejected stones. All the rest proved to be white and were taken up by the virgins, for, since they were white, they could be fitted into the building by the virgins themselves. Moreover, they were placed on the outside, because they turned out to be sound and able to support those placed in the middle. For none of them was completely chipped. 6 Then he examined the hard and rough. A few of these were rejected, because they could not be trimmed and turned out to be very hard. However, the rest were trimmed and taken up by the virgins to be put into the middle of the tower-building, since they were rather weak. 7 Then he examined the stones that had spots. Very few of them had been blackened and had to be rejected with the rest; the balance were glistening and sound and were fitted into the building by the virgins. Because of their strength, they were placed on the outside.

IX. The Completion of the Tower

1 Then he went to look at the white, spherical stones and said to me: 'What are we to do with these stones?' 'How am I to know, sir?' I said. 'Do you not notice anything about them? he said. 2 'Sir. I am not familiar with this handicraft; I am not a stone-cutter and cannot know.' 'Do you not see,' he said, 'that they are very round? And, if I should wish to square them, I shall have to lop off a great deal? However, some of them have to be put into the building.' 3 'Well, sir,' I said, 'if some have to be put into the building, why do you

bother. Choose those you want for the building and fit them into it.' He then chose from these stones the larger, brilliant ones and trimmed them, and the virgins took them up and fitted them into the outside portions of the building. 4 And the rest were taken up and put away in the plain whence they had been carried. However, they were not rejected, 'because,' he said, 'there is still a small part of the tower to be built. The master of the tower is exceedingly anxious to have these stones fitted, because they are very brilliant.' 5 Twelve women of most beautiful form were then called. They were dressed in black and wore girdles; their shoulders were exposed and their hair was hanging loose. These women seemed to me to be savage. The shepherd gave orders to them to take up the stones rejected from the building and to carry them back to the mountains whence they had been taken. 6 They picked up and cheerfully carried away all the stones and put them in the place whence they had been taken. After all the stones had been picked up and there was not a single one lying around the tower, the shepherd said to me: 'Let us walk around the tower to see whether there is any defect in it.' So I walked around with him. 7 At the sight of the tower's beauty of structure he was exceedingly cheerful. In fact, it was so beautifully constructed that I yearned for it when I saw it. It was built as if it were a single stone with only one joining. The stone looked as if it had been hewn out of the rock, for it seemed to be of one piece.

X. The Cleansing of the Site About the Tower

1 As I was walking with him, I was happy at this beautiful sight. The shepherd said to me: 'Go and bring lime and fine clay to fill up the holes left by the stones taken up and put into the building. Everything around the tower must be

smooth.' 2 I did as he told me and brought these to him. 'Help me,' he said, 'and the work will soon be finished.' Then he removed the traces of the stones that had gone into the building and gave orders to sweep around the tower and to make it clean. 3 And the virgins took brooms and swept all the rubbish taken out of the tower, washed the site with water, and made it pleasant and most attractive. 4 Then the shepherd said to me: 'Everything,' he said, 'has been cleaned. Whenever the lord comes to inspect his tower, he will not have any reproach to make to us.' With these words he wished to go off. 5 But I took hold of him by his wallet and began entreating him in the Lord's Name to explain what he had shown me. He said to me: 'I am busy for a little while. Then I shall explain everything. Wait here until I return.' 6 I said to him: 'What shall I do here, all by myself?' 'You will not be alone,' he said, 'for these virgins will be with you.' 'Put me in their care,' I said. So the shepherd called them and said to them: 'I am entrusting this person to you until I return.' Then he left. 7 So I stayed alone with the virgins, who were quite cheerful and well-disposed to me, especially the four of superior dignity.

XI. Hermas Remains With the Virgins

1 The virgins said to me: 'The shepherd will not return today.' 'Then,' I said, 'what shall I do?' 'Wait for him until tomorrow. If he comes, he will speak with you; if he does not, stay with us here until he comes.' 2 I said to them: 'I shall wait for him until tomorrow. But, if he does not come, I shall go home and return early in the morning.' They answered and said: 'You have been put in our care. You cannot leave us.' 3 'Where shall I stay, then,' I said. 'You will pass the night with us, as a brother, not as a husband,'

they said, 'for you are our brother and in the future we intend to stay with you, because we love you dearly.' However, I was ashamed to stay with them. 4 Then the one who seemed to be the leader began to kiss and embrace me. And when the others saw her kiss and embrace me they also began to kiss me and to chase me around the tower in play. 5 At this I also became like a young man and played with them. Some danced; some gavotted; others sang. I kept silent as I moved in their company around the tower, thrilled to be with them. 6 When evening came, I wished to go home; however, they did not let me, but restrained me. So I stayed with them for the night and slept near the tower. 7 The virgins spread their linen tunics on the ground and made me lie down in the midst of them. Yet they did absolutely nothing else except pray. I also, every bit as much as they, prayed without ceasing. The virgins were gladsome at such a prayer on my part. I remained there with them until the next day at seven o'clock. 8 Then the shepherd came back and said to the virgins: 'Have you done him any wrong?' 'Ask him,' they said. 'Sir,' I said, 'I was delighted to stay with them.' 'What have you had for supper?' 'Sir, I said, 'our supper all night was the words of the Lord.' 'Did they treat you well,' he asked. 'Yes, sir,' I said. 9 'What do you want to hear now before anything else?' he asked. 'Sir,' I said, 'I would like to ask you questions in the order in which you pointed things out to me and to have you give explanations in the order of my questions.' 'Just as you please,' he said. 'I shall give you explanations and I shall conceal absolutely nothing from you.'

XII. THE SIGNIFICANCE OF THE ROCK AND THE DOOR

1 'In the very first place,' I said, 'tell me this: What is the rock and the gate?' 'This rock and this tower,' he said,

'is the Son of God.' 'But, sir,' I said, 'how is it that the rock
is ancient, whereas the gate is new?' 'Listen to me,' he said.
'You will know why, foolish man. 2 The Son of God is born
before all His creation and, so, is counsellor to His Father in
His creation. For this reason He is ancient.' 'But, sir, why is
the gate new?' I said. 3 'Because,' he said, 'He has manifested[1]
Himself in the last days of the consummation of things, and
for this reason the gate is new. In this way those who are
destined to be saved enter the Kingdom of God through the
gate. 4 Do you not see,' he said, 'that the stones that have
entered through the gate go into the building of the tower,
whereas those that have not so entered are cast off and sent
back to their original place?' 'Yes, sir,' I said. 'For that reason
also, nobody enters the Kingdom of God without receiving
the Name of His Son.[2] 5 For, if you desire to enter some city
that has a wall all around it and only one gate, you cannot
possibly enter without going through the available gate.' 'How
else, sir,' I said, 'could one enter?' 'In the same way that
you cannot enter a city, except through this gate, so no human
being can enter the Kingdom of God, except by means of the
Name of His Beloved Son. You see,' he said, 'the crowd of
tower-builders?' 'Yes, sir,' I said. 'These persons,' he said,
'are all glorious angels. By them the Lord is walled about.
But the gate is the Son of God, the only entrance to the Lord.
Therefore, no one goes in to Him except through His Son.
7 You have seen,' he said, 'the six men and the noble, tall
man in their midst, the one who walked around the tower
and rejected the stones from the building?' 'Yes, sir,' I said.
8 'The noble man,' he said, 'is the Son of God, and the six
are the glorious angels who guard Him on the right and on

1 1 Pet. 1.20.
2 Acts 4.12

the left. None of these angels,' he said, 'will go before God, except in His company. Anyone who fails to receive His Name will not enter into the Kingdom of God.'

XIII. The Significance of the Tower and the Virgins

1 'Now about the tower,' I said, 'what is it?' 'This tower,' he said, 'is the Church.' 2 'And the virgins?' I said, 'who are they?' 'They,' he said, 'are holy spirits. It will be found that no man will enter the Kingdom of God in any other way, unless they clothe him with their raiment. For, if he only receives the Name, without receiving raiment from them, it is of no avail to him. The virgins are the powers of the Son of God. If you bear the Name, without His power, you are bearing the Name to no purpose. Now, the stones you saw rejected,' he said, are those who bore the Name, but did not put on the virgins' raiment.' 'What kind of garment is this raiment of theirs?' I said. 'The names themselves,' he said, 'are the garment. Anybody who bears the Name of the Son of God is also bound to bear their names. 3 Even the Son of God Himself bears the names of these virgins. 4 All the stones,' he said, 'that you saw going into the building of the tower and distributed by the hands of the virgins to remain in the building are clothed with the power of the virgins. 5 For this reason you see that the tower has been made in one piece from the rock. And so, those who believe in the Lord through His Son, and have clothed themselves with these spirits, will be one spirit, one body,[3] with a single color to their raiment.' 6 'Now, sir,' I said, 'these rejected stones— why are they rejected? They have come through the gate and have been set in the building by the hands of the virgins.'

---

3 Eph. 4.4.

'Since you show interest,' he said, 'and enquire accurately, I shall tell you about the rejected stones. 7 They all received the Name of the Son of God, as well as the power of the virgins. So, on receiving these spirits, they obtained power and were associated with the servants of God; theirs was one spirit, one body[4] and one raiment, for they had the same mind and practiced justice. 8 However, after some time they were led astray by the beautiful women you saw dressed in black garments, with bare shoulders and hair hanging down loosely and beautiful in form. At their sight they were filled with desire for them, clothed themselves with their power, and shed the power of the virgins. 9 Therefore, they were ejected from the house of God and handed over to the women. But, those who were not led astray by the beauty of these women remained in the house of God. There you have the interpretation of the rejected stones.'

XIV. THOSE LED ASTRAY CAN DO PENANCE

1 'Now, sir, suppose,' I said, 'that these men, in spite of their condition, should repent and put off their desire for these women and return to the virgins? And suppose, also, that they walk in their power and in their deeds: Will they not enter the Kingdom of God?' 2 'They will enter,' he said, 'if they cast off the works of these women and assume the power of the virgins, so as to walk in their deeds. That is the reason there was a pause in the building, so they could repent and return to the building of the tower. However, if they do not repent, then others will enter and they themselves will be finally rejected.' 3 At all this I gave thanks to the Lord that He had had mercy on all who invoke His Name and that He

---

4 *Ibid.*

had sent the angel of repentance to us who had sinned against Him. I gave thanks that He had renewed our spirit and that now, when we were lost without hope of life, He had renewed our life. 4 'Now, sir,' I said, 'explain why it is that the tower is not erected on the ground, but on the rock and the gate.' 'Are you still foolish and without understanding?' he said. 'I have to ask all the questions, sir,' I said, 'because I am unable to understand anything. All these matters are awesome, glorious, and difficult for human beings to understand.' 5 'I shall tell you,' he said. 'The Name of the Son of God is great, and incomprehensible, and supports the whole world. Now, if the whole of creation is supported by the Son of God, what do you think of those called by Him, who bear His Name and walk in His commandments? 6 Do you see the kind of persons He supports? Those who bear His Name with their whole heart. Therefore, He has been made their foundation and gladly gives them support, because they are not ashamed to bear His Name.'

XV. The Names of the Women and the Virgins

1 'Sir, let me know,' I said, 'the names of the virgins and of the women dressed in black raiment.' 'I shall tell you,' he said, 'the names of the virgins standing at the corners, the stronger ones. 2 The first one is Faith, the second is Continence, the third is Fortitude, and the fourth is Long-suffering. The others standing between them, in the middle, are called: Simplicity, Innocence, Purity, Cheerfulness, Truth, Understanding, Concord, and Love. The person who bears these names and that of the Son of God can enter into the Kingdom of God.[5] 3 Let me also tell you,' he said, 'the names of

---

5 Apoc. 7.3.

the women with the dark raiment: The first is Unbelief, the second is Incontinence, the third Disobedience, and the fourth Deceit. Their companions are called: Grief, Wickedness, Licentiousness, Irascibility, Lying, Foolishness, Slander, and Hatred. The servant of God who bears these names can, indeed, see the Kingdom of God, but cannot enter it.' 4 'Now these stones, sir,' I said, 'that have been taken out of the abyss and fitted into the building—what are they?' 'The first ten put into the foundations,' he said, 'are the first generation; the twenty-five are the second generation of just men; the thirty-five are God's prophets and His ministers; while the forty are the Apostles and the teachers who proclaimed the Son of God.' 5 'Then, why, sir,' I said, 'did the virgins carry these stones also through the gate and pass them on for the building of the tower?" 6 'These first stones,' he said, 'bore these spirits. They were never at all separated from one another, neither the spirits from men, nor the men from the spirits. No! Their spirits remained with them until their decease. Unless these spirits had persisted with them, they would not have been useful for the building of this tower.'

XVI. Even the Prophets and Apostles Must Receive Baptism

1 'Sir, tell me another thing,' I said. 'What is it?' he said. 'Why,' I said, 'did the stones that had borne these spirits go up from the abyss, and why were they put into the building?' 2 'They had to ascend,' he said, 'by means of water in order to be made living. Otherwise, if they had not shed the death of their former life, they could not enter the Kingdom of God. 3 Those, also, who were deceased so received the seal

of the Son of God[6] and entered the Kingdom of God. For, a man is dead before he receives the Name of the Son of God, but, when he receives the seal, he puts off death and receives life. 4 The seal, therefore, is water. The dead go down into the water and come out of it living. Therefore, this seal was proclaimed to them and they put it to use to enter the Kingdom of God.' 5 'Then, why, sir,' I said, 'did the forty stones come out of the abyss with them, if they already had the seal?' 'Because' he said, 'the Apostles and teachers who preach the Name of the Son of God, after having been laid to rest in power and faith in the Son of God, preach also to those who have been laid to rest before them. To the latter they themselves passed on the seal they proclaimd. 6 So, they went down with them into the water and came up again. But, the Apostles and teachers, though they were alive, went down and returned alive. But those who had been laid to rest before them went down dead and came up alive. 7 With the help of the Apostles and teachers they were made to live and came to the knowledge of the Name of the Son of God. For the same reason they returned in their company and were fitted into the building of the tower along with them, built into it without having been trimmed. They went to their rest in justice and great purity. They merely did not have the seal. Now you have the solution of this matter also.' 'Yes, sir,' I said.

XVII. The Meaning of the Mountains

1 'Now, sir, tell me,' I said, 'about the mountains. Why are some of one shape and color and others of other shapes and colors?' 'I shall tell you,' he said. 'These twelve mountains

---

6 *Ibid.*

are the twelve tribes that inhabit the whole earth. To them
the Son of God was proclaimed by the Apostles.' 'But,' I said,
'why are they varicolored? 2 Explain to me, sir, why the
mountains are some of one shape and others of another.'
'I shall tell you,' he said. 'These twelve tribes that inhabit
the earth are twelve nations. They are varied in understanding
and in mind. The varieties of mind and understanding among
the nations correspond to the varicolored mountains. I shall
explain the conduct of each.' 3 'First of all, sir,' I said, 'show
why, though the mountains are of such different colors, when
their stones are fitted into the building they all become of one
color, brilliant, like those that come up out of the abyss.'
4 'The reason is,' he said, 'that all the nations that dwell
under the heavens, after hearing and believing, are called by
one Name, that of the Son of God. So, when they receive the
seal, they have one understanding and one mind. Their faith
and love make them one and, along with the Name, they
bear the spirits of the virgins. Consequently, the tower-building becomes bright as the sun and of one color. 5 But, after
they had entered the same place and had become one body,
some of them sullied themselves and were banished from the
society of the just to become what they formerly were—only
worse.'

XVIII. The Sins of Believers Are the More Serious

1 'Sir,' I said, 'how did they become worse, after having
known God?' 'The person who has not known God,' he said,
'and commits wickedness receives some punishment for his
wickedness, but the person who has known God is required to
do no wicked actions and must do good. 2 The person who
ought to do good, having known God, and still acts wickedly
certainly seems to commit a greater wickedness than the per-

son who does not know God. For this reason, then, those who have not known God and act wickedly are sentenced to death, whereas those who have known God and have seen His mighty works, and yet act wickedly for the second time, will be punished and will die forever. In this manner the Church of God will be cleansed. 3 Just as you have seen the stones removed from the tower and handed to the wicked spirits, to be cast out along with them, and so to leave one body of the cleansed, so also did the tower become as one stone after its cleansing. In the same way it will be with the Church of God after the cleansing, after the wicked have been cast out—the hypocrites, blasphemers, persons who are doubters, and perpetrators of various crimes. 4 After the banishment of these people, the Church of God will become one body, one understanding, one mind, one faith and one love. Then, too, the Son of God will be glad and rejoice in their midst because He has received His people clean.' 'All this, sir,' I said, 'is awesome and glorious. One more thing, sir,' I said. 'Explain to me the power and conduct of each of the mountains, so that every soul that trusts in the Lord may hear and praise His mighty, marvellous, and glorious Name.' 'I shall explain,' he said, 'the variety of the mountains and of the twelve nations.

XIX. THE FIRST AND SECOND MOUNTAINS

1 'Out of the first mountain, the black one, come believers of this kind: apostates and blasphemers against the Lord, betrayers of the servants of God. Repentance is impossible for them; death is their destiny and, for that reason, also, they are black, because their race is lawless. 2 From the second mountain, the bare one, this kind of believer comes: hypocrites and teachers of wickedness. These, also, are like the first, without fruits of justice. Just as their mountain is with-

out fruit, so men of this kind have the name of believer, but
are devoid of faith. There is no fruit of truth in them. To
these, then, repentance is offered, if they repent promptly;
but, if they dally, their portion will be death along with the
former.' 'Sir, why is repentance possible for these, but not
for the former? Their actions are practically the same.' 'The
reason why repentance is possible for the second class,' he
said, 'is that they have not blasphemed their Lord, nor have
they betrayed God's servants. But, from a desire of gain they
each taught in accordance with the lusts of sinful men. But,
pay the penalty they must. However, repentance is offered
them, because they have not blasphemed, nor have they betrayed.

XX. The Third Mountain

1 'Out of the third mountain, with the thorns and thistles,
this type of believer comes: the rich and those involved in
too much business. The thorns are the rich and the thistles
are those involved in varied business affairs.[7] 2 These persons
who are involved in many varied business affairs do not stay
with the servants of God, but wander off and are choked[8]
by their business preoccupations. The rich have difficulty
remaining with the servants of God, because they fear that
they may ask them for something. Such persons, then, will
enter the Kingdom of God[9] only with difficulty. 3 So, for these
persons it is just as hard to enter into the Kingdom of God
as it is to walk among thorns without shoes. 4 However,
repentance is possible for all these persons, but it has to be
swift. Since they were formerly idle, they now have to hasten

---

7 Matt. 13.18 ff.
8 Matt. 13.22.
9 Matt. 19.23.24.

back to former days and do something worthwhile. After they repent and do good, they will live to God. But, if they persist in their conduct, they will be handed over to those women who will put them to death.

XXI. The Fourth Mountain

1 'From the fourth mountain, with the many weeds, some green at the top, but dried at the roots, and some scorched by the sun, come believers like this: doubters who have the Lord on their lips but not in their hearts. 2 For this reason their foundations are dry without strength; only their words are living, but their works are dead. Persons like this are neither alive nor dead. They resemble the persons who are doubters. The latter are neither green nor dry; they do not live, neither are they dead. 3 Just as their weeds wither at the sight of the sun, so also do persons who are doubters worship idols in their cowardice and are ashamed of the Name of their Lord when they hear of persecution. 4 Thus, persons like this are neither alive nor dead. But, they also, provided they hasten to repent, can live. But, if they do not repent, they are already in the hands of the women who take away their life from them.

XXII. The Fifth Mountain

1 'From the fifth mountain with green plants, which is rough, this kind of believer comes: believers but hard learners, opinionated and self-satisfied; though they wish to know everything, yet they know nothing. 2 Because of their presumption, understanding has left them and foolishness and stupidity has entered into them. They praise themselves, as though they had wisdom, and they wish to magnify their

office, though they are senseless. 3 So, because of this pride, many who exalt themselves have been made empty by their haughtiness. For, stubbornness and vain self-confidence is a mighty demon. Of this group many have been rejected, although some have understanding, once they realized their own senselessness. 4 For the rest of this type repentance is possible. For, they are not wicked; rather, they have become senseless and foolish. Provided they repent, these persons will live to God. But, if they do not repent, they will dwell with the women who devise evil against them.

XXIII. The Sixth Mountain

1 'The believers that come out of the sixth mountain, with the great and small clefts and fading plants in the clefts, are of this kind: 2 Those with the same clefts are persons at odds with one another who from their backbiting have faded in the faith. However, many of this group have repented. The rest will repent when they hear my commandments, for their backbitings are small and they repent quickly. 3 Those with large cracks persist in their backbitings and hold grudges in their rage against one another. These have been thrown out of the tower and have been pronounced unworthy of the building. This kind of person will live with difficulty. 4 Now, our God and Lord, who is Lord of all things and has power over all His creation, holds no grudge against those who have confessed their sins, but is indulgent. How is it, then, that a corruptible man, full of sins, holds a grudge as if he were able to destroy and to save? 5 I, the angel of repentance, declare to you that live in such disunion: Put this away, repent! And the Lord will heal your former sins, provided you are cleansed of this demon. If you are not, you will be handed over by Him to death.

XXIV. The Seventh Mountain

1 'From the seventh mountain, in which there are green and pleasant plants and which is flourishing in all its extent, where every kind of cattle and the birds of the heavens feed on the plants, and where the plants on which they feed become ever more flourishing—from this mountain comes this kind of believer: 2 persons at all times simple, innocent and happy, without a grudge against one another; who, on the contrary, always rejoice in God's servants and have clothed themselves with the holy spirit of these virgins; who, merciful to every human being lend assistance to them, without reproach and without hesitation. 3 The Lord, then, on seeing their simplicity and childlike guilelessness, has given them abundance in the labor of their hands and favored them in their whole conduct. 4 I, the angel of repentance, declare to you who belong to this group: Remain as you are, and your offspring will never be wiped out till the end of time. For, the Lord has passed favorably on you and has written you down in our number. All your descendants will dwell with the Son of God, for you have received from His Spirit.

XXV. The Eighth Mountain

1 'From the eighth mountain, where the fountains are those that watered all the Lord's creation, this is the kind of believer that came: 2 Apostles, and the teachers who preached to the whole world, and those who teach with reverence and purity; persons who do not turn one whit aside for evil desire, but walk at all times in justice and in truth in accordance with the Holy Spirit that they received. So the entrance of this group [into the Kingdom] is with the angels.

XXVI. The Ninth Mountain

1 'From the ninth mountain, which is deserted and has serpents and wild beasts that destroy human beings, this kind of believer comes: 2 The stones with spots are the deacons who administered their óffice wickedly and robbed widows and orphans of livelihood; who make profit for themselves out of the ministry they received to administer. If they persist in the same [evil] desire, they die and there is no hope of life for them, but, if they turn from their ways and fulfill their ministry with probity, they can live. 3 The stones that are mildewed are those that denied their Lord and did not turn back to Him. Shrivelled and wasted, they did not cling to the servants of God, but went their lonesome ways and are destroying their own souls. 4 These men are like a vine. Left by itself behind a fence, it gets no care and is wasted by weeds. In time, it goes wild and is no longer of any use to the master. In the same way these men have given themselves up in despair and, in their wildness, have become useless to their Lord. 5 Penance, then, is possible for these men, provided it turns out that they have not denied from the heart. But if it is found that one of these men has denied from the heart, I do not know whether he can live. 6 This I say not with regard to the present, namely, that one who denies obtains repentance; for it is impossible for a man to be saved who now intends to deny His Lord. But, there does seem to be a possibility for those who denied Him in the past to obtain repentance. So, if one intends to repent, let him hurry before the tower is completed. Otherwise, he will be done to death by the women. 7 Now, the chipped stones are deceitful persons and backbiters. They are the wild beasts you saw on the mountain. The remarks of these men hurt and slay a man

just as the wild beasts hurt and kill with their venom. 8 These persons are chipped in their faith, because of their conduct toward one another. However, some of them have repented and have been saved. The others of the same kind can be saved. If they do not repent, they will be slain by those women who have the power.

XXVII. The Tenth Mountain

1 'From the tenth mountain, where there were trees affording shelter to some sheep, comes this kind of believer: 2 bishops friendly to strangers and who receive the servants of God into their homes gladly, without sham. They have given shelter constantly by their own ministrations to the indigent and widows, and their conduct has always been pure. 3 Therefore, they will be given shelter by the Lord forever. Those who act in this way are glorious in God's sight and their place is now with God's angels, provided they persist to the end in their service to the Lord.

XXVIII. The Eleventh Mountain

1 'From the eleventh mountain, where are the trees laden with the weight of all kinds of fruit, come the following kinds of believers: 2 those who have suffered for the sake of the Name of the Son of God, who bore sufferings readily with their whole heart, and who have given up their lives.'[10] 3 'But, sir,' I said, 'why do all the trees bear fruit, but some of them more beautiful fruit than others?' 'I shall tell you,' he said. 'All those who have ever suffered for His Name are glorious in God's sight and all their sins are remitted, because they suffered for the Name of the Son of God. Now I shall

---

10 James 4.12.

tell you why their fruits are different and why some of them
surpass others. 4 All who were tortured and did not deny
when called before the magistrates, but suffered with alacrity,
are decidedly more glorious in the Lord's sight and their fruit
is superior. But, those who were cowardly and lost in uncer-
tainty, who debated in their hearts whether to deny or confess, yet finally suffered—the fruit of these persons is inferior,
because this deliberation occurred to them. 5 Take care, if you
have had such deliberation, not to allow it to remain and you
die to God. You who have suffered for His Name ought to
praise God, because He has deemed you worthy of bearing
His Name and of healing all sins. 6 Therefore, count yourselves blessed. Consider that you have performed a mighty
deed, if one of you suffers for God. The Lord is bestowing
life upon you and you are not aware of it. For, your sins have
weighed you down and, if you have not suffered for the Name
of the Lord, you would have died to God for these sins. 7 This
I declare to those who have hesitated between denial and
confession: Confess that you hold fast to the Lord, lest you
be handed over and put in prison for your denial. 8 What
do you think the Lord who has power over all things will
do to you, if pagans punish their slaves for denying their
master? Remove such deliberation from your hearts to live
forever to God.

XXIX. THE TWELFTH MOUNTAIN

1 'From the twelfth white mountain these are the believers
that come: They are innocent as babes into whose hearts no
guile enters and they do not know what wickedness is, constant
in their innocence. 2 These believers, then, undoubtedly live in
the Kingdom of God, because they have not sullied the commandments of God in any regard; all the days of their lives

they have innocently persisted in the same resolution. 3 You who will remain constant,' he said, 'and will be like babes, without evil guile, will be more glorious than all the aforementioned. Every child is glorious in God's sight and comes to Him before all others. Blessed are you, then, who removed wickedness and clothe yourselves with innocence. You will live to God before all the rest.' 4 When he had finished the parables of the mountains, I said to him: 'Now, sir, give me an explanation of the stones removed from the plain and put in the building in place of the stones taken out of the tower. Explain, also, the spherical stones put into the building and those that are still spherical.'

XXX. The Meaning of the Stones from the Plain

1 'I shall tell you about all this,' he answered. 'The stones removed from the plain and placed in the tower-building, instead of those that were rejected, are the base of this white mountain. 2 Since it was found that the believers from this mountain were all innocent, the Lord gave orders that the believers from the base of this mountain be used for the tower-building, for He knew that these stones will remain brilliant and not one of them will become black when they go into the building.[11] 3 Whereas, if he had taken and put them in from some other mountains, it would have been necessary for Him to come back to the tower to cleanse it. However, it was found that all these persons who believe and are destined to believe are white, for they are of the same kind. Blessed are they and innocent. 4 Now I shall tell you about those brilliant spherical stones, all taken from this white mountain. First, I must tell you why they were found spherical.

---

11 The Greek text ends here.

Their riches clouded their minds to the truth and obscured it. However, they never fell away from the true God and no evil word came from their lips, but all was justice and the virtue of truth. 5 So, when the Lord saw their frame of mind and that they could help the truth and remain virtuous, He had their riches cut off from them. But, He did not remove their riches altogether; hence, they could do some good with what was left them. They will live to God, for they come from a good stock. Consequently, they have been trimmed a little and placed in the tower-building.

XXXI. The Meaning of the Spherical Stones

1 'However, the other stones that still remained spherical and were not fitted into the building, because they have not yet received the seal, were put back in their original place, for it turned out that they were round. 2 This world and its empty riches have to be cut away from them. Then they will dwell in the Kingdom of God. They must enter God's Kingdom; God has blessed this innocent kind. Not a single one of this group will perish. For, though one or the other may sin because of the Devil's temptation, he will quickly return to His Lord. 3 I, the angel of penance, consider you all happy, you who are innocent as babes, because your part is good and in honor in God's sight. 4 To all of you who have received the seal I make this declaration: Retain your guilelessness, do not recall injuries, do not persist in your wickedness or in the bitter memory of your past offenses. Be of one spirit and heal those evil dissensions. Remove them from your midst, that the Lord of the flock may rejoice in His sheep. 5 And He will, if He finds all the sheep in good health. But, woe to the shepherds if He finds any of the sheep scattered. 6 And, if the shepherds themselves are scat-

tered, how will they answer for their flocks? They cannot say that they were in distress because of the flock. No one will believe them. It is past credence that a shepherd should suffer at the hands of the flock. His punishment will be all the greater because of his lie. I, also, am a shepherd, and I have the gravest obligation to give an account for you.

XXXII. Exhortation to Live in Innocence and Peace

1 'So, mend your ways while the tower is still in the building. 2 The Lord has His dwelling among the peace-lovers. The Lord prizes peace and He is far from the quarrelsome and from those who are given up to wickedness. Return to Him that spirit entire, as you received it. Suppose you give to the dyer a new garment, whole. You want to get it back, whole. Will you take it if the dyer returns it torn? You will instantly blaze up, cover him with reproaches, and say: "I gave you a whole garment. Why did you tear it and make it useless? Because of the rent you made in it, it cannot be used." Surely you will say all this to the dyer for the rent he made in your garment? 4 Now, if you are so annoyed about your garment and complain about not receiving it whole, what do you think the Lord will do to you? He gave you His spirit whole and you return it to Him altogether useless, so that it cannot be put to use. For it began to be useless after it had been spoiled by you. Surely the Lord of that spirit will punish you with death for this deed of yours.' 5 'Evidently,' I said, 'He will punish all those He finds continuing to bear malice.' 'Do not trample His mercy,' he said. 'Pay honor to Him for His patience with your sins. He is not like you. Do penance, then, that is useful for you.

XXXIII. The Meaning of the Filled-in Plain

1 'All that is written above, I, the shepherd, the angel of penance, manifested and spoke to God's servants. So, if you believe and hear my words and walk according to them, correcting your ways, you can live. But, if you persist in wickedness and continue to bear malice, remember no one of this type will live to God. All that I had to say has been told you.' 2 The shepherd in person had this, also, to say to me: 'Have you asked all your questions?' 'Yes, sir,' I said. 'Why, then, did you not ask me about the marks left by the stones put back in the building? We filled up the marks.' I said: 'I forgot, sir.' 3 'I shall tell you about this now. They are those who have heard my commandments in the present time and have done penance with their whole heart. After the Lord saw that they had done sound and thorough penance, and that they were able to continue in this disposition, He gave orders that their former sins be wiped out. These marks are their sins which have been levelled off so that they could not show.'

Tenth Parable

I. The Power and Dignity of the Shepherd

1 After I had written this book, the messenger who had handed me over to the shepherd came to the house I was in and sat on my bed. On the right stood the shepherd. Then he called me and said: 2 'I handed you over with your household to this shepherd, so you could be protected by him.' 'Yes, sir,' I said. 'So, if you want protection from all annoyance and cruelty; if you want success in every good work and

in every word; if you want power of justice—walk in the commandments of this shepherd, the commandments I gave you. With them you can overcome all iniquity. 3 For, if you keep the commandments of this shepherd, all the lusts and pleasures of this world will be under your control and, in every good undertaking of yours, success will follow you. Imitate his gravity and self-restraint, and let all know that he is highly regarded and this his dignity is great in the sight of the Lord. Tell all, likewise, that he is a ruler of great authority and powerful in his office. Over the whole earth authority over penance has been put in his hands exclusively. Surely you see that he is powerful. However, you make little of the restraint and modesty he shows you.'

II. The Testimony of the Shepherd in Favor of Hermas

1 I said to him: 'Ask him, sir, whether I have done anything against his command, anything offensive to him since he came to my house.' 2 'I also know,' he said, 'that you have done and are going to do nothing against his command. For your perseverance I speak: His report on you has been good. Tell this to others: Those who do penance or who are going to do penance should have the same sentiments as you. Then he will give a good report of them to me, and I to the Lord.' 3 'Sir,' I said, 'I also make known to everybody the glories of the Lord; it is my hope that all who committed sin in the past will readily do penance on hearing this, and thus recover life.' 4 'Continue in this ministry,' he said, 'and fulfill its requirements. All who fulfill His commandments will have life; yes, such a person will be held in high esteem by the Lord. Anyone who does not keep His commandments runs away from his own life, besides acting against Him. Furthermore, he who does not keep His commandments delivers him-

self to death. He is guilty of his own blood. I tell you: Keep His commandments and you will have a cure for sin.

III. HERMAS IS PUT IN THE KEEPING OF THE VIRGINS

1 'Now, I sent these virgins to live with you, because I saw that they were friendly to you. So, now you have helpers to be better able to keep His commandments. For the observance of these commandments is impossible without [the help of] these virgins. Though I see they are glad to be with you, I shall, nevertheless, bid them not to leave your house at all. 2 As for you, clean your house thoroughly, for they will be glad to live in a clean dwelling. They are pure, chaste, and industrious, and are highly regarded by God, all of them. So, if they have a clean dwelling in your house, they will stay with you. On the other hand, if the slightest taint creeps in, they will instantly go away from your house, for these virgins have not the slightest love for any taint whatever.' 3 'Sir,' I said to him, 'I hope that I shall find favor with them and that they will always be glad to live in my house. Just as this person, to whom you have handed me over, has no complaint against me, so neither will they.' 4 He said to the shepherd: 'I am sure that the servant of God wishes to live, and is going to keep these commandments, and that he is going to house these virgins in a clean dwelling.' After saying this, he handed me over again to the shepherd and called in the virgins. To them he said: 'Because I am sure that you are glad to dwell in this man's house, I entrust him to you and his household also. So, do not go away from his house at all.' These remarks of his they were glad to hear.

IV. Exhortation to Hermas to Remain True to His Calling

1 Then he said to me: 'Acquit yourself manfully of this office. Tell every human being of God's wonders and you will find favor in this office. Thus, everybody who walks in these comandments will live and will be happy during his life. But, anyone who disregards them will not live and will be unhappy in his life. 2 Tell all who can perform charitable acts not to lag in good works and that this is helpful to them. Now I say that every man should be relieved in his difficulties. For, a person who is in need and endures inconveniences in his daily life is in torment and want. 3 The person who rescues from want the life of a man who is in want draws great joy for himself. For, the man who is harrassed by this kind of misfortune suffers the same torture and affliction as the man in prison. Indeed, many incapable of enduring such misfortunes lay violent hands on themselves. Therefore, the one who knows the misfortune of such a person, and does not release him, commits a serious sin and is guilty of that man's blood. 4 So, all you who have received from the Lord, perform works of charity, lest, while you are delaying, the building of the tower be finished. For your sakes, the building of the tower has been interrupted. So, if you do not hurry to do right, the tower will be finished and you will be left out of it.' 5 After speaking to me, he got up from the bed and left, taking along the shepherd and virgins. However, he assured me that he would send the shepherd and the virgins back to my house.

LETTER
TO
DIOGNETUS

Translated

by

† GERALD G. WALSH, S.J., M.A. (Oxon), Ph.D., ST.D.
Fordham University

IMPRIMI POTEST:

F. A. McQUADE, S.J., PRAEP. PROV.

Neo Eboraci

die 8 Sept., 1946

INTRODUCTION

HE DOCUMENT which is here translated consists of two quite disparate parts. The first ten chapters constitute one of the most exquisite pieces of early Christian literature. They were written by an unnamed master of Greek style, a fervent Christian filled with Pauline convictions, a humanist who had achieved a remarkable harmony of supernatural faith and charity, with a highly cultivated intelligence, literary taste, conscience and social sense. The calm and clarity of his thought reveal a master of logic, the deep convicitions of a serious thinker, the eloquence of a trained rhetorician, the breadth of mind and warmth of heart, the poise of an educated gentleman.

The second part, Chapters 11 and 12, was obviously written by a different sort of a person. The author describes himself as a 'disciple of the Apostles.' His style lacks the calm and clarity of the Letter. The tone is more Oriental than Hellenic. According to one guess, the writer was Hippolytus, author of the *Philosophumena,* who died as a martyr about A.D. 236.

The first part has been assumed to be a letter, but it may well have been a formal written defense presented to a judge. It is difficult to determine the date of its composition. The fact that Christianity is alluded to in the opening chapter as 'this *new group* or institute' suggests an early date, but the attribution to Clement of Rome or to Apollos is merely conjecture. The fact that Diognetus was the name of a tutor of Marcus Aurelius led some to think that Justin Martyr was the author, but the style of Justin is quite unlike the style of this Letter. Like the homily (Chapters 11 and 12), the Letter is incomplete. The treatment of the Father in Chapter 10

355

supposes a corresponding treatment of the Son, which is not given.

It is curious that so beautiful a composition appears to have left no impression on any writer of the patristic or medieval period. The single manuscript of the thirteenth or fourteenth century which contains the Letter was discovered in the sixteenth century and published in 1592. It was destroyed during the siege of Strasburg in 1870.

LETTER TO DIOGNETUS

Y DEAR[1] DIOGNETUS: I see that you are eagerness itself to learn about the religion of the Christians. Your questions in regard to them have been drawn up with great clarity and care. You ask: In what God do they trust? How does their worship of Him help them—all of them—to care so little for the world and to despise death? Why do they neither esteem the gods that are considered as such by the Greeks nor keep the observances of the Jews? What is the character of the love that links them one with another? And, finally, why is it that this new group or institute has come into existence[2] in our time and not earlier? I welcome this earnestness in you, and I pray to God who gives us power both to speak and to listen that I may be given the grace so to speak that you may profit by what you hear, and that you may be given the grace so to listen that, after I have spoken, I may not be disappointed.

(2) The first thing, then, is to clear away all the prejudices that clutter your mind and to divest yourself of any habit of thought that is leading you into error. You must begin by being, as it were, a new man,[3] ready, as you yourself put it, to give ear to a new story. You must take a look not only with your eyes, but with your mind, at what you call and consider gods, and ask: What substance or form can they really have?

---

1 Literally, 'most-excellent,' as in Acts 23.26; 24.3; 26.25, where the word *krátistos* is applied to Felix and Festus. If the present document is a defense presented to a pagan judge, 'most excellent' would have the sense of 'Your Honor.'
2 *Bios* may here be rendered by 'world.'
3 Cf. St. Paul to the Ephesians 4.22-24: 'You must be quit now of the old self . . . you must be clothed in the new self.'

Is not this one made of stone, like the pavement under our feet, and that one of bronze, no better than what is in the pots and pans in daily use? Is not a third made of wood and already rotting, and a fourth of silver and in need of a custodian, lest it be stolen? Is not another made of iron that is corroded with rust, and still another of clay that is no more distinguished than what is made into a vessel for the lowliest use? Are not all of them perishable matter, or forged with iron and fire? Did not a sculptor make this one, a coppersmith that one, a silversmith a third, and a potter another of them? Is there any one of them that could not have been changed into any other shape before it was given this or that form by one or another of these arts? And, even now, given the right craftsmen, could not any of these utensils be turned into gods of the same material just like these? And could not any of these gods that are now worshipped by you be once more turned by man into pots and pans like the rest? Are they not all deaf and blind, without soul or sense or power to move? Are not all of them subject to rot and decay? You call these things gods; you serve them; you bow down before them; and, in the end, you become no better than they are. This is the reason why you hate the Christians—because they refuse to take these things for gods. But the fact is that you who now esteem and worship them despise them much more than the Christians do. When you leave the gods of stone and clay which you worship unguarded, while you lock up at night the gods of silver and gold, and set a guard over them by day, lest they be stolen, do you not mock and insult them much more than the Christians do? And so with the honors you imagine you pay them: If they are sensible of them, you insult them; if they are insensible, you convict them [of insensibility],

while you are propitiating[4] them with blood and fumes of fat.
Imagine one of yourselves submitting to this, or allowing anything of the sort to happen to him! There is not a single
human being who would willingly put up with such treatment—for the simple reason that he can feel and think. A
stone endures it, because it feels nothing. And so, you dis-
believe in its power of perception.[5] There are many other
things I might say on this matter of the Christians not being
enslaved to such gods as these. But, if anyone finds what I
have said insufficient, it is useless, I think, to say more.

(3) The next question, which I think you are very eager
to have discussed, is why the Christians do not worship in the
same way as the Jews. As for the Jews, in so far as they keep
away from the service of idols I have just mentioned, they
are right in claiming to revere one God and Lord over all;
but, in so far as they worship God in ways like the ones already mentioned, they are in the wrong. If the Greeks offer
a proof of their folly in making offerings to gods that can
neither see nor hear, then the Jews, in making the same offerings to God, as though He were in need of them, should think
this ridiculous rather than religious. For, He who made
heaven and earth and all that is in them, and has provided us
all with what we need, could not Himself have any need of
the very things which He gives to those who think they are
giving something to Him. As for those who think they can
offer Him sacrifices with blood and fat and holocausts, and
by such rites honor Him, they differ in nothing, so it seems
to me, from those who show the same devotion to deaf idols.
The latter think they can give to beings unable to take; the
former to one who is in need of nothing.

---

4 The Greek text reads: 'convicting them . . . you propitiate'; the
words 'of insensibility' have been added.
5 Literally, 'Therefore, you convict his (i.e., the god's) sensibility.'

(4) But, now, as to certain ridiculous matters that call for no discussion—such as their scruples in regard to meat, their observance of the Sabbath days, their vain boasting about circumcision, and the hypocrisy connected with fasting and the feasts of the new moon—I do not suppose you need any instructions from me. For, how can it be other than irreligious to accept some of the things which God has created for men's use and to reject others, as though some were created to good purposes and others were useless and superfluous? And how can it be other than profane to lie against God, pretending that He has forbidden us to do a good deed on the Sabbath day? And is it not ridiculous to boast of a mutilation of the flesh as a sign of the chosen people, as though on account of this they were particularly loved by God? Take again their constant watching of the stars[6] and the moon in order to make sure of the observance of months and days, and to commemorate the dispensations of God and the changes of the seasons according to their own whims, making this season a time of feasting and that one a time of fasting.[7] Who would look on all this as evidence of religion and not, rather, as a sign of folly? And so, I hope I have said enough to show you how right the Christians are in keeping away from the plain silliness and error, the fussiness and vaunting of the Jews. But, as to the mystery of their own worship, you must not expect that any man fully instruct you.

(5) Christians are not different from the rest of men in nationality, speech, or customs; they do not live in states of their own, nor do they use a special language, nor adopt a

---

6 The Jewish Sabbath began on Friday evening, as soon as three stars of moderate size were visible in the sky. The order of words, 'stars . . . moon . . . months . . . days,' is an illustration of the rhetorical figure, *chiasmos*.

7 Literally, 'mourning,' i.e., the Day of Atonement.

peculiar way of life. Their teaching is not the kind of thing that could be discovered by the wisdom or reflection of mere active-minded men; indeed, they are not outstanding in human learning as others are. Whether fortune has given them a home in a Greek or foreign city, they follow local custom in the matter of dress, food, and way of life; yet the character of the culture[8] they reveal is marvellous and, it must be admitted, unusual. They live, each in his native land—but as though they were not really at home there. They share in all duties like citizens and suffer all hardships like strangers. Every foreign land is for them a fatherland and every fatherland a foreign land. They marry like the rest of men and beget children, but they do not abandon the babies that are born. They share a common board, but not a common bed.[9] In the flesh as they are, they do not live according to the flesh. They dwell on earth, but they are citizens of heaven.[10] They obey the laws that men make, but their lives are better than the laws. They love all men, but are persecuted by all. They are unknown, and yet they are condemned. They are put to death, yet are more alive than ever.[11] They are paupers, but they make many rich. They lack all things, and yet in all things they abound. They are dishonored, yet glory in their dishonor. They are maligned, and yet are vindicated. They are reviled, and yet they bless. They suffer insult, yet they pay respect. They do good, yet are punished with the wicked. When they are punished, they rejoice, as though they were getting more of life. They are attacked by the Jews as Gentiles

---

8 Or, perhaps, 'the constitution of their polity' *katástasin tês heautôn politeías;* although the verb *endeíknuntai* suggests more an inner than an outward way of life.
9 The Greek text has *koinén,* 'common,' in the sense of 'unclean,' but the emendation *koíten* makes much better sense.
10 Cf. Phil. 3.20.
11 For this and what follows cf. 2 Cor. 6.9-10; 4.12.

and are persecuted by the Greeks, yet those who hate them can give no reason for their hatred.

(6) In a word, what the soul is to the body Christians are to the world. The soul is distributed in every member of the body, and Christians are scattered in every city in the world. The soul dwells in the body, and yet it is not of the body. So, Christians live in the world, but they are not of the world. The soul which is guarded in the visible body is not itself visible. And so, Christians who are in the world are known, but their worship remains unseen. The flesh hates the soul and acts like an unjust aggressor, because it is forbidden to indulge in pleasures. The world hates Christians—not that they have done it wrong, but because they oppose its pleasures. The soul loves the body and its members in spite of the hatred. So Christians love those who hate them. The soul is locked up in the body, yet it holds the body together. And so Christians are held in the world as in a prison, yet it is they who hold the world together. The immortal soul dwells in a mortal tabernacle. So Christians sojourn among perishable things, but their souls are set on immortality in heaven. When the soul is ill-treated in the matter of food and drink, it is improved. So, when Christians are persecuted, their numbers daily increase. Such is the assignment to which God has called them, and they have no right to shirk it.

(7) For, as I said, it was no earthly discovery that was committed to them, nor is it mortal wisdom that they feel bound to guard so jealously, nor have they been entrusted with the dispensation of merely human mysteries. The truth is that the Almighty Creator of the Universe, the invisible God Himself, scattered from heaven among them the seed of truth and of holy thought which is higher than men's minds, and He made it take firm root in their hearts. He did not send a servant (whether angel or principality, whether of those that

direct the affairs of earth or of those entrusted with arrangements in heaven), but He sent the very Artificer and Maker
of the cosmos, by whom He created the heavens, Him by
whom He enclosed the ocean in its proper bounds, Him whose
mysterious laws all the elements faithfully observe, and by
whom the measures of the length of days were given to the
sun to guard, Him whom the moon obeys when it is bidden
to shine by night and whom the stars obey when they follow
the course of the moon, Him by whom all things are put in
order and given their bounds and told to obey—the heavens
and the things in heaven, the earth and the things in the
earth, the sea and the things in the sea, fire and air and
peace, the things in the heights and in the depths and those
that are in between. To them He sent Him. Do you really
think—as might be humanly possible—that He sent Him
to impose His power with fear and terror? Certainly not. He
came in gentleness and humility. He sent Him as a King
would send a son and king; He sent Him as God for the sake
of men. In sending Him, He acted as a Savior, appealing to
persuasion and not to power—for it is not like God to use
compulsion. He acted as one inviting, not as one pursuing;
as a lover, not as a judge. Later on, indeed, He will send Him
as a Judge;[12] and then who will be able to withstand His
coming? . . . [13] [Do you not see] them thrown to wild beasts
to make them deny their Lord—and yet they are not con-
quered? Do you not see that the more of them who are punished, the more they grow in number? Such things do not
look like the works of men; they are the power of God; they
are signs of His coming.

---

12 Cf. John 3.17.
13 Cf. Mal. 3.2. After this there is an obvious break in the text. The
words, 'Do you not see,' were supplied by Henri Etienne (Stephanus)
who first edited the MS.

(8) Was there one among all mankind who knew what God was before He came? Or, perhaps, you prefer to accept the vacuous and silly professions of those specious philosophers? One group of them said that God was fire—what they call God is the place to which they are likely to go. Another group said God was water; a third, one of the other elements that God created. The trouble is that, if any one of these propositions is acceptable, there is no reason why any one of the other created things should not have an equal claim to be considered God. The fact is that all this stuff is the sham and deceit of tricksters. God showed Himself to men; not one of them has seen or known Him. He revealed Himself by means of faith; for by this alone it is possible to see God. For, God, the Lord and Creator of all, who made all things and set them in order, was not merely a lover of mankind, but was full of compassion. Mild and good calm and true— He always was and is and will be; He alone is good. The great and ineffable Idea which He conceived He communicated to His Son alone. For a time, indeed, He kept the plan of His wisdom to Himself and guarded it as a mystery; and thus He seemed to have no care and thought for us. But when, through His beloved Son, He removed the veil and revealed what He had prepared from the beginning, He gave us all at once—participation in His gifts, the graces of being able to see and understand things beyond all our expectations.

(9) In Himself and with His Son, His providence had all things arranged. If, for a time before He came, He allowed us to be carried along by our own whims and inordinate desires, to be led astray by pleasures and lusts, it was in no sense because He took any joy in our sins—He merely permitted them. He did not approve of the period of our wickedness in the past; He was merely preparing the present reign of grace. He wanted us who, in times past, by our own sins,

were convicted of being unworthy, to become now, by the goodness of God, worthy of life. He wanted us who proved that, by ourselves, we could not enter into the kingdom of God, to become able, by the power of God, to enter in. Once the measure of our sin had become full and overflowing, and it was perfectly clear that nothing but punishment and death could be expected as the wages of sin, the time came which God had foreordained. Henceforth He would reveal His goodness and grace—and Oh! how exceeding great is God's love and friendship for men. Instead of hating us and rejecting us and remembering our sins, He was compassionate and patient and took upon Himself our sins. He gave us His own Son for our redemption.[14] For us who were sinful, He gave up the Holy One; for the wicked the Innocent One; the Just One for the unjust; the Incorruptible One for corruptible men; and for us mortals the Immortal One. For, what else but His righteousness could have concealed our sin? In whom, if not in the only Son of God, could we lawless and sinful men have been justified? What a sweet exchange! What an inexplicable achievement! What unexpected graces! that in One who was just the sin of many should be concealed, that the righteousness of One should justify many sinners. In the former time He proved the inability of our nature to obtain life, and now He has revealed a Savior capable of saving the incapable. For both these reasons He wanted us to believe in His goodness and to look upon Him as guardian, father, teacher, adviser, and physician, as our mind, light, honor, glory, strength, and life, and to have no solicitude about what we wear and eat.[15]

---

14 Cf. 1 Peter 3.18.

15 Lightfoot omits the last phrase from his text, but the phrase has the authority of the MS.

(10) This faith, if only you desire it, you can have, and, first of all, the knowledge of the Father. For, God loved men, and for their sake made the world and made all things on earth subject to them. He gave them their reason and their mind. Them alone He allowed to look up to heaven. He fashioned them in His own image. To them He sent His only-begotten Son.[16] To them He promised the kingdom which is in heaven and He will give it to those who love Him. And with what joy do you think you will be filled when you come to know these things? And how you will love Him who first loved you so much! And, when you love Him, you will be an imitator of His goodness. And do not be surprised that a man may become an imitator of God. He can do so because God wills it. You know, there is no real happiness in getting the better of your neighbors, in wanting to have more than weaker men, in being rich and able to order your inferiors about. It is not in such ways that a man can imitate God, for these things are no part of His greatness. On the other hand, any man can be an imitator of God, if he takes on his own shoulders the burden of his neighbors, if he chooses to use his advantage to help another who is underprivileged, if he takes what he has received from God and gives to those who are in need—for such a man becomes God to those who are helped. When you have faith, you will see that God rules in heaven, even though you are on earth; you will begin to speak of the mysteries of God; you will love and admire men who suffer because they refuse to deny God; you will condemn the deceit and error of the world as soon as you realize that true life is in heaven, and despise the seeming death in this world, and fear the real death which is reserved for those who are to be condemned to eternal fire which shall torment

16 Cf. 1 John 4.9.

forever those who are committed to it. When you have faith, you will admire those who, for the sake of what is right, bear the temporal fire, and you will think them blessed when you come to know that fire. . . .

* * *

(11) I have no strange doctrines to preach, nor any queer questions to ask, but, having been a disciple of the Apostles, I have become a teacher of the Gentiles. To those who have become learners of the truth I try to be a worthy minister of the teaching that has been handed down. Is there any man who, once he has been properly taught and admitted as a friend of the Word, is not anxious to master as clearly as he can the lessons openly taught to the disciples by the Word? Unperceived by the unbelieving, but speaking at length to the disciples, the Word appeared and declared the truth, speaking freely of His mysteries. Further, those who were considered by Him to be faithful learned the mysteries of the Father. It was for this reason that He sent the Word, that He might appear to the world. Dishonored by the populace, He was preached by the Apostles and was believed in by the Gentiles. He was from the beginning. He appeared as new, but was found to be old and ever young, when He is born in the hearts of the saints. He is the Eternal One, who in our day is accounted to be the Son. Through Him the Church is enriched, and in the saints His unfolded grace is multiplied. This grace gives understanding, makes mysteries clear, announces the acceptable times, rejoices over the faithful, is granted to those who seek, that is to say, to those by whom the promises to believe are not broken and the limits set down by the fathers are not overstepped. And so the fear of the Law is hymned, and the grace of the Prophets is acknowledged, and the faith of the Gospels is made firm, and the tradition of the Apostles is guarded, and the joy of the Church exults. If you do not

reject this grace, you will understand what the Word says by the tongues of those whom He chooses, when He wills. We have been moved to utter with difficulty whatever it was the will of the Word to command us, and out of love of the things revealed to us we became sharers of them with you.

(12) Now that you have come to know and have given earnest attention to these truths, you will learn how much God bestows on those who love Him properly. These men become a paradise of delight, a tree bearing every fruit and flower, growing up in themselves and adorned with various fruits. For, in this place there were planted a tree of knowledge and a tree of life. It is not the tree of knowledge, but disobedience, that kills. For, the Scriptures are not silent on how God from the beginning planted a tree of knowledge and a tree of life in the middle of Paradise, revealing life through knowledge. Those who did not use it properly in the beginning were made naked by the deceit of the serpent. For, there is neither life without knowledge, nor sound knowledge without true life. Hence, the one tree was planted near the other. The Apostle saw the force of this and, blaming the knowledge which is exercised without the truth of the command leading to life, he says: 'Knowledge only breeds self-conceit, it is charity that binds the building together.'[17] For, the man who thinks he knows something, apart from the true knowledge to which witness is borne by life, knows nothing. He is deceived by the serpent, because he has not loved life. But, the man who with fear acknowledges and pursues life plants in hope and can expect fruit. Let your heart be knowledge and your life be true reason, properly understood. And so, bearing the tree of this truth and plucking the fruit, you will forever gather the harvest which God desires and which

---

17 1 Cor. 8.1.

the serpent does not touch. Eve is not deceived nor destroyed by deception and is trusted as a virgin. Salvation is set forth and the Apostles are given understanding, and the Pasch of the Lord goes on, and the candles[18] are brought together and arranged in order. In teaching the saints the Word is gladdened. Through Him the Father is glorified. To Him be glory forever. Amen.

---

18 Keeping the reading *keroi;* Lightfoot's text has the conjecture, *kléroi*, and he translates: 'the congregations are gathered together.'

THE FRAGMENTS

OF

PAPIAS

Translated

by

JOSEPH M.-F. MARIQUE, S.J., Ph.D.

Holy Cross College
Worcester, Massachusetts

Imprimi Potest:

F. A. McQuade, S.J., Praep. Prov.

Neo Eboraci
die 24 Oct., 1946

THE FRAGMENTS OF PAPIAS

INTRODUCTION

THE FOLLOWING tantalizing short *Fragments of Papias*[1] are all citations from writers, principally from the second to the fourth century. Yet, the interest in them, on the part of both Christian antiquity and modern Scripture scholars, has been intense and sustained.[2] The reason is that Papias, Bishop of Hierapolis, has something to tell us about the authors of three Gospels, especially St. John and St. Mark. St. Luke is not mentioned by name in any of the quotations. St. Matthew is briefly—even with reference to the brevity of the other portions—dismissed.[3] What that 'something' is which Papias has to tell has been the subject of voluminous current criticism.[4]

---

1 For an exhaustive treatment of the *Fragments of Papias* and a bibliography cf. Bardenhewer, *Geschichte der altkirchlichen Literatur* (Freiburg 1913) 1 and K. Bihlmeyer, *Die apostolischen Väter* (Tübingen 1924). Two English works will repay reading: The article 'Papias' in *Catholic Encyclopedia* XI, by Dom John Chapman, and (revision and condensation of the article in the old work by Wace and Smith) in the *Dictionary of Christian Biography and Literature* (D.C.B.), pp. 779 ff. Most of the modern studies on the subject are mentioned in these books, with the exception of occasional items cited in the notes.
2 Cf. the bibliography in the *Catholic Encyclopedia* article.
3 Eusebius *Hist. eccl.* 3 39; cf. Fragment II.16.
4 Among the very latest is the sober and painstaking discussion of the Mark Fragment by James A. Kleist, S.J., in the St. Louis University Studies, Series A. Humanities Series No. I, *Rereading the Papias Fragment on Mark*. This is a scholarly evaluation of the evidence, the appraisal of the 'difficulties,' and the solution of the remarks of Eusebius in Fragment II.15. On the John Fragment, Dom Chapman's *John the Presbyter and the Fourth Gospel* (Oxford 1911) can still be read with profit.

In the translation submitted in the following pages, the purpose has been merely to enable the reader to judge for himself what the *ipsissima verba* are and not to pronounce judgment for him. Much less is a commentary on the writings of Papias in place here; notes are added to indicate where such information may be obtained. The fragments themselves are the only solid basis of information on Papias' life, just as they also must be the starting point of all exegetical attempts. From these we are warranted in saying that he was a native of Phrygia and that he flourished toward the end of the first century and, perhaps, as late as the middle of the second.

The revised translation of the *Fragments of Papias* in this second printing of *The Apostolic Fathers* is based on the text of Funk, *Opera Patrum Apostolicorum*, (Tubingae 1881)2. The arrangement is the same as Funk's except that after Fragment X of Funk's edition, Bihlmeyer's Fragment XI has been introduced. The last Fragment (XIX), relegated to a footnote by Funk (p. 299, n.2), though under suspicion, has been included because it has frequently entered into discussions of Papias.

THE FRAGMENTS OF PAPIAS

I

HEN CREATION, reborn and freed from bondage, will yield an abundance of food of all kinds from the heaven's dew and the fertility of the earth,[1] just as the seniors recall. Those who saw John, the Lord's disciple [tell us] that they heard from him how the Lord taught and spoke about these times: Days will come when vines will grow each with ten thousand shoots, and on each shoot ten thousand branches, and on each branch ten thousand twigs, and on each twig ten thousand clusters, and on each cluster ten thousand grapes. Each grape, when pressed, will yield twenty-five measures of wine. And, when anyone of these saints will take hold of a cluster, another cluster will cry out: 'I am a better cluster. Take me and give thanks to the Lord through me.' In the same way, also, the grain of wheat will produce ten thousand grains, and every single grain will produce ten pounds of flour, fine and clean. And other fruits, seeds, and grass also will produce in similar proportions. And all the animals who use the products of the soil will be at peace and in harmony with one another, completely at man's beck and call.

Papias, a disciple of John and companion of Polycarp, a man of the first ages, also bears written testimony to this in the fourth of his books, for he is the author of five books.

For believers, this is credible. For, according to him, when

---

1 Gen. 27.28.

Judas the traitor refused to believe, and asked how such crops would be produced by the Lord, He answered: 'Those who reach these times will see.'

Irenaeus, *Haer.* V. 33.3.4. (ed. Stieren 1853) 1. 809 ff.

II

1 We still have the books of Papias, five in number, entitled *Expositions of the Oracles of the Lord.* Irenaeus also records that these were his only writings, in words more or less to this effect: 'Papias, who had heard John and been a companion of Polycarp, a man of the first ages, bears witness to this in his fourth book; as is known, he composed five books.' 2 So much for Irenaeus. Papias himself, however, in the introduction to his treatises, brings out clearly that he never was a hearer or eye-witness of the holy Apostles. By the language used he tells us that he received the doctrines of the faith from acquaintances of theirs. 3 'So far as you are concerned, I shall not hold back a single thing I carefully learned from my seniors and carefully remember, and shall thoroughly guarantee the truth of these matters. For I do not delight in wordy accounts, as many people do, but in accounts that tell the truth. Furthermore, I do not take delight in the commandments of anybody else, but in those mentioned as having been given by the Lord for our belief and which proceed from Truth[1] itself. 4 Whenever anyone came my way, who had been a follower of my seniors, I would ask for the accounts of our seniors: What did Andrew or Peter say? Or Philip or Thomas or James or John or Matthew, or any other of the Lord's dis-

[handwritten in margin: Non Sequitur]

---

1 The expression 'Truth itself' is distinctly Johannine; cf. Gospel according to St. John, Prologue and *passim.* 'Wordy accounts' and 'commandments of anybody else' most probably refer to the rigoristic sects of Gnostics; cf. D.C.B.

ciples? I also asked: What did Aristion[2] and John the Presbyter,[3] disciples of the Lord, say. For, as I see it, it is not so much from books as from the living and permanent voice that I must draw profit.' 5 At this point it is worth noting that he twice includes the name John in his enumerations. In the first list he puts him down along with Peter, James, Matthew, and the rest of the Apostles, clearly meaning the Evangelist. In the other list, after an interval, he puts John in the class of those who are not Apostles, with Aristion ahead of him, and 6 he definitely designates him 'the Presbyter.' This proves that the account of those who state there were two persons of the same name in Asia is true, as also that there are two tombs in Ephesus, each still called 'John's.' It is important to keep this in mind, for, if the former is not accepted, it is probable that the latter is the person who saw the Apocalypse which bears the name 'John'. 7 Now, the Papias of whom I am here speaking declares that he received the discourses of the Apostles from persons who were their followers, and he furthermore states that he himself actually heard both Aristion and John the Presbyter. In any case, he repeatedly mentions them by name in his writings and also records their traditions. These items presumably have not been mentioned uselessly. 8 It is worth adding to these remarks of Papias other statements of his, in which he recounts some extraordinary events and other matters that allegedly came to his knowledge by tradition. 9 In the foregoing an account was given of Philip the Apostle's stay in Hierapolis with his daughters. At this point attention must be called to the miraculous story which, Papias their contemporary relates, was told him by Philip's

---

2 Little more is known from literary sources about the identity of this person than what Papias tells us; cf. D.C.B.
3 On John the Presbyter, cf. the articles by Dom John Chapman, O.S.B. and his book *John the Presbyter and the Fourth Gospel* (Oxford 1911), besides the literature mentioned by Bihlmeyer, cf. Introduction, p. XLV f. n.1.

daughters. He says that a man rose from the dead in his time. Another extraordinary story is about Justus, surnamed Barsabbas, to the effect that someone drank a deadly poison and, by the Lord's grace, did not suffer any injurious effect. 10 The Acts of the Apostles record[4] that after the Ascension of the Savior the holy Apostles put forward this Justus with Matthias, and prayed for the choice to round out their number: 'And they put forward two, Joseph named Barsabbas, whose surname is Justus, and Matthias, and after prayer they said.' 11 The same author also includes in his narrative other information allegedly from oral tradition, some strange parables and teachings of the Savior, as well as other statements of a rather mythical character. 12 Among other things he says that a thousand years will elapse after the resurrection of the dead and there will be a corporeal establishment of Christ's Kingdom on this earth. This assumption of his is due, I think, to the fact that he misunderstood the Apostolic accounts, not realizing that what they said in figures was meant in a mystical sense. 13 For, he was very obviously a man of small intelligence, as one can say on the basis of his own remarks. Nevertheless, he was responsible for the same opinion[5] as his own among all the ecclesiastical writers, who urged in their support his antiquity. An example is Irenaeus, and whosoever else has appeared [on the scene] holding the same views. 14 In his writings he has also given us other ac-

---

4 Acts 1.23.

5 The belief in the millenium played an important part throughout the Middle Ages, both in the West and in the East of Europe. Bardenhewer, *op. cit.*, lists among Chiliasts, besides Irenaeus, no less a person than Justin Martyr, and perhaps Melito of Sardes. For further details on Chiliasm in Christian antiquity, cf. L. Atzberger, *Geschichte der christlichen Eschatologie innerhalb der vornicänischen Zeit* (1896) and J. Rohr, *Die geheime Offenbarung und die Zukunftserwartungen des Urchristentums* (Bibl. Zeitfragen IV 5 1922). Cf. J. P. Kirsch, Millenium and Milleniarianism, *Cath. Encycl.* X 307.

counts of the discourses of our Lord on the authority of the above-mentioned Aristion and traditions of John the Presbyter. I refer the curious to these. For the present, I shall add to the words quoted above the tradition on Mark, the writer of the Gospel, which he records in these words: 15 'The Presbyter also said this: Mark,[6] the interpreter of Peter, wrote down carefully what he remembered, both the sayings and the deeds of Christ, but not in chronological order, for he did not hear the Lord and he did not accompany Him. At a later time, however, he did accompany Peter, who adapted his instructions to the needs [of his hearers], but not with the object of making a connected series of the discourses of our Lord. So, Mark made no mistake in writing the individual discourses in the order in which he recalled them. His one concern was not to omit a single thing he had heard or to leave out any untruth in this account.' Such is Papias' statement on Mark. 16 About Matthew he says this: 'So Matthew composed the discourses in Hebrew and everyone interpreted them to the best of his ability.' The same writer makes use of testimonies from the first letter of John and, likewise, from Peter's letter. He also sets down another account of the woman who was accused of many sins before our Lord, an

---

6 Cf. the competent treatment of this section of Eusebius' quotation by James A. Kleist, s.g. The translation, which Father Kleist submits after painstaking examination of all aspects of the question, follows:
This, too, the Old Man said: 'When Mark became (sc. by writing his Gospel) the interpreter of Peter, he wrote down, though by no means with full detail (though not without gaps in his narrative), as much as he accurately remembered of the words and works of the Lord: for he had neither heard the Lord nor followed Him, but he subsequently joined Peter, as I said. Now, Peter did not intend to give a complete exposition of the Lord's ministry, but delivered his instructions to suit the varying needs of the people. It follows, then, that Mark was guilty of no blunder if he wrote, simply to the best of his recollections, an incomplete account. For, of one matter he took forethought—not to omit anything he had heard or to falsify in recording anything.'

account contained in the Gospel according to the Hebrews.[7] And let these observations of ours, the indispensable minimum, stand in addition to what has been set forth.

Eusebius, *Hist. Eccl.* III 39, ed. Heinichen.

III

Apollinarius:[1] 'Judas did not die by hanging, but continued to live, for he was taken down before he choked to death. The Acts of the Apostles makes this clear, for, "falling headlong, he burst asunder in the midst: and all his bowels gushed out."' Papias, the disciple of John, tells this story more clearly, when he says as follows in the fourth book of the *Expositions of the Oracles of the Lord*: Judas was a dreadful, walking example of impiety in this world, with his flesh bloated to such an extent that he could not walk through a space where a wagon could easily pass. Not even the huge bulk of his head could go through! It is related that his eyelids were so swollen that it was absolutely impossible for him to see the light and his eyes could not be seen by a physician, even with the help of a magnifying glass, so far had they sunk from their outward projection. . . . He died after many tortures and punishments, in a secluded spot which has remained deserted and uninhabited up to our time. Not even to this day can anybody pass by the place without shielding his

---

7 The first mention of the Gospel according to the Hebrews occurs in the *Stromata* 2.9.45 of Clement of Alexandria. Modern 'Higher Criticism' has shown considerable interest in this work. Cf. Bardenhewer, *op. cit.* 513. The story of 'the woman accused of many sins' is the same as the one found in John 8.1-11.

---

1 Apollinaris (in Greek more often written *Apollinarios* than *Apollinaris*, Cf. Bardenhewer, *op. cit.* 289), of Laodicea, was read by Photius. Excerpts from his work were given by him and also by Eusebius; cf. Bardenhewer, *op. cit.* 286 ff.

nostrils with his hands! Such is the afflux that goes through his flesh [and even pours] out on the ground.

> Compiled from Cramer, *Catena² ad Acta SS. Apost.* (1838) 12 ff. and other similar sources mentioned by Bihlmeyer, *op. cit.* 137.

IV

Papias word for word says the following:[1] 'To some (*obviously he means some of the angels who in the beginning were holy*) He gave dominion over the proper arrangement of the world and He enjoined them to exercise their dominion well.' *Right after this he says:* 'But it turned out that their battle-array came to no good end. And the great dragon, the immemorial serpent, also called Devil and Satan, was cast out. So he wanders over the whole world and is banished to earth along with his angels.'

> Andrew of Caesarea, *On the Apocalypse* Ch. 34. Serm. 12 (Migne, PG 106.325).

V

However, I do not think I have to linger any more on the inspiration of the book [the Apocalypse], since Saints Gregory[1] (the Theologian, I mean) and Cyril[2] have borne witness to

---

2 The Catena literature of the medieval times and earlier is treated in a masterly fashion by H. Jordan, *Geschichte der altchristlichen Literatur* 412 ff. Catenas are, basically, reference books for dogmatic, moral, or ascetical purposes.

---

1 The words of Papias are not italicized; what is italicized is the statement of Andrew of Caesarea.

---

1 Gregory of Nazianzus is meant; cf. D.C.B. 406 ff.
2 Cyril of Alexandria, cf. D.C.B. 236 ff.

its genuineness. Furthermore, the ancients Papias, Irenaeus, Methodius,[3] and Hippolytus[4] add their testimony on this point.

> Andrew of Caesarea,[5] *Preface of the Apocalypse* (Migne, PG 106. 217).

VI

Drawing their inspiration from the great Papias of Hierapolis, who lived in the company of the [Apostle] who leaned on [Christ's] breast, from Clement[1], Pantaenus,[2] priest of Alexandria, and the great scholar Ammonius,[3] the venerable first interpreters who are in mutual agreement and refer to Christ and His whole Church the work of six days. . . .

> Anastasius of Sinai,[4] *Contempl. Anagog. in Hexaëmer.* 1 (Migne, PG 89.860).

VII

Now, the more ancient interpreters in the Church, I mean Philo, the philosopher and contemporary of the Apostles, and the famous Papias of Hierapolis, the disciple of John the

---

3 A Lycian bishop of the latter part of the fourth century, martyred under Diocletian, cf. D.C.B. 724 ff., especially 725 where the citation from Anastasius of Sina is referred to.

4 This is the famous Hippolytus, most learned member of the Roman Church in the first years of the third century; cf. D.C.B. 482 ff., but especially the article by J. P. Kirsch, *Cath. Encycl.* VII 360 ff.

5 Editors waver in calling this commentary on the Apocalypse Andreas' or Arethas'. Arethas succeeded Andreas in the See of Caesarea in Cappadocia after 907; cf. Krumbacher, *op. cit.* 233, substantially repeated in *Cath. Encycl.* I 701. D.C.B. 39 has valuable material, especially the comment on the role played by the work of Andreas. But the *floruit* of these men is strangely placed in the 'last 30 or 40 years of the fifth century.'

---

1 Clement of Alexandria is referred to; cf. D.C.B. 176 ff.

2 Pantaenus was the head of the catechetical school at Alexandria and master of Clement; cf. D.C.B. 797 ff.

3 Also of Alexandria, author of the 'Ammonian Sections' of the New Testament. Cf. *Cath. Encycl.* I 431.

4 It is not surprising that Clement, Pantaenus, and Ammonius should be cited by Anastasius, since he himself was an Alexandrian. His *floruit* extends from the middle of the seventh century to the beginning of the eighth. Cf. *Cath. Encycl.* I 455 and references given there.

Evangelist . . . as well as their associates, took a spiritualistic view of the passages on Paradise and referred them to Christ's Church.

> Anastasius of Sinai, *Contempl. Anagog. in Hexaëmer.*, 7 (Migne, PG 89.962).

VIII

Those who exercise innocence in their relations to God were called children, as both Papias makes clear in the first book of his *Lord's Expositions* and Clement of Alexandria does in his *Paedagogus*.

> Maximus Confessor,[1] *Schol. in libr. Dionys. Areop. De caelesti hierarchia*, 2, (Migne, PG 4.48-49).

IX

I think, when he says this, he is hinting at Papias, who had once been Bishop of Hierapolis in Asia and flourished in the times of John the Divine, the Evangelist. For Papias himself, in the fourth book of his *Discourses of the Lord*, mentioned the pleasures [that come] from eating in the resurrection . . . and Irenaeus of Lyons in the fifth book *Against Heresies* says the same, quoting in support of his statements the above-mentioned Papias.

> Maximus Confessor, *Schol. in Libr. Dionys. Areopag. De eccl. hierarchia*, 7, (Migne, PG 4.176).

---

1 Cf. *Cath. Encycl.* X 78.

X

And Stephen[1] does not accept Papias, the Bishop of Hierapolis, and martyr, either, nor Irenaeus, the holy Bishop of
Lyons, when they say that the Kingdom of Heaven consists
in the enjoyment of material food.

> Photius, *Biblioth. cod.* 232, speaking of Stephen
> Gobarus, ed. Bekker (1824) 291.

XI

Papias, Bishop of Hierapolis, a disciple of John the Theologian and a companion of Polycarp, wrote five books of
oracles of the Lord. In these books, when making a list of the
Apostles after Peter, John, Philip, Thomas and Matthew, he
includes among the disciples Aristion and another John, whom
he also called the Presbyter. According to him, some think that
the latter John is the author of the two short *Catholic Epistles*
under John's name, on the ground that the Christians of the
first age consider only the first [to be John's]. Some also
mistakenly considered that the Apocalypse had John the
Elder for author. Papias is likewise mistaken about the millenium and, because of him, Irenaeus. In the second book
Papias says that John the Theologian and James his brother
were put to death by the Jews. The above-mentioned Papias
told a story, alleging that he learned it from the daughters of
Philip, that Barsabbas, surnamed Justus, drank snake's poison
on a challenge by unbelievers, but was preserved free from
harm in the name of Christ. He tells other miraculous tales,
also, in particular the one about Manaimus' mother who rose

---

1 The Stephen mentioned by Photius is Stephen Gobarus, the Tritheist;
cf. *Cath. Encycl.* X 492, col. 2.

from the dead. About those who were raised from the dead
by Christ he says that they lived to the time of Hadrian.

> Philippus Sidetes,[1] *Hist. Christ.* (published by De
> Boor, *Texte und Untersuchungen* V. 2 p. 170).[2]

XII

After Domitian, Nerva reigned one year. It was he who recalled John from the Island [of Patmos] and allowed him to
live in Ephesus. He was the only one of the twelve Apostles
still living at the time and, after composing the Gospel that
bears his name, he was deemed worthy of martyrdom. Papias,
Bishop of Hierapolis, an ocular witness [of him], says in the
second book of his *Oracles of the Lord* that he was put to
death by the Jews.[1] In this way, together with his brother, he
manifestly fulfilled the prophecy of Christ, both their confession of Christ and their accomplishment in His behalf.[2] For,
the Lord had said to them: 'Can you drink the chalice which
I drink?' At their ready assent and agreement [the Lord
said]: 'You shall drink My chalice and you shall be baptized
with the baptism with which I am baptized.' Naturally, this
must be so, for God can utter no falsehood! In his exegesis
of Matthew, the encyclopedic Origen also vouches for the
martyrdom of John on the strength of information to this

---

1 Philip of Side (in Pamphylia) was author of a *Christian History*. For
the general circumstances of his life, cf. D.C.B. 841. The more probable
view that Philip of Side took his information from Eusebius, and not
from Quadratus the Apologist, is presented by Dom John Chapman,
O.S.B., in *John the Presbyter and the Fourth Gospel;* cf. Bardenhewer,
op. cit. 186. The original version has not reached us. Philip of Side
flourished at the beginning of the fifth century. Cf. Bardenhewer,
op. cit. 450.
2 Funk omits this selection in his edition, but Bihlmeyer, *op. cit.,* p. 138,
includes it and M. G. Lagrange, *L'Evangile selon Saint Jean,* p. 40
(Paris 1924), deems it pertinent to the discussion.

---

1 There is no way of judging whether Papias says that St. John 'was put
to death by the Jews.' This probably is another mistake of transmission and misreading of earlier manuscripts; cf. D.C.B. 803.
2 The reference is to the ambitions of the sons of Zebedee in Mark
10.38,39.

effect that he received from successors of the Apostles. Besides, the widely-read Eusebius says in his *Ecclesiastical History*: 'Parthia fell by lot to Thomas; Asia to John. There he lived, dying at Ephesus.'

> Georgius Hamartolus,[3] *Chronicon* (published by Nolte in *Tüb. Theol. Quartalschr.* [1862] 466 ff., from *Cod. Coisl.* 305).

XIII

A person to achieve distinction throughout Asia in those times was Polycarp, a companion of the Apostles, who had been invested with the government of the Church of Smyrna at the hands of 'the eye-witnesses and ministers' of the Lord. In the times of Polycarp, Papias of the Bishopric of Hierapolis,[1] and actually its Bishop, became famous.

> Eusebius, *Hist. Eccl.* III 36.1.2.

XIV

Irenaeus[1] and other writers mention the fact that John, the theologian and Apostle, remained alive until the time of

---

3 Cf. Fortescue in *Cath. Encycl.* VI 435 f., summarizing Krumbacher, *Geschichte der byzantinischen Literatur* 128 ff.

1 The Hierapolis here meant is Hierapolis of Greater Phrygia. Pertinent references and illuminating sidelights will be found in Sir William M. Ramsay's *The Church in the Roman Empire* and *Luke* the *Physician*. This country had early been visited by St. Paul.

1 St. Irenaeus, Bishop of Lyons, the author of Fragment I, was an Oriental Cf. D.C.B. 520-535 and *Cath. Encycl.* VIII 130 ff. The date of his birth is between 126 and 136; his death occurred in 202 or 203. 'The time of Trajan' would mean between the years 97 and 117.

Trajan. It was after this that Papias, Bishop of Hierapolis, and Polycarp,[2] Bishop of Smyrna, who both had heard him, became well known.

> Eusebius,[3] *Chronicon* (Syncell.[4] 655, 14) for Olymp. 220.

XV

Papias, Bishop of Hierapolis in Asia and disciple of John, wrote only five books, which he entitled *Expositions of the Discourses of the Lord.* While declaring in the foreword that he is not following promiscuous statements, but using the Apostles as sources, he says: 'I used to weigh what Andrew, Peter, Philip, Thomas, James, John, Matthew or any other disciple of the Lord said, likewise, what Aristion and John the Elder, disciples of the Lord [said]. For, books to read are not useful to me as the living voice that rings out to the present day [in the person of] their authors.

Hence, it is clear in the list itself that there is one John placed among the Apostles and another, John the Elder, whom he names after Aristion. Attention is called to the fact, because of the foregoing view, transmitted, as mentioned above, by a considerable number—that the two last letters are not those of John the Apostle, but of John the Elder. He it is, so they say, who originated the Jewish tradition of a millenium. The same view is shared by Irenaeus, Apollinarius and others who declare that, after the resurrection, our Lord is to reign in the flesh with His saints.

> Jerome,[1] *De Vir. Illust.* 18 (Migne, PL 23.670).

---

2 On St. Polycarp cf. *Cath. Encycl.* XII 219 ff. and D.C.B. 846 ff.

3 Cf. *Cath. Encycl.* V 617 ff. and D.C.B. 318-334. On Eusebius' *History Chronicle,* cf. *Cath. Encycl.* V 616 ff.

4 Georgius Syncellus, author of one of the more important Byzantine chronicles, based primarily on Eusebius for times after the time of Christ. He died after 810. Cf. *Cath. Encycl.* VI 463.

---

1 St. Jerome, who often has much new information not elsewhere found on pagan and Christian antiquity, does not seem to give any more than what he could have drawn from Eusebius; cf. D.C.B. 843 and *Cath. Encycl.* VIII 341 ff., especially 342.

XVI

Moreover, the report to reach you, that the Books of Joseph and the writings of Saint Papias[1] and Polycarp had been translated by me, is without foundation, for I have neither the leisure nor the strength to translate with corresponding grace matters of such importance.

> Jerome, *Ad Lucinium* (CSEL 65, Epist. 71.5, p. 6, 11. 2.5).

XVII

Irenaeus, the disciple of Papias, who had heard John the Evangelist, relates. . . .

> Jerome, *Ad Theodoram Ep.* 75 (29) c.3. (CSEL 55, Epist. 75.2, p. 32).

XVIII

The content of the Gospel according to St. John begins here. The Gospel of John was made known and given to the Churches by John, while he still remained in the body, as a certain Papias by name, of Hierapolis, a disciple dear to John, has related in his five esoteric[1] books. . . . However, he copied the Gospel correctly under John's dictation.

> *Cod. Vatic. Alex.* 14 of the 9th cent., ed. by J. M. Thomasius Card. Opp. I 344 (Rome 1747); Pitra, *Analecta Sacra* II 160.

XIX

The last of these [Evangelists], John, surnamed son of Thunder, at a very advanced age, according to the tradition from Irenaeus, Eusebius and a series of other trustworthy

---

1 One solid basis for designating Papias as 'Saint' Papias is that of Photius, *Bibl. cod.* 232; cf. Bardenhewer, *op. cit.* 448, and D.C.B, 843,

1 I.e., exegetical.

historians, dictated his Gospel about the time when dreadful heresies had cropped up. It was to his own disciple, the virtuous Papias of Hierapolis, that he dictated, to fill out his predecessors' preaching of the word to the peoples of the whole world.

> *Catena Patr. Graec. in S. Joan.* Proem. (first published by B. Cordier [Antwerp 1630]).

INDEX

INDEX